MW01247415

ANIMAL RIGHTS
The Inhumane Crusade

Daniel T. Oliver
Capital Research Center

Second Edition, Revised

*a publication of the
Capital Research Center*

Merril Press
BELLEVUE, WASHINGTON

Animal Rights: The Inhumane Crusade

Second Edition
Published by Merril Press

Typeset in Times New Roman by Excelsior Graphics, New York, New York. Cover design also by Excelsior Graphics.

Animal Rights: The Inhumane Crusade is distributed by Merril Press, P.O. Box 1682, Bellevue, Washington 98009. Additional copies of this book may be ordered from Merril Press at $14.95 each. Phone 425-454-7009.

PHOTO CREDITS:
Man fishing: Arthur Tilley
Dog: Daniel T. Oliver
Elephants: Clyde Beatty-Cole Bros. Circus
Man hunting: Eric Crosson
Turkey: Robert M. Huberty
Giraffes: Chris Summers
Bull: International Professional Rodeo Association
Aquarium: Lewis Kemper
Women in Fur: Fur Information Council of America

LIBRARY OF CONGRESS CATALOGING-IN-PUBLICATION DATA
Oliver, Daniel T., 1963
    Animal Rights: The Inhumane Crusade / Daniel T. Oliver. – 2nd ed., rev.
        p.   cm. – (Studies in Organization Trends; #13)
    Includes bibliographic references and index.
    ISBN 0-936783-23-0
        1. Animal rights movement—United States—History. 2. Animal rights movement—Moral and ethical aspects—United States. 3. Animal rights move-ment—Economic aspects—United States. 4. United States—Politics and govern-ment. 5. United States—Social conditions. I. Title. II. Series.
HV4764.045 1999
179' .3—dc21
                                                                                    99-14005
                                                                                    CIP

PRINTED IN THE UNITED STATES OF AMERICA

Acknowledgments

I wish to thank Capital Research Center Research Director Robert Huberty for his excellent editing of the second edition of this book. Mary Tang, a 1998 Koch Foundation Fellow, also deserves thanks for her help in updating the appendices.

The following people, listed alphabetically by organizational affiliation, reviewed parts of the first edition to ensure accuracy and thoroughness and also made many invaluable suggestions: Ken Cheatham, American Veal Association; Irvin C. Mohler, Circus Fans Association of America; Tim Sulltvan, Fur Farm Animal Welfare Coalition; Shelia Lehrke, International Professional Rodeo Association; Janice S. Henke, National Trappers Association; Terri Greer, Professional Rodeo Cowboys Association; and Gary M. Kolesar, National Shooting Sports Foundation. Staff of United Egg Producers also reviewed and commented on parts of the manuscript. Patti Strand of the National Animal Interest Alliance reviewed parts of the second edition draft.

Some of the material for this revised edition was original published in three issues of the Capital Research Center's monthly newsletter *Alternatives in Philanthropy*: "Animal Welfare vs. Animal Rights: The Case of PETA" (July 1997), "The Humane Society of the United States: It's Not about Animal Shelters" (October 1997), and "The ASPCA: From Animal Welfare to Animal Rights" (August 1998). These articles can be viewed at CRC's website: www.capitalresearch.org.

The Capital Research Center is an independent, nonpartisan education and research organization classified by the IRS as 501(c)(3) public charity. CRC did not receive support from any animal-use trade association, business, or concern to research and publish this book.

About the Author

DANIEL T. OLIVER is a research associate at the Capital Research Center and editor of CRC's monthly newsletter *Alternatives in Philanthropy.* He received his undergraduate degree in sociology from the University of Akron. His writings have appeared in publications including the *Wall Street Journal,* the *Cleveland Plain Dealer,* the *Minneapolis Star Tribune,* the *Washington Times,* the *Chronicle of Philanthropy,* the *NonProfit Times,* and *Human Events.*

Preface

Over the last one hundred years, the United States and other Western societies have experienced one of the most dramatic transformations in human history: rural, agricultural societies have become urban, technological ones. As recently as the late 19th century, more than 80 percent of American families lived in rural areas, and 40 percent lived on farms. Today, only 27 percent live in the country, and less than two percent live on farms.

Consequently, many of us lack a basic understanding of animal husbandry. We do not know how farmers raise the animals we depend on for food, clothing, and countless animal byproducts. Nor do we understand the need for hunting and trapping. We probably have heard that animals are used in biomedical research, but we don't know exactly what this entails. Our hands-on experience with animals today consists almost entirely of pet ownership.

Today's pet-owning public is naturally concerned about humane animal treatment. We are angered by stories of animal abuse and want to see perpetrators punished. But some modern methods of livestock and poultry farming, wildlife conservation, and biomedical research can disturb us, especially when sensationalized by a ratings-hungry media. Given our unfamiliarity with animals, we sometimes accept as gospel truth exaggerated media portrayals of animal abuse. Unfortunately, our ignorance has become an exploitable resource for a newly emergent protest industry—the animal rights movement.

Some leaders of this movement may genuinely believe that there is widespread abuse of animals in the United States today. But there have always been people who are ready and willing to capitalize on any perceived problem, who deliberately foster misunderstanding, and who offer simple panaceas—often self-serving—for complex issues. They use whatever means are necessary to achieve their purpose—legal or otherwise.

Leaders of the animal rights movement fit that profile. They camouflage their radical agenda—ending all use and ownership of animals—leading the public to believe instead that they wish only to improve animal welfare. They have organized a powerful, highly sophisticated, and media-savvy international movement that cashes in on a public that is concerned yet uninformed about animal treatment.

Daniel Oliver shows that the animal rights movement has seriously affected our society. Raids on biomedical research laboratories and the destruction of life-saving research have almost certainly cost lives. Millions of dollars have been diverted from research that could save lives to tightened security. Meat-processing plants, mink farms, and countless other enterprises have been vandalized and firebombed. Those who use and depend on animals have received hate mail and death threats, and some live in constant fear. Animal rights campaigns to stop seal and whale hunting have even destroyed the centuries-old cultures of indigenous peoples.

Animal rights organizations raise millions of dollars each year by doing little more than defaming individuals and industries that use animals. Unlike traditional humane organizations, they do not work with animal users to improve the treatment of animals. Instead, they attack them. Ironically, many responsible animal users, some of whom have spent their lives working to improve animal welfare, now find themselves targeted as "animal abusers." Many of them—farmers, biomedical researchers, pet breeders—bravely defend themselves, but often at considerable cost. Their work suffers, and they lose time, money, and public credibility.

I believe this book speaks for them. By describing the tactics of animal rights groups, it will help the public understand their massive misinformation campaign. It will also help them see how the animal rights movement seriously affects us all. Not everyone can connect the dots that link the animal rights movement to the loss of human rights and dignity. Daniel Oliver has.

Rod and Patti Strand
National Animal Interest Alliance
Portland, Oregon
March 1999

Table of Contents

Introduction

PETA and the Huntingdon Life Sciences Lawsuit

In early 1997, the animal rights group People for the Ethical Treatment of Animals (PETA) began a campaign against Huntingdon Life Sciences, an East Millstone, New Jersey firm that uses animals to test products for other companies. An undercover PETA investigator named Michelle Rokke had spent several months working at Huntingdon, using a camera hidden in her glasses to make 50 hours of videotape inside its laboratories. She also photocopied 8,000 company documents, many of them containing trade secrets.

When PETA announced it had evidence that Huntingdon had abused dogs in tests it had done for Colgate-Palmolive, that company and more than half of Huntingdon's other clients cancelled their contracts. PETA also alleged that monkeys were roughly handled and improperly anesthetized during tests for Procter & Gamble.

In response, Huntingdon filed a civil lawsuit under RICO statues, contending that PETA had engaged in a pattern of criminal behavior that included harassing scientists and companies and making unsubstantiated allegations that harmed scientific careers and company reputations. Moreover, it alleged that the information Rokke had gathered constituted trade secrets that could be used by competitors. Huntingdon lost $1 million in business and its president, Alan Staple, said he and his family received death threats.

When federal marshals arrived at PETA's headquarters in Norfolk, Virginia with a temporary restraining order, PETA employees initially denied knowing or having any involvement with Rokke. The marshals returned when they learned PETA had misled them. Despite a court-imposed gag order, PETA celebrity spokesman Kim Basinger appeared at a PETA-sponsored media event, covered by *Entertainment Tonight* and *Access Hollywood,* outside Huntingdon's headquarters, where she pleaded for the release of the research dogs. Four days later, Federal Court Judge Rebecca B. Smith ruled that the event and a PETA news release on the Huntingdon case violated the gag order. While she imposed no punishment, she warned of "very heavy monetary fines and potential jail time" for future violations.[1]

Federal Judge Robert G. Doumar, who took over the case (but later removed himself because of a possible conflict of interest), ruled in favor of Huntingdon in a preliminary hearing. He laid down several findings of fact, including that Rokke had engaged in "fraudulent misrepresentation" and acted "surreptitiously;" that she had signed and broken a confidentially agreement outlined in Huntingdon's employee manual; and that she had taken property that "she knew was not hers to take." He also noted that Rokke had failed to report alleged violations of animal-care statutes to her supervisor as stipulated in the employee manual, and that her primary objective thus appeared to be to put Huntingdon out of business rather than improve animal welfare.

In December of 1997, PETA and Huntingdon settled out of court. In return for Huntingdon's agreement to drop all charges, PETA agreed to destroy or return all the documents, videotapes, and audiotapes related to the investigation. It also agreed not to interfere again with Huntingdon's business relationships and to forgo undercover investigations at Huntingdon for five years. Nonetheless, PETA president Ingrid Newkirk boasted in a fundraising letter that PETA "will pay *no* damages or costs to HLS. . . . Their expensive attack on PETA *backfired.* . . . I'm so excited to share with you the good news about our victory over Huntingdon Life Sciences. . . ."[2]

No independent third party found evidence that Huntingdon had violated the Animal Welfare Act, a set of federal rules that regulates the use of animals in research. Moreover, the Association for Assessment and Accreditation of Laboratory Animal Care International, an independent agency that evaluates and accredits 600 laboratory programs, had inspected Huntingdon's facilities for years and declared them in compliance with all regulations. AAALAC International's Dr. John G. Miller concluded, "the site-visit team saw nothing that supported any of the allegations made by PETA."[3]

Criminal Actions and Terrorism

This incident is not unusual. As shown throughout this book, animal rights organizations raise millions of dollars annually by making allegations of animal abuse that cannot be substantiated. Their targets are biomedical researchers, farmers, pet breeders, hunters, trappers, fishermen, and others who use and depend on animals. Moreover, since the early 1980s, a radical fringe of the animal rights movement, led by the Animal Liberation Front, has been suspected of hundreds of acts of vandalism, theft, and arson directed at biomedical research laboratories, chicken farms, meat-processing plants, mink ranches, fur stores, and similar concerns.

The American Medical Association notes that break-ins at biomedical research laboratories "have led to the interruption, delay, and even abandonment of research, and . . . have increased the costs of conducting research by requiring more security at laboratories, the replacement of stolen animals, and the repetition of experiments."[4] In addition, these incidents have generated fear among biomedical researchers and deterred students from careers in science. In terms of possible treatments or cures foregone, the cost of this destruction is incalculable.

In response, Congress in 1992 passed the Animal Enterprise Protection Act, making the theft or damage of equipment, records, or other property (including animals) at research laboratories, farms, businesses, zoos, aquariums, circuses, rodeos, and related concerns a federal offense, with penalties ranging from one year to life imprisonment and restitution for damages.[5] In addition, the Federal Bureau of Investigation and U.S. Bureau of Alcohol, Tobacco and Firearms have conducted grand jury investigations into activities of the Animal Liberation Front, including the subpoenaing of PETA officials Ingrid Newkirk and Alex Pacheco, two animal rights leaders with ties to ALF.[6]

Regulatory Costs

Only time will tell how effective these efforts will be. However, one observer notes that activists' "potential for substantial injury to our national research program [through criminal actions and illegality] is minuscule compared to the adverse consequences to research that can occur from political decisions arrived at in a perfectly legal manner."[7] Through lobbying and litigation, animal rights groups have persuaded government at all levels to tighten regulations governing medical research and other animal-use concerns. The U.S. Department of Agriculture estimated that laboratories, zoos, animal dealers, and auction operators spent over $1 billion in 1990 complying with new federal rules covering the housing, feeding, watering, sanitation, and ventilation of animals. The National Association for Biomedical Research, an association of universities, research institutes, and companies that use animals in biomedical research, estimated the cost at as much as $2 billion—roughly 15 percent of the $14 billion spent on medical research that year.[8]

Many critics doubt that these regulations have done much, if anything, to improve animal well-being. But animal rights groups have nonetheless increased the cost of biomedical research and other animal enterprises. As biomedical researcher David H. Hubel remarks, "Their tactics are clear. Work to increase the costs of research, and stop its progress with red tape and lawsuits."[9]

An Animal Non-Use Movement

In addition to animal research, the animal rights movement would end all the following:

• Raising farm animals for food, clothing, and animal byproducts of which many Americans are unaware, such as antifreeze, photographic film, and pet food.

• Hunting, trapping, and fishing.

• Using animals in education and entertainment, including zoos, aquariums, circuses, rodeos, and stage acts.

• Breeding and owning pets.

The animal rights movement is, quite simply, an animal non-use movement. *Unlike traditional humane organizations, which seek to prevent cruelty and improve the treatment of animals, animal rights organizations seek to end the use and ownership of animals.* Some people mistakenly believe that animal rights groups are just humane organizations that have "gone overboard" in their concern for animals—that they care so deeply for animals that they overlook human welfare. But as animal rights "philosopher" Tom Regan says, "It is not larger, cleaner cages that justice demands . . . but empty cages; not 'traditional' animal agriculture, but a complete end to all commerce in the flesh of dead animals; not 'more humane' hunting and trapping, but the total eradication of these barbarous practices."[10]

Animal lovers who wish to support organizations that express a concern for animals should consider the implications of Regan's remarks. If it is wrong to use animals, as animal rights groups claim, the issue of how well animals are treated is irrelevant. If an organization believes it is fundamentally wrong to use animals, it will have little or no interest in improving animal treatment. Instead, it will use donations in campaigns to end animal use.

Many animal rights groups are no doubt aware that the goal of ending animal use, if stated openly, would be rejected by most Americans. Not surprisingly, they often portray their efforts as part of the traditional humane movement, saying they seek only to improve animal treatment. Janice Henke, who has studied the movement's opposition to whaling and sealing, says that "most supporters of 'animal rights' organizations are Americans who still believe that the 'movement' is primarily interested in increasing awareness about the need for increased animal welfare. They do not realize that the leaders of this . . . philosophy are actually working toward a goal of the total elimination of animal use, and are selling the concept through initial campaigns which use 'cruelty' as a marketing tool."[11]

Size of the Animal Rights Movement

There are no definite figures on the total number of animal rights organizations, their level of funding, and their combined memberships. The largest is the Humane Society of the United States (HSUS), often mistaken for a traditional humane association. Although it has nearly two million members, it is likely that many of them do not realize they are supporting an animal rights organization since HSUS presents itself to the public as an animal welfare organization. Likewise, many of the 425,000 members of the American Society for the Prevention of Cruelty to Animals (ASPCA), the third largest group in terms of membership, may believe they are supporting a traditional humane organization since ASPCA fundraising letters often convey this impression (see Chapter VIII). People for the Ethical Treatment of Animals (PETA), which openly announces its animal rights agenda, is the second largest group with 600,000 members. Most other organizations have memberships well below these levels. Since many supporters of animal rights groups likely belong to more than one, simply adding together the memberships of the largest organizations would overcount the total number of Americans who support animal rights groups.

In 1996, ten of the largest animal rights organizations had combined budgets of $125 million. These were the Humane Society of the United States (budget: $37.8 million), the Massachusetts Society for the Prevention of Cruelty to Animals ($24.2 million), the American Society for the Prevention of Cruelty to Animals ($19.3 million), the International Fund for Animal Welfare ($11.7 million), PETA ($11.5 million), the World Society for the Protection of Animals ($5.2 million), Friends of Animals ($4.9 million), the Fund for Animals ($4.1 million), the Doris Day Animal League ($2.5 million), and the Animal Legal Defense Fund ($1.9 million).[12]

Some observers note that these budgets are relatively small compared to those of other nonprofit organizations. For example, among environmental groups, the largest—the Nature Conservancy—had a 1997 income of over $400 million. However, it would be a mistake to conclude that animal rights groups could never significantly affect public policy. As noted, they have already helped to shift significant amounts of biomedical research money into compliance with burdensome animal-care regulations. And they are in the midst of campaigns to end livestock and poultry farming, hunting, trapping, fishing, zoos, aquariums, circuses, rodeos, and pet breeding and ownership. Some of these campaigns have achieved limited success. Moreover, many animal rights groups use their resources to carry out what can only be called campaigns of harassment, such as the one against Huntingdon Life Sciences. For the companies and individuals targeted, these campaigns are time-consuming, costly, demoralizing, and even terrifying, involving hate mail, threatening phone calls, and death threats.

Past Its Peak?

A survey of animal rights activists conducted by University of Oregon researchers Wesley V. Jamison and William M. Lunch in 1992 concluded that "the activists we interviewed often demonstrated extraordinary levels of commitment, which could help them to maintain their efforts despite repeated frustration in the incremental legislative arena.... The movement has thus far been able to adapt to organizational and societal demands without disintegrating. The resiliency and sophistication of the movement should not be lost on scientists who would dismiss the movement as transitory."[13] The researchers found that 38 percent of activists had campaigned for political candidates who support animal rights. "Compared to the general public, or even campaign contributors, this level of political activity is truly extraordinary.... [Activists are] characterized by profound commitment to the movement and to continued action within the political system."[14]

On the other hand, there is some evidence that the animal rights movement, which was one of the fastest growing social movement in the United States in the 1980s, may be waning. Membership in animal rights groups grew by five times between 1984 and 1993[15] and letters concerning animals comprised the third largest volume of mail to Congress in 1992 (exceeded only by those concerned with social security and the federal deficit.)[16] But a 1996 survey of activists by researchers Shelley L. Galvin and Harold A. Herzog found that the median age of respondents had increased since 1990 (from 32 to 34) and that the average respondent had been involved in the movement for six years, compared to three years in 1990. "This suggests the movement may not be attracting new recruits in sufficient numbers to maintain the growth witnessed in the 1980s."[17] Moreover, associations of biomedical researchers, livestock and poultry farmers, hunters and trappers, and others who rely on animals have become increasingly organized—and successful—in opposing recent animal rights campaigns.

Outline

About 20 percent of Americans have given money to animal rights and traditional animal welfare organizations.[18] This book seeks to encourage potential donors to look beyond the rhetoric of organizations that express a concern for animals and to consider their actual agendas. Above all, donors should question allegations of animal cruelty often found in these organizations' fundraising letters, newsletters, and other materials. If these allegations cannot be substantiated, donors should put their money to better use.

Chapter I is an historical overview that traces the modern animal rights movement to the British and American antivivisection (anti-animal research) movements of the late-19th and early-20th centuries. It also examines animal rights "philosophy" and the implications of this view.

Chapters II through VI respectively examine biomedical research involving animals, livestock and poultry farming, hunting and trapping, the use of animals in education and entertainment (zoos, circuses, etc.), and pets. They examine the claims that animal rights groups make against these types of animal use, the strategies they use to build public opposition, and the resulting costs to humans and animals.

Chapter VII examines the strategies animal rights groups use to raise funds, attract media attention, and recruit supporters. The use of false and unsubstantiated charges of animal cruelty is highlighted.

Chapter VIII examines what critics Rod and Patti Strand call the "hijacking of the humane movement,"[19] whereby animal rights groups take over long-established—and sometimes wealthy—humane organizations. It also discusses how other humane organizations, of their own accord, have adopted the animal rights agenda.

Chapter IX examines the criminal actions and terrorism that the public often associates with the animal rights movement. It also assesses the cost of these activities and considers possible remedies.

Appendix I features short profiles of several organizations that promote improved animal treatment and responsible animal use. Animal lovers may wish to support some of them.

This new edition features four new profiles of prominent animal rights groups: the Animal Protection Institute of America, In Defense of Animals, the International Fund for Animal Welfare, and the Physicians Committee for Responsible Medicine. Appendices II through XV also examine the leadership, activities, and funding sources of the American Society for the Prevention of Cruelty to Animals, the Animal Legal Defense Fund, the Animal Liberation Front, Animal Rights International, the Animal Welfare Institute, the Farm Animal Reform Movement, Friends of Animals, the Fund for Animals, the Humane Society of the United States, and People for the Ethical Treatment of Animals.

Appendix XVI is a list of major animal rights groups and Appendix XVII lists prominent animal rights leaders. Appendix XVIII is a sample of quotes—some rather startling—by these leaders.

Finally, Appendix XIX describes the results of a 1992 survey of animal rights activists.

Notes
1. Judge Rebecca B. Smith, quoted in Americans for Medical Progress, *AMP News,* September 26, 1998.
2. Ingrid Newkirk, quoted in PETA fundraising letter dated January 16, 1998.
3. John G. Miller, quoted in "Tough Tactics in One Battle over Animals in the Lab," *New York Times*, March 24, 1998.
4. American Medical Association, "Use of Animals in Biomedical Research," white paper, 1992, p. 9.
5. Putting People First, facsimile transmissions dated August 5, 20, 26, 28, and September 1, 1992.
6. Americans for Medical Progress, news release, July 21, 1992, and "Accidental Hero," *Los Angeles Times,* May 10, 1993.
7. Larry Horton, "The Enduring Animal Issue," *Journal of the National Cancer Institute*, May 22, 1989, vol. 81, no. 10, p. 739.
8. "Animal Rules Uncage Scientists' Complaints," *Washington Post*, July 9, 1989.
9. David H. Hubel, quoted in John G. Hubbell, "The 'Animal Right's' War on Medicine," *Reader's Digest,* June 1990, p. 75.
10. Tom Regan, *The Philosophy of Animal Rights,* quoted in Fur Farm Animal Welfare Coalition, "Animal Rights . . . in the Words of Its Leaders," undated sheet, p. 3.
11. Janice S. Henke, quoted in Russ Carman, *The Illusions of Animal Rights* (Krause Publications: St. Iola, Wisconsin, 1990), pp. 147-148.
12. *Animal People,* December 1997, cited in Foundation for Biomedical Research, "Animal Rights Funding Continues to Rise," website: www.fbre-search.org.
13. Wesley V. Jamison and William M. Lunch, "Rights of Animals, Perceptions of Science, and Political Activism: Profile of American Animal Rights Activists," *Science, Technology, & Human Values*, Vol. 17, No. 4, Autumn 1992, p. 454.

14. Jamison and Lunch, p. 452.

15. Rod and Patti Strand, *The Hijacking of the Humane Movement* (Wilsonville, Oregon: Doral Publishing, Inc., 1993), p. 55.

16. Jamison and Lunch, p. 439.

17. Shelley L. Galvin and Harold A. Herzog, study cited in "The Watchdog," *Animal People*, April 1998, p. 13.

18. Geoffrey S. Becker, "Humane Treatment of Farm Animals: Overview and Selected Issues," Congressional Research Service, report dated May 1, 1992, p. 3.

19. Rod and Patti Strand.

CHAPTER I

Overview of the Movement

The animal rights movement can be traced as far back as the second half of the 19th century, when Western societies underwent significant change and people's relationship to nature was also transformed. In Great Britain and the United States, these changes prompted a small faction of individuals to challenge and break away from an animal welfare movement that had begun some 50 years earlier. As Larry Horton, a critic of the animal rights movement, says, "as much as current activists like to think that they are the vanguard of a new movement, suffused with new ethical insights, . . . the truth is that the current debate is a rehash of a very old dispute. . . ."[1]

The 19th-Century Humane Movement

Before 1800 in Great Britain, animal abuse was legally regarded as a property crime. Convictions for abuse were based on the concept of damage to another person's property. By the late 18th century, however, attention began to center on the cruelty inflicted on animals themselves. Due largely to concerns expressed in sermons, pamphlets, and articles of the time, Great Britain in 1822 passed the first law against cruelty to animals, the Martin's Act. Named after "Humanities Dick" Martin, M.P. for Galway (1754-1834), the act prohibited the mistreatment of horses, mules, cattle, and sheep.[2]

Two years later, a group of lawyers, abolitionists, and aristocrats met in London to form the first animal welfare group, the Society for the Prevention of Cruelty to Animals. An 1829 tract defined the SPCA's main concerns: "sheep driven to market in a cruel way, slaughterhouse conditions, cruel driving of oxen, horses, and donkeys, inhumane slaughter, calve-carting [using calves as beasts of burden], and bull-baiting" (setting dogs on a chained or confined bull for amusement).[3] Through a network of inspectors who examined the treatment of animals at markets, slaughterhouses, and in the streets, the SPCA helped secure the arrest and conviction of violators of the Martin's Act. In 1835, Princess Victoria (who in 1837 became queen) extended royal patronage to the SPCA, which in 1840 changed its name to the Royal Society for the Prevention of Cruelty to Animals.

In the United States, the American Society for the Prevention of Cruelty to Animals was founded in New York City in 1866 by humanitarian Henry Bergh. Just after its founding, it helped pass America's first anti-cruelty bill in the New York state legislature. The law stated, "every person who shall by his act or neglect maliciously kill, maim, wound, injure, torture, or cruelly beat any horse, mule, cow, cattle, sheep or other animal belonging to himself or another, shall upon conviction, be adjudged guilty of a misdemeanor."[4]

Like the RSPCA, the ASPCA used a team of field inspectors to monitor compliance with the law. By 1888, it had prosecuted 13,000 cases of alleged animal cruelty.[5] By 1869, humane societies had also formed in Boston, Philadelphia, and San Francisco. (See Chapter VIII and Appendix II for a discussion of the ASPCA's recent adoption of animal rights ideas.)

The British Antivivisection Movement

Several changes in the latter half of the 19th century helped create an ideological rift between the humane movement and a faction of persons opposed to using animals in biomedical research. Among these were the growing prominence of science, the increasing use of scientifically based technology, and a growing sense that life was becoming "impersonalized" and "detached" from nature.

Anthropologist Susan Sperling notes that the newly emerging field of research-based medicine, which used animals as experimental subjects, was seen by some as an example of "the increasing domination by science and medicine of the body and of nature . . . [of setting] the concerns of the body above those of the spirit and technological expertise above compassion:"[6]

Antivivisection in Victorian England was a movement addressing trends in society that are richly symbolized by the act of vivisecting an animal but that go far beyond this basic issue. . . . The underlying critique was of the perceived dominance of nature by impersonal and technologically oriented institutions. For the antivivisectionists, the animal experiment was the key symbol of the oppression of living beings. Antivivisection was a powerful movement because it drew on deeply felt anxieties that found their symbolic focus in vivisection.[7]

From its inception in the 1870s, the antivivisection movement was closely tied to both evangelicalism, which "preached the value of revelation and natural faith and emotion over theoretical logic,"[8] and to feminist thought, which drew parallels between scientists' experiments on animals and women's subjugation in patriarchal society—strains of thought that persist in the animal rights movement today. Like many of her contemporaries, the British antivivisectionist leader Frances Power Cobbe was a feminist and evangelical. As Sperling notes,

Cobbe's explicit feminism was important in linking feminist values and

2

activism to the antivivisection movement. The remodeled and idealized animal of the Victorian period represented the emotional and spiritual values of the heart and of natural instinct as opposed to the ruthless rationalism of science and logic. As women were also symbolically linked to these values, it was felt by many that the two formed an appropriate partnership for returning society to an alignment with natural laws.[9]

By the mid-1870s in Great Britain, sharp ideological differences had emerged between generally pro-science humane societies and newly formed antivivisection groups such as the British Anti-Vivisection Society and Victoria Street Society. Following a series of highly publicized cases of alleged abuse of laboratory animals, a royal commission was formed to "establish the extent of experimentation on living animals . . . the amount of cruelty that might be taking place . . . and the best means of preventing such cruelty."[10]

In 1876, the Cruelty to Animals Act was passed, requiring all persons experimenting on living vertebrates to be licensed. Laboratories were also subject to investigation without notice, and all experiments had to have government approval in advance. "Moreover, the investigator was required to adhere strictly to the protocol, irrespective of the finding of interesting or unexpected results, which, as all investigators recognize, frequently changes the course of true research."[11]

The Antivivisection Movement in the U.S.

In the United States, the first major clash between antivivisectionists and supporters of animal research occurred between 1896 and 1900 when the Washington Humane Society lobbied Congress to pass the Gallinger-D.C. bill, an effort to severely restrict animal research in the District of Columbia. Physicians affiliated with the American Medical Association

> organized a massive letter-writing campaign to enlist the aid of medical school faculty, state and county medical society officers, practicing physicians, and others in educating the public and elected officials regarding [the importance of animal research]. . . . Practicing physicians across the country responded and wrote to newspapers, circulated petitions, and enlisted their patients' support. These actions were instrumental in securing Senate opposition to the bill.[12]

While the bill failed, some antivivisectionists in the years immediately following broke into research laboratories, destroying property and threatening biomedical researchers—actions remarkably similar to those carried out by fringe elements of the animal rights movement today.

Antivivisectionist activity peaked between 1908 to 1922. Most antivivisectionists concentrated their efforts at the state level, spearheading bills to restrict animal research in California, Colorado, Maryland, Massachusetts, Minnesota, New York, and Pennsylvania. In 1920, a statewide referendum to ban animal research in California was defeated by a two-to-one margin after physicians, scientists, and concerned citizens mounted a massive campaign.

In 1908, the American Medical Association issued guidelines to allay the public's fear of possible animal abuse in laboratories. These read in part:

• "Vagrant dogs and cats brought to this Laboratory and purchased here shall be held at least as long as at the city pound and shall be returned to their owners if claimed and identified."

• "Animals in the Laboratory shall receive every consideration for their bodily comfort; they shall be kindly treated, properly fed, and their surroundings shall be kept in the best possible sanitary condition."

• "In any operation likely to cause greater discomfort than that attending anesthetization, the animal shall first be rendered incapable of perceiving pain and shall be maintained in that condition until the operation is ended."[13]

Between 1929 and 1945, antivivisectionists continued to challenge animal research, but were unable to achieve any significant legislative victories. From 1960 to 1965, however, increases in federal funding for biomedical research resulted in a rapid expansion of animal research and an increase in the number of animals used. According to the American Medical Association,

> In direct response to this expansion, the animal welfare movement also grew in size and strength and intensified its efforts to win congressional approval of animal welfare legislation. In the past, demands for outright . . . abandonment of animal research had not won much legislative or public support. Consequently, antivivisectionists shifted their strategy to . . . winning public support of legislation that restricted and regulated animal research. Among the active organizations that helped draft these bills were the Humane Society of the United States, the Society for Animal Protective Legislation, and the Catholic Society for Animal Welfare.[14]

In February 1966, a pictorial essay in *Life* entitled "Concentration Camps for Dogs" convinced many members of Congress and the public that animal cruelty and the theft of pets were common among animal dealers who sold dogs to research laboratories. Lobbying by animal welfare organizations led to the passage of the Laboratory Animal Welfare Act, which regulates the sale and transport of animals by dealers and requires research laboratories, circuses, and some pet stores to be licensed and inspected by the U.S. Department of Agriculture.

Reinvigorating the Antivivisection Movement

The American antivivisection movement has been reinvigorated during the last 30 years as a result of at least three events:

• In the late 1960s, the International Fund for Animal Welfare, Greenpeace, the Fund for Animals, and several smaller organizations began a campaign to end the Canadian harp seal hunt, which for centuries had been conducted each spring in the Gulf of St. Lawrence and off the coast of northeastern Newfoundland. Through the distribution of films, photographs, and other materials alleging that killing baby harp seals was cruel, unnecessary, and morally wrong, many Americans, Canadians, and Europeans were convinced that the hunt should be ended. About the same time, activists launched a similar (and on-going) campaign to "Save the Whales." (See Chapter VII for a discussion of these campaigns.)

• In 1975, Australian author Peter Singer published a book entitled *Animal Liberation: A New Ethics for Our Treatment of Animals* that restated and helped to repopularize antivivisectionist ideas.[15] Singer's claim that biomedical researchers and farmers routinely abused animals helped to mobilize a growing network of activists opposed to animal research and the raising of animals for food. "In the U.S., some activists were veterans of the civil rights, women's rights and antiwar movements of the 1960s and 1970s. They brought to the cause of animal rights the same commitment, zeal, and tactics that they employed in support of those movements."[16] Alex Pacheco, chairman and co-founder of People for the Ethical Treatment of Animals, says that "I read one chapter [of *Animal Liberation*] and it gave me the nuts and bolts of how to put your beliefs into action. It connected my guts with my brain."[17]

• In 1981, Pacheco himself accused a biomedical researcher in Silver Spring, Maryland, of abusing chimpanzees. In a series of widely read news accounts that came to be known as the "Silver Spring Monkeys Case," leaders of the burgeoning animal rights movement sought to introduce Americans to the notion of animal rights, bring supporters into the movement, and legitimize animal rights as an area of public policy concern. (See Chapter VII for a discussion of the Silver Spring Monkeys Case.)

In addition to these events, certain facets of late-20th century American life—in particular increasing urbanization—are also likely reasons for the resurgence of the antivivisection movement. Surveys show that the typical animal rights activist is a young, white, middle-class, college-educated urban woman who owns at least one pet but who has little or no experience raising farm animals or dealing with wildlife. (See Appendix XIX for the results of one such survey.) For many activists, the ownership of tamed animals, a relatively comfortable urban lifestyle, and a relative unfamiliarity with rural life may make an anthropomorphic view of animals seem plausible while the reality of nature as "red in tooth and claw" can be easily discounted.[18] Activist Mariela Gordon says, "I understand, you know, we're basically an urban movement anyway. The people in the country think we're a bunch of nuts. . . . It's an urban kind of middle-class movement. I don't like to generalize but it's basically kind of young people, who really don't know a lot about actually dealing with animals. They just deal with them on a philosophical level. . . ."[19]

Another factor that has likely helped reinvigorate the antivivisection movement is the recent emergence of a cadre of scientists, academics, and journalists who warn that new technologies and the "overuse" of natural resources present a growing threat to humans, animals, and the environment. As Sperling notes,

> the impact of technology is all around us . . . as it was increasingly in the Victorian era. Anxiety about the incursion of human industry into the natural environment is a feature of both periods. . . . A high degree of concern about pollution and technological manipulation of the environment and living organisms is expressed by most adherents of the modern animal rights movement. Many increasingly view our species as subject to materialistic technological forces antithetical to nature. . . . Animal rights has emerged in recent years as a response to these anxieties about the human relationship to nature much as occurred in theVictorian era.[20]

Activist Michael Fox believes that "the natural world will become transformed into a toxic bioindustrial wasteland, run by a global technocracy caught in the down-spiral of human need and greed and the rising costs of adapting to an increasingly uninhabitable planet."[21] Similarly, animal rights author Tom Regan says that

> the major cause of environmental degradation, including the greenhouse effect, water pollution and the loss both of arable land and top soil . . . can be traced to the exploitation of animals. This same pattern exists throughout the broad range of environmental problems, from acid rain and ocean dumping of toxic wastes, to air pollution and the destruction of natural habitat. In all these cases, to act to protect the affected animals (who are, after all, the first to suffer and die from these environmental ills), is to act to protect the earth.[22]

Activist L. J. Barillaro believes that

> to destroy the environment is wrong, and we are paying the price in increasing violent crime, immorality and diseases such as cancer, heart disease, multiple sclerosis, muscular dystrophy, diabetes, AIDS, leukemia, lupus, etc., etc. Then we think we can solve those problems by further destruction of animals in experiments. . . . Respect for animals and the environment is the only hope for a bright future for the human race.[23]

Restoring "Paradesia"

Not surprisingly, these views are often accompanied by a condemnation of modern man and society. Dave Foreman, co-founder and former leader of the environmental and animal rights group Earth First!, says that "we're not the brain, we are a cancer on nature."[24] Ingrid Newkirk, president of People for the Ethical Treatment of Animals, believes that "mankind is the biggest blight on the face of the Earth. We should just stop our pushing and prodding, and let nature take care of itself."[25]

The theme of "leaving nature alone" appears repeatedly throughout animal rights literature, along with the warning that we must live more "in harmony" with nature or face dire consequences. Sperling notes that

> Both [Victorian] antivivisection and animal rights activists have been concerned with the revitalization of societies that they have perceived as morally diseased and dangerous . . . and have suggested redemption through a realignment of the entire relationship between our species and the world of nature. . . . In both periods, adherents have referred to an earlier time when humans lived in a state of nature, without disease or strife, a common theme of millennium sects throughout European history. This state of nature will be restored with the abolition of animal abuse and the achievement of animal rights.[26]

Newkirk says that "as I get older, I seem to become more a Luddite. . . . And now I think that Ned Ludd had the right idea, and we should have stopped all the machinery way back when, and learned to live simple lives. It's very hard to stop the process now. I think that we're not only digging our own graves in our conduct, but that we could make a more peaceful society for the whole earth if we did live simply. . . ."[27] Tom Regan believes that "those who respect the rights of animals are embarked on a journey back to Eden—a journey back to a proper love for God's creation."[28] Michael Fox contends that "human salvation is wholly dependent upon the liberation of nature from our selfish treatment. Human liberation will begin when we understand that our evolution and fulfillment are contingent on the recognition of animal rights. The dawning of a New Eden is to come. . . . [Animal rights entails] the restoration, dressing, and keeping of the Garden of Eden: Paradesia."[29] Newkirk similarly envisions "a world where the lion will lie down with the lamb, where man will live in harmony with nature, where when two animals fight, human beings will intervene."[30]

Sperling and others note that the animal rights movement in many ways resembles a charismatic cult, which often "[appeals] to the disenfranchised and alienated during periods of social upheaval. . . . It appears that today many middle-class people in American society feel as alienated and removed from power over their lives as have tribal peoples facing the incursions of technological cultures that destroyed their traditional ways of life."[31]

CHAPTER I

"Absolutist, Impossibilist, Bizarre"

The thesis that animals have rights is probably most fully explored by Peter Singer, whose *Animal Liberation*[32] has sold over 300,000 copies and helped bring thousands of supporters into the movement.[33] Singer reformulates the utilitarian principle that all human action should help bring about the greatest happiness for the greatest number (or conversely, the least suffering for the fewest number). He argues that since animals (or at least vertebrates) can also feel pleasure and pain, their "interests," such as their desire to avoid pain, must "be counted equally with the suffering . . . of any other being," including man.[34]

Singer does not argue, as traditional animal welfare advocates have, that animals' ability to feel pain makes them *morally considerable* beings, i.e., that humans should try to minimize their suffering whenever possible. Rather, he believes that animals' capacity to suffer makes them *morally equal* to humans in terms of rights possessed: "the capacity for suffering [is a] vital characteristic that gives a being the right to equal consideration."[35]

As many critics have noted, this view presents many problems—even for animal rights adherents. One PETA spokesman is a diabetic who uses insulin, a treatment developed through animal research and for decades available only from the pancreas glands of slaughtered animals. (Insulin derived from humans recently became available.)[36] Countless other activists also benefit from medical treatments and cures derived largely or in part through animal research. And despite advocates' claim that vegetarianism saves animals' lives, many wild animals are killed in the process of creating farmland and growing and harvesting vegetables, fruits, and grains. Billions if not trillions of insects are killed annually in the U.S. to produce "vegetarian" foods.

One activist seems to understand the implications of Singer's thesis, saying that animal rights requires "[pulling] down the big cities and [returning] to small communities, to make room for the animals to roam free. . ."[37] But in fact, any type of human subsistence—even the simplest agrarian or gathering society—would result in at least some animal deaths. Singer himself acknowledges that "we need to grow crops of vegetables and grain to feed ourselves [and] these crops may be threatened by rabbits, mice, and other 'pests.'"[38] While this is certainly true, a prior problem is that bringing land under cultivation or building "small communities" requires clearing land of brush, trees, and other wildlife habitat. Even a tribe of nomadic vegetarians subsisting on berries, nuts, and other wild foods would deprive *some* animals of sustenance, and the loss of these animals would affect other species higher in the food chain.[39]

Ecologist Walter E. Howard suggests that the appeal of animal rights is partly due to "a steadily growing percentage of the public [that] no longer understands the basic biological principles responsible for the so-called balance of nature."[40] Critic Robert James Bidinotto succinctly notes that animal rights actually means that *"only* animals have rights: since nature consists entirely of animals, their food, and their habitats, to recognize 'animal rights' man must logically cede to them the entire planet."[41] Indeed, a recent book entitled *A Declaration of War: Killing People to Save Animals and the Environment* argues unabashedly that the only hope for animals is the extinction of the human race.[42] Such implications have prompted journalist Polly Toynbee to call animal rights "probably the most revolutionary movement the world has ever known—absolutist, impossibilist, bizarre."[43]

Notes

1. Larry Horton, "The Enduring Animal Issue," *Journal of the National Cancer Institute*, Vol. 81, No. 10, May 22, 1989, p. 736.

2. Susan Sperling, *Animal Liberators: Research and Morality* (Berkeley: University of California Press, 1988), pp. 31-32.

3. Sperling, p. 33.

4. S. Coleman, *Humane Society Leaders in America*, cited in Sperling, p. 34.

5. American Society for the Prevention of Cruelty to Animals, "Some Milestones: Early Years to the Present," undated historical overview of ASPCA activities.

6. Sperling, pp. 51, 53.

7. *Ibid.*, p. 47.

8. *Ibid.*, p. 45.

9. *Ibid.*, p. 44.

10. David C. Sabiston, Jr., "The Antivivisection Movement: A Threat to Medical Research and Future Progress," *North Carolina Medical Journal*, Vol. 48, No. 12, December 1987, p. 653.

11. Sabiston, p. 653.

12. Steven J. Smith, R. Mark Evans, Micaela Sullivan-Fowler, William R. Hendee, "Use of Animals in Biomedical Research," *Arch Intern Med*, Vol. 148, August 1988, p. 1850.

13. American Medical Association, "Guidelines for Laboratory Animal Care, 1908," cited in Smith *et al.*, p. 1851.

14. *Ibid.*

15. Peter Singer, *Animal Liberation: A New Ethics for Our Treatment of Animals* (New York: Avon Books, 1977).

16. American Medical Association, "Use of Animals in Biomedical Research: the Challenge and Response," white paper, 1992, p. 7.

17. John Farley, "He Wrote the Bible on Animal Rights," *USA Today*, March 7, 1990, p. 7D.

18. Alfred Lord Tennyson, quoted in Sperling, p. 71.

19. Mariela Gordon, quoted in Sperling, p. 117.

20. Sperling, p. 200.

CHAPTER I

21. Michael W. Fox, *Inhumane Society: The American Way of Exploiting Animals* (New York: St. Martin's Press, 1990), p. xvii.

22. Tom Regan, "The Philosophy of Animal Rights," undated booklet published by Culture & Animals Foundation.

23. L. J. Barillaro, member of People for Reason in Science and Medicine, "Humans vs. their Animal Instinct," *Wall Street Journal*, Aug. 6, 1990, p. A13.

24. Dave Foreman, quoted in "Only Man's Presence Can Save Nature," *Harper's*, April 1990, p. 48.

25. Ingrid Newkirk, quoted in Katie McCabe, "Beyond Cruelty," *Washingtonian*, February 1990, p. 191.

26. Sperling, pp. 19, 155.

27. Ingrid Newkirk, speech at Loyola University, Oct. 24, 1988.

28. Regan.

29. Michael W. Fox, *Returning to Eden* (New York: Viking Press 1980), p. xiv., and Fox, *Inhumane Society*, p. 103.

30. Ingrid Newkirk, quoted in McCabe, p. 190.

31. Sperling, pp. 194-195.

32. Singer, *op. cit.*

33. Sperling notes that many of the activists she interviewed "underwent a personal and revelatory moment in their sudden apprehension of the concept of speciesism," a key notion in *Animal Liberation*. Sperling, p. 198.

34. Singer, pp. 8-9.

35. *Ibid.*, p. 8.

36. Mary Beth Sweetland, PETA spokesman, cited in Putting People First, facsimile transmission dated November 10, 1992.

37. *Manchester Guardian,* June 10, 1985, cited in National Trappers Association, p. 38.

38. Singer, p. 246.

39. Singer seems aware of this problem when he says early in *Animal Liberation* that we have generally "ignored the interests of wild animals as we extend our empire of concrete and pollution over the surface of the globe;" but in a later section intended to address "the various arguments and excuses that are still used in defense of animal slavery," this issue, interestingly, is nowhere addressed. Singer, "Speciesism Today . . . defenses, rationalizations, and objections to Animal Liberation" (Chapter 6), *ibid.*, pp. 23, 223.

40. Walter E. Howard, *Animal Rights vs. Nature* (Walter E. Howard: Davis, California: 1990), p. 8.

41. Robert James Bidinotto, "Environmentalism: Freedom's Foe for the '90s," *Freeman*, November 1990, p. 412; emphasis in original.

42. "Screaming Wolf" (pseudonym), *A Declaration of War: Killing People to Save Animals and the Environment* (Patrick Henry Press, 1991).

43. Polly Toynbee, quoted in National Trappers Association, p. 38.

CHAPTER II

Research Animals

Animals have been used in experiments for more than 2,000 years. In the third century B.C., the Greek philosopher Erisistratus studied the bodily functions of animals. Aristotle is believed to have performed vivisection and, five centuries after Erisistratus, the Roman physician Galen used apes and pigs to prove that veins, not air, carry blood.[1] In 1622, the British physician William Harvey demonstrated the circulation of blood in animals. Two hundred years later, the French physiologist Magendie discovered the localization of function in the nervous system.[2] In 1846, animal experiments documented the effects of anesthesia, and in 1878, clarified the relationship between bacteria and disease.[3]

Animal rights leaders often claim that animal research is fundamentally wrong. Priscilla Feral, president of Friends of Animals, says that "animal experimentation is just plain wrong. Human beings have no right to the knowledge gained from experimentation on animals. . . ."[4] Ingrid Newkirk, president of People for the Ethical Treatment of Animals, calls animal research "fascism" and "supremacism."[5]

Animal rights groups have sought to bring about the demise of animal research by imposing increasingly burdensome regulation. They usually claim that this is needed to ensure the humane treatment of animals. But if it is morally wrong to use animals in experiments, the question of how humanely they are treated is irrelevant. As researcher David H. Hubel says, "Their tactics are clear. Work to increase the costs of research, and stop its progress with red tape and lawsuits."[6]

Building Opposition to Animal Research

Insofar as animal rights groups have been unable to convince the public that animal research is inherently wrong, they have sought to create opposition by saying that its results are unreliable, misleading, or useless. However, as critic Larry Horton notes,

> antivivisection has always rested on two fundamentally distinct arguments: (a) a moral argument that concludes that research with animals is morally wrong no matter how beneficial the results and (b) a utilitarian argument that animal experimentation ought not to be done because it is bad science, its results worthless. These two arguments . . . do not logically fit well together. Adopting the moral argument makes the utilitarian argument irrelevant; conversely, using the utilitarian argument implies that vivisection

11

could be accepted if its efficacy could be demonstrated, thus contravening the moral argument.[7]

These arguments are often mingled with other claims and accusations intended to discredit animal research and biomedical researchers. Activist Michael Fox says that

> the validity of research conclusions are [*sic*] dubious at best and probably of little relevance to the real-life conditions that actually cause health and disease. . . . Most research is . . . supported ideologically by those who lack vision or conscience, or who are greedy for acclaim or profit. . . . From all indices of well-being, modern medicine is not enhancing the quality of human life. The deep causes of sickness, greed, anguish, insecurity, and their consequences of violence, oppression, unethical domination of animals and nature, violation of human and animal rights, and the destruction and pollution of the planet are the diseases of civilization. . . .[8]

Because of the vagueness of many of these claims, this chapter examines only those arguments concerning the alleged immorality and uselessness of animal research.

Research Benefits to Humans

In claiming that animal research yields unreliable results, activists often point to the drug thalidomide. In the 1950s, the West German pharmaceutical company Chemie Grunenthal claimed that this "wonder drug" could cure impotence and insomnia, remove acne, and help children teethe. Several drug companies in other countries also manufactured and marketed thalidomide under license.

In the early 1960s, thalidomide gained worldwide attention when some women using the drug gave birth to severely deformed babies. Activists say that although thalidomide had been tested on animals, this did not prevent "thalidomide babies" and in fact gave parents a false sense of security.

However, thalidomide had not been tested on pregnant animals to determine its possible effects on fetuses. After the appearance of deformed babies, researchers found that thalidomide did indeed cause similar defects in newborn animals, including rabbits and several types of monkeys. Parents used the results of those tests in their lawsuit against Chemie Grunenthal. Researchers say the thalidomide incident shows the importance of thorough animal testing.[9]

The alleged uselessness of animal research is discredited by the crucial role it has played in developing treatments or cures for many infectious diseases and chronic conditions, including AIDS, Alzheimer's, anthrax, beriberi, cancer, cholera, coronary heart disease, diabetes, diphtheria, histamine shock, influenza, leprosy, Lyme disease, measles, pellagra, poliomyelitis, rabies, rheumatoid arthritis, rickets, rubella, smallpox, tetanus, yellow fever, and whooping cough.[10] Animal research has also led to numerous medical breakthroughs, including:

- Improved understanding of infection control and pain relief and the management of heart failure (pre-1900s).
- Electrocardiography (for diagnosing heart disease) and cardiac catherization (early 1900s).
- Intravenous feeding (1920s).
- The development of anticoagulants (to prevent blood clotting), modern anesthesia, and neuromuscular blocking agents (1930s).
- The therapeutic use of antibiotics such as penicillin, aureomycin, and streptomycin (1940s).
- The development of cancer chemotherapy, open heart surgery, and cardiac pacemakers (1950s).
- Corneal transplantation and coronary bypass surgery, the therapeutic use of cortisone, and the development of radioimmunoassay for the measurement of minute quantities of antibodies, hormones, and other substances (1960s).
- The modern treatment of coronary insufficiency, heart transplantation, and the development of non-addictive pain killers (1970s).
- The use of cyclosporine to aid in organ transplants, artificial heart transplantation, the identification of psychophysiological factors in depression, anxiety, and phobias, the development of monoclonal antibodies for treating diseases, and the discovery of HIV as a probable causative agent of AIDS (1980s).
- Pancreas and liver transplantation, thrombolytic therapy for acute myocardial infarction (inadequate blood flow), and human gene therapy (1990s).[11]

In addition, psychological and behavioral research involving animals has led to the rehabilitation of patients with neuromuscular disorders, behavior therapy for eating disorders, the treatment of enuresis (bed-wetting), and increased understanding of deficits in memory that occur with aging.[12] Many biofeedback techniques were developed through animal research, allowing patients to reduce their risk of heart attack by controlling their blood pressure, to assist paralyzed persons in sitting up, and to relieve the discomfort of migraine headaches, insomnia, and lower back pain."[13]

The life span of the average American has increased roughly 30 years since the turn of the century, and much of this increase is attributable to medical advances gained through animal research.[14] Ironically, many critics note that because of animal research, those protesting against it will live to protest longer.

13

CHAPTER II

Research Benefits to Animals

Interestingly, the benefits to animals of animal research are rarely, if ever, noted by activists. Yet animal research has revolutionized veterinary medicine, leading to such advances as:

• Over 80 medicines originally developed for humans that are now used to treat pets, farm animals and wildlife, including anesthetics, tranquilizers, and pain killers.

• Ultrasound, magnetic resonance imaging, and CAT scans to remove brain tumors and correct birth defects in animals.

• Cataract removal, hearing aids, and pacemakers for animals.

• Immunization against distemper, rabies, parvo virus, infectious hepatitis, anthrax, and tetanus.

• Treatment for parasites.

• Orthopedic surgery for horses.

• Surgery to correct hip dysplasia in dogs.

• Experimental radiation techniques and immunotherapy for cancer in dogs.

• Identification and prevention of brucellosis and tuberculosis in cattle.

• Treatment of feline leukemia.

• Improved nutrition for pets and farm animals.[15]

Pathologist Robert W. Leader notes that "millions of animals have . . . benefited from research developments that use splints, antibiotics, vaccines, immunology, surgical advances, insulin, and other therapies, developed by the use of experimental animals. These benefits are realized not only by the present population but for all future generations of human beings and animals."[16] Richard L. Fink, former president of the American Veterinary Medical Association, observes that "the difference between animal care [fifty years ago] and now is like night and day. Sick animals put to sleep years ago aren't being euthanized today because of our diagnostic capabilities, the way we can handle diseases and the surgical techniques. It is an extreme joy going to work these days."[17]

In addition, "imprinting"—the tendency of animals to identify with the first species they encounter—has been used to train captive-bred animals to relate to members of their own species. This has helped the endangered California condor to survive and propagate in the wild. Animal research is also helping to save the endangered musk ox in Alaska. And research done on the sexual behavior of other endangered animals has led to their successful reproduction in captivity, a first step in restoring their numbers in the wild.[18]

Pain in Animal Research

Animal rights groups often say that animal research causes pain. The Physicians Committee for Responsible Medicine speaks of "the millions of helpless creatures who are made to suffer terribly—and we believe, needlessly—in animal experiments day after day."[19] Yet the most comprehensive study of pain in animal research, conducted by the U.S. Department of Agriculture in 1984, found that 61 percent of research animals are not subjected to painful procedures. Another 31 percent receive anesthesia or pain-killers while the remaining 8 percent do experience some pain, usually because improved understanding and treatment of pain, including chronic pain, is the purpose of the experiment.[20]

The federal Animal Welfare Act, which regulates animal research, requires that a veterinarian be consulted in planning any experiment where an animal might experience pain. Anesthesia, tranquilizers, and analgesics must be used except when they would compromise the results of the study. While the AWA does not cover rats, mice, and birds bred specifically for research, all biomedical research facilities that receive funding from the National Institutes of Health and all that are certified by the Association for Assessment and Accreditation of Laboratory Animal Care International must adhere to humane standards of care outlined in the National Research Council's "Guide for the Care and Use of Laboratory Animals," which includes these three species.

The American Medical Association notes that

> chronic pain is a challenging health problem that costs the United States about $50 billion a year in direct medical expenses, lost productivity, and income. . . . More than 300,000 Americans suffer severe traumatic injuries each year from car accidents and other causes that leave them permanently disabled. If experiments seeking a better understanding of these injuries and ways to treat them are banned . . . those and future victims will have to live without hope of improvement in their condition. . . .[21]

Critics contend that ending animal research because it sometimes causes pain would be morally wrong to those who benefit from such research. Laurence McCullough of Georgetown University's Kennedy Center for Bioethics asks, "Are you ready to say to the thousands of human beings in this country who have heart attacks every year that we're more obligated not to use those dogs than we are to you and everybody else to try to reduce the long-term consequences of heart attack?"[22] The American Medical Association says that "depriving humans (and animals) of advances in medicine that result from research with animals is inhumane and fundamentally unethical. [Depriving] patients with dementia, stroke, disabling injuries, heart disease, and cancer . . . of hope and relief by eliminating animal research is an immoral and unconscionable act."[23]

Alleged Alternatives to Animal Research

Animal rights groups often say that there are alternatives to animal research that make experiments on animals unnecessary. These include the study of organ cultures (used in vaccine production and cancer and virus research), cell cultures (to test substance toxicity), bacterial cultures (to study birth defects, heart disease, and aging), chemical tests (to screen cosmetics and household products for safety), and computer simulations (to predict the likely effects of a substance or treatment on a living organism). PETA president Ingrid Newkirk says that in the search for a polio vaccine, "we were all cheated" because researchers killed over one million rhesus monkeys (most sources put the figure at 100,000) when cell cultures could have been used to develop a vaccine.[24]

Nearly all biomedical researchers, however, see the use of these techniques as adjuncts rather than alternatives to animal research. Neurosurgeon Robert J. White asks, "How can researchers using cell cultures, which do not have bones, develop a treatment for arthritis or other bone diseases? How can cell cultures help us to perfect the surgical techniques used in organ transplantation?"[25] The American Medical Association notes that cell cultures "do not act or react the same as cells in an intact system." Moreover,

> the validity of any [computer simulation] depends on how closely it resembles the original in every respect. Much about the body and the various biological systems of humans and animals is not known. . . . Therefore, they cannot be programmed into any model. Until full knowledge of a particular biological system is developed, no model can be constructed that will in every case predict or accurately represent the reaction of the system to a given stimulus.[26]

Regulatory and Other Costs
In 1997, 45 bills that would negatively affect animal research were introduced at the state level and another four at the federal level. In the states, animal rights groups have most often spearheaded legislation to prohibit the use of unwanted shelter animals in research. In 1986, Massachusetts became the first state to adopt such a law after the New England Anti-Vivisection Society launched an anti-"pound seizure" campaign. Since then, 13 states—Connecticut, Delaware, Hawaii, Maine, Maryland, Massachusetts, New Hampshire, New Jersey, New York, Pennsylvania, Rhode Island, Vermont, and West Virginia—have enacted similar legislation.[27] At the federal level, the 1998 Pet Safety and Protection Act (H.R. 594), sponsored by Charles Canady (R-FL), would enact a nationwide ban on the use of unwanted shelter animals in research. It attracted 65 co-sponsors as of late 1998.

Such bans increase the cost of biomedical research by requiring dogs and cats to be specially bred for research or transported from other states. In Massachusetts, however, an addendum prohibits the transport of dogs and cats from other states for research, so medical schools and other facilities must breed a separate population of animals at significant cost while thousands of unclaimed animals are killed at shelters.[28] Since most shelter and research animals are eventually euthanized, such laws result in more animal deaths.

Probably the most significant regulations hindering biomedical research are 1985 amendments to the federal Animal Welfare Act (AWA). Enacted in 1966 and revised in 1970 and 1975, the AWA sets standards for the housing, feeding, watering, sanitation, ventilation, anesthetizing, and provision of veterinary and postoperative care for animals housed by universities, medical schools, hospitals, and research centers. The U.S. Department of Agriculture enforces the act through periodic inspections. In addition, the Association for Assessment and Accreditation of Laboratory Animal Care International, a Rockville, Maryland-based organization, regularly inspects 600 member animal laboratories to ensure compliance with its own guidelines. Other federal legislation, including the 1985 Health Research Extension Act, requires the National Institutes of Health to create guidelines for laboratory animal use and to develop a research plan for alternatives to animal testing at all federally funded research facilities. These read in part:

> [Vertebrate animals] selected for a procedure should be of an appropriate species and quality and the minimum number required to obtain valid results. . . . Procedures with animals that may cause more than momentary or slight pain or distress should be performed with appropriate sedation, analgesia, or anesthesia. Surgical or other painful procedures should not be performed on unanesthetized animals paralyzed by chemical agents.[29]

In addition, the Health Research Extension Act requires that animal-care committees, which monitor research protocols and ensure that all experiments comply with federal guidelines, include at least one veterinarian, one scientist, one non-scientist, and one individual not affiliated with the research institution. Other federal regulations, including the Good Laboratory Practices Regulations and the Public Health Services Animal Welfare Policy, also set standards for veterinary care and housing of research animals.

Two amendments to the 1985 AWA—one requiring dogs to be exercised and socialized and another requiring researchers to provide an environment that promotes the "psychological well-being" of primates—account for much of its regulatory cost. Interestingly, no hearings were held in either the House or Senate on these provisions; they were added to the omnibus Farm Bill in December 1985 by then-Senate Majority Leader Robert J. Dole (R-KS), a Watergate neighbor of Animal Welfare Institute president Christine Stevens. The amendments require that:

- Dogs be housed "in cages four times as large as the current requirements."
- Animals "immobilized in a chair" have "an hour of exercise both

before and after the immobilization."

• Primates be released for at least four hours a week for "exercise and social interaction."

• Primates living in "solo housing" have "positive physical contact or other interaction with their keeper or other familiar and knowledgeable person" for at least an hour a day.

• Primates in separate housing be able to "see and hear other members of the same species."

• Primates have a "physical environment . . . enriched by . . . means of expressing species-typical behavior," such as perches, swings, mirrors, and "other cage complexities;" manipulatable objects; "foraging or task-oriented feeding methods;" and a "method of feeding" that varies daily in order to promote . . . psychological well-being."[30]

The U.S. Department of Agriculture estimated that these and other revisions, which comprise 133 triple-columned pages of the *Federal Register,* would cost laboratories, zoos, animal dealers, and auction operators over $1 billion in 1990. The National Association for Biomedical Research estimated the cost at as much as $2 billion[31]—nearly 15 percent of the $14-billion budget for biomedical research that year and more than the entire 1989 budget for research on AIDS, Alzheimer's, and heart disease combined.[32] Many critics doubt that these changes have done much if anything to improve animal well-being.

In addition to legislative initiatives, animal rights groups have used litigation to delay and increase the cost of animal research:

• In 1988, People for the Ethical Treatment of Animals filed a lawsuit to stop federally funded research at 17 San Francisco Bay-area research laboratories, claiming that animal research was having adverse impacts "on air quality, traffic congestion, land use, noise, waste disposal, [etc.]," which violated national environmental laws.[33] The suit was dismissed for lack of legal standing.

• In 1992, the Animal Legal Defense Fund won a joint federal lawsuit to force the U.S. Department of Agriculture to include mice, rats, and birds under provisions of the Animal Welfare Act.[34] However, the case was later overturned, also for lack of standing.

• On behalf of several animal rights groups, the Animal Legal Defense Fund also sought unsuccessfully to limit AIDS-related animal research by petitioning the U.S. Department of the Interior to list chimpanzees as an endangered species, thus prohibiting their use.[35]

• When Stanford University recently tried to build a state-of-the-art animal research facility and new biology building, a coalition of animal rights groups lead by the radicalized Palo Alto Humane Society delayed the effort for over a year through county building permit laws, causing the university to pay an additional $3 million in project expenses.[36] Other animal rights groups have used similar laws to delay construction of research facilities at the University of Georgia, the University of California at Berkeley, and in Boston.

In addition, activists have staged hundreds of demonstrations at bio-medical research facilities around the country, increasing security costs and intimidating biomedical researchers. During the 1998 World Week for Animals in Laboratories, 100 activists descended on the Yerkes Primate Research Center at Emory University (Georgia) and blocked traffic. Seven demonstrators were arrested. During the 1997 Week, as many as 65 activists were arrested in violent confrontations with police.

Critic Larry Horton notes that animal rights activism "is having an impact *now* at a variety of levels of government. . . . Very real burdens are being placed on research, and many of them in incremental and almost invisible ways, so that it is difficult to attract public or government attention to the cumulative effects."[37] James Wyngaarden, former director of the National Institutes of Health, notes that the cost of regulation is ultimately "levied against those who wait for better treatments or preventive measures for disease and disability—whose very lives may be at stake."[38] Former Congressman Vin Weber says that "we're talking about cures for cancer, AIDS and heart disease that are being delayed because the money that should be spent on them is being spent on complying with the animal welfare regulations. . . ."[39]

Countervailing Trends

Larry Horton notes that for antivivisectionists, ending animal research "is above all a moral issue—the rationalizations about bad science and unnecessary research notwithstanding. . . . An antivivisectionist program will continue to be pushed by all available means. . . . Most sophisticated activists are quite satisfied to take one step at a time while keeping their ultimate objective firmly in mind."[40]

But the history of the antivivisection movement shows that physicians, animal researchers, and concerned citizens have effectively defeated anti-vivisectionists in the past. The following trends are noteworthy:

• Recent public opinion polls show that most Americans believe that animal research is necessary for progress in medicine. In one recent poll, Americans for Medical Progress, an Arlington, Virginia-based organization, found that when both sides of the animal research issue are presented, two-thirds of women and an even greater share of men support animal research.[41]

• When the public is informed about the cost of anti-"pound seizure" laws, they have through public referenda supported the use of shelter animals for research. Voters in Sierra Vista, Arizona, and Hillsborough County, Florida, recently supported the use of shelter animals for research by margins of two-to-one.[42]

• Since the early 1980s, the Washington, D.C.-based Foundation for Biomedical Research has provided the public with information about the benefits of animal research and "the commitment of researchers to humane and appropriate animal use."[43]

• Since 1990, Americans for Medical Progress has educated the public, including students and government officials, about the importance of animal research to human health.

Moreover, in the last two years, an unusual coalition of mainstream organizations and radical AIDS activist groups has emerged in support of animal research. Their basic message: there will be no cure for AIDS without animal research. In December 1996, some 25 patients who have survived serious illnesses demonstrated outside PETA's annual Animals' Ball and Humanitarian Awards gala, held at Paramount Studios in Los Angeles. Protestors, who carried signs praising animal research and urging celebrities not to attend, included members of Americans for Medical Progress, the Los Angeles chapter of ACT-UP (a national activist group that uses "street theater" tactics to advocate more government funding of AIDS research), and incurably ill For Animal Research (iiFAR), a Lansing, Michigan-based group promoting animal research.

During the 1996 Animal Awareness Week in Washington, D.C., which brought together animal rights groups from around the world, the Foundation for Biomedical Research held press conferences and distributed stacks of materials to reporters that challenged the allegations of animal rights groups. Hecklers from ACT-UP Washington, D.C. also followed PETA to its press conferences, demonstrations, and celebrity galas.

AMP recently launched a project called the Hollywood Information Project to dissuade celebrities from supporting PETA. Following the birth of a baby girl to Alec Baldwin and his wife Kim Basinger, two long-time animal rights supporters, AMP ran a full-page ad in the Hollywood trade paper *Variety* depicting a baby on a life-support system. It read, "Dear Alec Baldwin and other celebrity supporters of animal rights: when you help PETA this is who you hurt the most."[44] Baldwin has since broken with PETA over the issue of using animals in breast cancer research (his mother is a breast cancer survivor). In fact, several Hollywood celebrities who formerly supported PETA, including Naomi Campbell, Joan Collins, Melissa Etheridge, and Betty White, no longer do so.

Jacquie Calnan, president of Americans for Medical Progress, notes that "since the public, for the main, doesn't know much about the true nature of animal research, these messages [of animal rights groups] do have some resonance. . . . Large national groups with huge budgets are working hard to poison the public attitude against research." Moreover, "a small core of young activists" is engaged in criminal actions against this research.[45] How successful animal rights groups will be in their effort to end animal research will depend largely on whether legislators and the public understand what is at stake.

Notes

1. American Medical Association, "Human v. Animal Rights: In Defense of Animal Research," white paper, 1990, p. 2716.

2. Susan Sperling, *Animal Liberators: Research and Morality* (Berkeley: University of California Press, 1988), p. 36.

3. American Medical Association, p. 2716.

4. Priscilla Feral, quoted in Katie McCabe, "Beyond Cruelty," *Washingtonian*, February 1990, p. 76.

5. Ingrid Newkirk, quoted in Katie McCabe, "Who Will Live, Who Will Die?" *Washingtonian*, August 1986, p. 115.

6. David H. Hubel, quoted in John G. Hubbell, "The 'Animal Rights' War on Medicine," *Reader's Digest*, June 1990, p. 75.

7. Larry Horton, "The Enduring Animal Issue," *Journal of the National Cancer Institute*, vol. 81, no. 10, May 22, 1989, p. 737.

8. Michael W. Fox, *Inhumane Society: The American Way of Exploiting Animals* (New York: St. Martin's Press, 1990), pp. 59, 72, 87.

9. incurably ill For Animal Research (iiFAR), newsletter, Spring 1989, pp. 1-2.

10. *Journal of the American Medical Association*, June 23 / 30, 1989, p. 3602; Americans for Medical Progress, 1991 annual report, pp. 4-7; and American Medical Association, "Use of Animals in Biomedical Research: the Challenge and Response," white paper, 1992, p. 12.

11. American Medical Association, "Use of Animals in Biomedical Research: the Challenge and Response," p. 12.

12. Robert W. Leader and Dennis Stark, "The Importance of Animals in Biomedical Research," *Perspectives in Biology and Medicine* (Chicago: University of Chicago, Summer 1987), p. 479.

13. American Medical Association, "Use of Animals in Biomedical Research: the Challenge and Response," p. 13.

14. See, for example, Americans for Medical Progress, 1991 annual report, pp. 1 and 2; American Council on Science and Health, "America's Health: a Century of Progress," pamphlet dated 1988; and John A. Krasney, "Some Thoughts on the Value of Life," *Buffalo Physician*, Vol. 18, No. 3, September 1984.

15. Foundation for Biomedical Research, "Animal Research for Animal Health," undated pamphlet, and American Medical Association, "Use of Animals in Biomedical Research: the Challenge and Response," p. 12.

16. Leader (quoted) and Stark, p. 479.

17. Foundation for Biomedical Research.

18. American Medical Association, "Use of Animals in Biomedical Research: the Challenge and Response," p. 13.

19. PCRM, undated fundraising letter signed by president Neal D. Bernard.

20. *Alternatives to Animal Use in Research, Testing, and Education* (Washington, D.C.: Office of Technology Assessment, 1989), cited in American Medical Association, "Human v. Animal Rights: In Defense of Animal Research," p. 2719.

21. American Medical Association, "Human v. Animal Rights: In Defense of

Animal Research," p. 2719, and AMA, "Use of Animals in Biomedical Research: the Challenge and Response,"p. 18.

22. Laurence McCullough, quoted in McCabe, "Who Will Live, Who Will Die?" p. 155.

23. American Medical Association, "Human v. Animal Rights: In Defense of Animal Research," p. 2718.

24. Ingrid Newkirk, speech at Loyola University, October 24, 1988.

25. Robert J. White, "The Facts about Animal Research," *Reader's Digest,* March 1988, p. 131.

26. American Medical Association, "Use of Animals in Biomedical Research: the Challenge and Response," pp. 18-19.

27. Foundation for Biomedical Research, newsletter, September / October 1992.

In 1992, for example, bills to prohibit "pound seizures" were introduced in five states; none of these, however, passed. In Maryland, H.B. 1108 sought to ban accepting, using, or killing any dog or cat—or using any part thereof—for food or any manufactured good or product. In Missouri, H.B. 1587 would have prohibited any pound, shelter, animal control authority, or humane society from selling or giving any dog or cat to a research, testing, or experimentation facility or dealer. A New Jersey bill would have prohibited anyone from selling, supplying, or receiving a live dog or cat for research if the animal had been acquired from an entity not registered with the U.S. Department of Agriculture. Similar bills were defeated in Illinois and New York.

Since 1987, activists have also spearheaded dozens of state-level bills to limit the use of animals in product safety tests and to restrict the types of substances that can be tested on animals; thus far, however, none of these has passed. In 1992, for example, state legislatures in Arizona, Illinois, Massachusetts, New York, and Vermont introduced seven bills and one resolution to limit such tests. In Arizona, H.B. 2564 would have prohibited the use of live animals to test cosmetics. H.B. 1042 in Illinois would have prohibited the use of live animals in dermal and ocular irritancy tests in cosmetics research. H.B. 2690 in Massachusetts would have prohibited "a lethal death dose test or eye irritancy test on a living nonhuman vertebrate for purposes of testing cosmetic products." Three bills in New York would have prohibited manufacturers from performing tests that place "a cosmetic in an animal's skin to measure its irritating effects." In Vermont, H.B. 143 would have prohibited the use of ocular, dermal, and other animal tests to screen the safety of cosmetics and household products.

28. Krasney.

29. National Institutes of Health, "Public Health Service Policy on Humane Care and Use of Laboratory Animals," revised September 1986.

30. "Animal Rules Uncage Scientists' Complaints," *Washington Post*, July 9, 1989, and "Billion Dollar Price Tag for New Animal Rules," *Science*, Vol. 242, November 1988, p. 662.

The Animal and Plant Health Inspection Service (APHIS) of the U.S. Department of Agriculture estimated the total cost of the revisions to the private sector at $885 million in initial outlays and another $207 million a year in operating expenses, including: $447 million in new animal housing facilities at research institutes and surgical facilities; $138 million for renovations, new cages, and construction of dog runs and exercise areas; $138 million in initial capital expenditures for dog facilities and $111 million for primate facilities; $100 million in compliance costs for federally run facilities; $59 million in new rabbit housing; $40 million for new staff to enforce the law; and $16.5 million in operating costs for dog handlers. While APHIS conducted no study to assess the potential impact of these changes on biomedical research, it noted that this "remains an interesting empirical question."

31. "Animal Rules Uncage Scientists' Complaints."

32. McCabe, "Beyond Cruelty," p. 76.

33. *People for the Ethical Treatment of Animals v. U.S. Department of Health and Human Services, et al.*, civil no. C880818AJZ, filed U.S. District Court, San Francisco, March 4, 1988, p. 3, cited in Horton, p. 740.

34. Humane Society of the United States, *Close-Up Report,* June 1992.

35. Many researchers consider chimpanzees "ideal candidates" for AIDS research since they are one of few primates that can actually be infected with the HIV virus; however, they develop no symptoms, raising hopes that a vaccine might be developed that prevents humans from developing symptoms as well. Lisa Belkin, "After Serving Man, a Humane Home," *New York Times*, September 6, 1989, p. A14.

36. Horton, p. 740.

37. Horton, p. 741.

38. James Wyngaarden, director of the National Institutes of Health, quoted in "Notable / Quotable," *Wall Street Journal*, April 24, 1989, p. A14.

39. Vin Weber, quoted in Foundation for Biomedical Research, undated newsletter, p. 5.

40. Horton, p. 743.

41. Americans for Medical Progress, e-mail dated November 5, 1998, on file with author. Results of this poll are available from AMP.

42. "Animals in Research," p. 2007.

43. Frankie Trull, "The 'Animal Rights' Movement: Frankie Trull Looks at the Cost of Scientific Ignorance," *Philanthropy*, July / August 1990, p. 16.

44. "Red Badge of Courage Turns into Raw Deal," *Sunday Times,* January 19, 1997.

45. Jacquie Calnan, presentation made at meeting of the American Association of Laboratory Animal Science, Cincinnati, October 1998, on file with author.

CHAPTER III

Farm Animals

Animals were first domesticated around 8000 B.C. in the foothills of mountain ranges to the west, north, and east of the Tigris-Euphrates Valley. With the retreat of ice caps at the end of the last ice age and a resulting milder climate with regular rainfall, hunting-and-gathering tribes learned to grow wheat and barley and to tame wild goats, sheep, pigs, and cattle to feed themselves.

Over the next few thousand years, raising plants and animals for food became common throughout most of the world, sometimes borrowed from established agrarian societies and sometimes discovered anew by hunting-and-gathering tribes as a more reliable source of food. Many historians have noted that the domestication of plants and animals revolutionized man's way of life, allowing nomadic tribes to abandon a precarious day-to-day existence of foraging and hunting to create permanent agricultural villages, a more stable food supply, and a broad division of labor, thereby increasing human productivity, longevity, and wealth. Historians John B. Harrison and Richard E. Sullivan note that the achievements of early farmers "served as the basis upon which higher civilization was built; without them, further human advance would have been impossible."[1]

Activists' campaign to abolish livestock and poultry farming would not only end the consumption of meat, poultry, and dairy products, but eliminate the use of thousands of farm animal byproducts including antifreeze, blood fibrin, bone china, brake fluid, burn dressings, cellophane, cement, commercial feeds, cortisone, crayons, dyes, estrogen, fertilizer, glass, heart valves, insecticides, insulin, linoleum, pet food, photographic film, plasmin, plastic, porcelain enamel, protein supplements, putty, rubber, surgical sutures, thyroid extract, tires, water filters, water-proofing agents, and weed killers.[2]

While animal rights groups in the 1980s focused their efforts primarily on ending animal research, they have recently shifted more attention to farm animals, which they believe are more widely abused. The Farm Animal Reform Movement complains that each year in the United States approximately nine billion farm animals—or in its words, "victims"—are killed. Moreover, the number is rising, in part because a growing population is eating more chicken.[3] People for the Ethical Treatment of Animals claims that modern livestock and poultry farming is "the largest form of animal abuse in the world!"[4]

Activists hope to enact stringent regulations affecting the housing, feeding, handling, transport, and slaughter of farm animals, thereby making

25

animal agriculture prohibitively expensive. As with animal research, they argue that such laws are needed to ensure the humane treatment of animals. However, if it is morally wrong to raise animals for food, the issue of how humanely they are treated is irrelevant. Critic Russ Carman contends that "[while] these groups propose vegetarianism as the ultimate goal for their movement, they recognize it as being too radical a proposal for the public to accept at this time. Instead, they have decided to wreck the present livestock systems, and by so doing, force their vegetarian lifestyle onto the public."[5]

Unlike animal research, activists have not made significant legislative inroads in the area of animal agriculture. However, the late Henry Spira of Animal Rights International believes that "we are still in the opening hours of the campaign to liberate farm animals."[6]

Building Opposition to Livestock and Poultry Farming

Insofar as activists have been unable to convince potential supporters that raising animals for food is morally wrong, they have used several other approaches to build public opposition to animal agriculture and promote vegetarianism. These include:

• Portraying farms, slaughterhouses, and meat consumption as disgusting. Animal rights author Peter Singer says that "disguise it as we may, the fact remains that the centerpiece of our dinner has come to us from the slaughterhouse, dripping blood. Untreated and unrefrigerated, it soon begins to putrefy and stink."[7] He does not mention that "untreated and unrefrigerated" vegetables also begin to "putrefy and stink."

• Raising fears about the safety of meat, poultry, and dairy products. People for the Ethical Treatment of Animals contends that "animal products are a Pandora's box of undeniably harmful ingredients, such as: E. coli, growth hormones, campylobacter, salmonella, and antibiotics."[8] In fact, Western societies today have the safest and most nutritious supply of food in history.[9]

• Claiming that modern livestock and poultry farming is abusive. John F. Kullberg, former president of the American Society for the Prevention of Cruelty to Animals, says that "more cruelty, by far, takes place in the production of food animals than against all other animals taken together."[10]

As with animal research, the charge of "cruelty" is the primary argument activists use in efforts to increase government regulation of animal agriculture. Generally, such abuse is said to arise from two factors:

• The increasing use of scientifically based methods of animal agriculture, including antibiotics, specially formulated feeds, and indoor housing with separate stalls. Many of these methods were developed over the last 50 years at agricultural research colleges.

• The fact that farm animals are raised for profit.

Not surprisingly, allegations of cruelty are often intended to arouse anti-science and anti-business sentiments. The Humane Farming Association, an animal rights group that seeks to "eliminate the severe and senseless suffering to which farm animals are subjected,"[11] says that modern animal agriculture causes

> severe physiological as well as behavioral animal afflictions. Anemia, influenza, intestinal diseases, mastitis, metritis, orthostasis, pneumonia, and scours are only the beginning of a long list of ailments plaguing . . . farm animals. . . . By ignoring traditional animal husbandry methods such as exercise, fresh air, wholesome food, and proper veterinary care, [today's] farms are a breeding ground for countless infectious diseases. [Farmers] attempt to counter the effects of grossly deficient husbandry, overcrowding, and intensive confinement by administering continuous doses of antibiotics and other drugs to the animals. This 'cost effective' practice has a significant negative impact on the health of . . . the animal.[12]

In fact, the health of farm animals is continually improving. Tuberculosis, once a major killer of cattle, has been virtually eliminated by animal research. With a better understanding of the dietary needs of chickens and the now-common use of indoor sheds to protect the birds from the cold, diseases, predators, poisoning, and fighting once endemic to backyard flocks, mortality rates have fallen from near 40 percent in the 1920s to ten percent today.[13] The American Farm Bureau Federation notes that

> an animal's welfare is indicated by specific clinical criteria such as appetite; growth rate; reproduction and production levels; presence of disease; signs of abuse, neglect, or deprivation; and unnecessarily cruel or painful treatment at death. . . . Concern for the well-being of poultry and livestock . . . is best exemplified by the high levels of production and low mortality rates being achieved in modern livestock and poultry operations.[14]

The National Cattlemen's Association likewise notes that "health and reproductive and productive traits continue to be the most readily measurable and most practically useful indicators of compatibility between farm animals and the environments in which they reside. Feeds, management systems and disease control are now better than at any time in the past."[15]

The fact that farm animals are raised for profit is also said to lead to abuse, a problem activists say is compounded by the rise of huge "agribusinesses" that have forced small family farmers out of business. According to the American Society for the Prevention of Cruelty to Animals, small farms have been replaced by "factory farming, a practice that treats animals like inventoried machines with little or no attention to their basic needs."[16] The Farm Animal Reform Movement says that "the peaceful family farm of yesteryear," where animals were "treated as part of the

CHAPTER III

family," has become a "giant, impersonal, mechanized factory. . . ."[17] Animal Rights International claims that "the farms of yesterday with contented animals in natural surroundings are almost extinct. They have been replaced by corporate factories—cramped indoor facilities—where nature, biological necessity and any reasonable consideration towards animals are spurned in favor of the massive profits that can be realized by treating animals as a commodity."[18] Activist Michael Fox contends that traditional farmers have been replaced by "space-age farming biotechnology" and "agribusiness corporate managers and specialists in chemical farming, genetics, nutrition, and other disciplines." Animal agriculture has become a "jungle of atrocities—fueled by greed, indifference, and competitive pressures of the market economy."[19]

In fact, nearly all of America's farms are owned by individuals, married couples, or family partnerships actively engaged in day-to-day operations.[20] As for the notion that there was a time when farm animals were treated "as part of the family" rather than raised for food or profit, critic Russ Carman notes,

> for thousands of years, man raised cattle and hogs to eat. . . . After cleaning their dung, working hard in the hot fields to harvest their feed, feeding them morning and night and putting up with their often stubborn behavior, it was never hard to butcher them. After all, that is what they were raised for. . . . Until shortly after World War II, it was very common for [American] families, even in medium-sized cites, to produce their own meat, eggs and dairy products. Those who didn't raise their own animals could usually buy them from someone in the neighborhood. . . . Most chickens, ducks, geese and smaller animals were usually butchered just prior to eating them, and often by the lady of the house.[21]

As others have noted, the fact that farmers are businessmen who can incur either profits or losses provides strong incentives to ensure the health and well-being of their animals. As one farmer says, "If we don't take care of our animals, they don't take care of us."[22]

While activists sometimes concede that more nutritious food, better disease prevention, the use of climate-controlled housing and the like have improved the physical health and longevity of farm animals, they often contend that modern animal agriculture causes animals to feel sad and bored, or conversely, anxious and afraid. Such allegations of "emotional suffering" are usually coupled with calls to change common husbandry practices—for example, that chickens would be "happier" scratching for feed in a barnyard than receiving automatically dispensed food in an indoor shed, or that cows would be "more content" standing in a pasture and eating grass than standing in indoor stalls and eating scientifically formulated feed.[23]

In fact, little is known about farm animal psychology or how farm animals "feel" under different conditions. Very few researchers engage in full-time study of farm animal behavior. A report by the Council for Agricultural Sciences and Technology notes that because there are few ethograms (studies that seek to determine, measure, and interpret the emotional states of animals under different conditions) for farm animals, there is no scientific basis for making the kinds of animal husbandry changes activists seek.[24] A Congressional Research Service report similarly notes that "just because a sow or hen, if given the choice, might prefer to move outdoors to a 'free range' is not necessarily an indication that confinement housing . . . is causing her to suffer."[25] The CAST report warns that "the failure to apply scientific criteria to this most-contested area of animal welfare will likely lead to the adoption of government standards that might be well-intentioned but harmful to the animals they were designed to protect."[26] Ironically, learning more about farm animal psychology would require more animal research.

Chickens

Roughly eight billion broiler chickens, usually kept on floors in sheds that house about 20,000 birds, are raised annually in United States. Another 250 million layer hens, typically housed in rows of cages that hold four birds each, lay nearly 80 billion eggs a year.[27] A large egg-producing facility with an automatic feeding and watering system may house a million hens.

The chicken industry was one of the first areas of modern animal agriculture targeted by animal rights groups. In the late 1980s, they launched a series of full-page ads in major newspapers, charging that entrepreneur Frank Perdue's pioneer role in modern chicken farming has resulted in "misery," "violence," and "excruciating pain" for billions of chickens.[28] According to the late Henry Spira of the Coalition for Nonviolent Food, a project of Animal Rights International, "we chose Frank Perdue as a starting point in animal agriculture" because he was a "suitable target" who allegedly

A) personified a problem; B) would not be able to effectively dispute the facts, and C) had the potential for high media visibility. . . . Perdue has become an effective focal point for the initial effort, and the momentum continues to build. . . . We believe the Perdue campaign will become a catalyst for industry-wide change and will catapult factory farming onto the national agenda in the 1990s.[29]

As with other farm animals, activists say there was once a time when chickens were happier, healthier, and better treated. Stephen Zawistowski, vice president of the American Society for the Prevention of Cruelty to Animals, says that "the barnyard flock [once had] chickens scratching and clucking, a hen gathering her brood under her wing and a rooster oversee-ing all with an arrogant glance."[30] Author Peter Singer claims that "once chickens were individuals. . . . If a bird became sick or was injured it could be attended to, or if necessary killed quickly. . . ."[31]

Today, however, according to the Farm Animal Reform Movement, "layer hens are crammed up to five birds in a tiny 'battery cage' the size of a folded newspaper. . . . They are alternatively [sic] starved or overfed to adjust egg production. Their beaks are cut off with a hot iron to prevent stress-induced cannibalism."[32] Similarly, the Coalition for Nonviolent Food says that "life for the day-old . . . chick begins with brutal dismem-berment as its beak is burned off with a hot knife. . . . Each chicken is expected to struggle through life with less than one square foot of living space. . . . Unnatural overcrowding . . . leads to suffocating and unhealthy conditions which often result in death and disease."[33] The American Society for the Prevention of Cruelty to Animals likewise says that "chick-ens react to the intense confinement by mutilating and even killing each other. To help prevent this, their beaks are commonly burned off."[34]

As noted, the mortality rate for chickens has fallen from near 40 per-cent in the 1920s to ten percent today—a key indicator that health and well-being have improved. The beaks of chicks are not "cut off" or "burned off," but are trimmed to remove their sharp tips so that feather picking, infighting, and cannibalism—all natural behaviors for chickens—are minimized. This kind of behavior occurs among backyard and "free-range" flocks. Layer chickens are not "alternately starved or overfed," but are given less feed once a year to induce simultaneous feather loss or "molting." This gives the birds a rest from laying eggs. Molting occurs naturally each year whether chickens are raised in cages, sheds, or outdoor ranges.

Regarding the claim that chickens live in "overcrowded" conditions, the Council for Agricultural Science and Technology notes that

> the current floor space allowance in the commercial broiler / fryer industry is generally 0.8 square foot per bird and in some environmentally controlled houses it may be 0.7 square foot per bird. Scientists have determined through numerous studies that the minimum floor space allowance required for broilers to achieve optimum productivity while maintaining the welfare of the bird is 0.50 to 0.67 square foot per bird, well below the current industry practice.

> Studies have shown that most broilers made little use of [additional perching areas] until they were obliged to do so by shortages of floor space. Birds were found to adjust their number on the floor to about 0.63 square foot per bird, and with a space allowance of 0.7 square foot or more per bird, perches were little used. . . . The space allowed in the current broiler practices is well above that suggested by feasible scientific research."[35]

The National Broiler Council concludes that

> Due to the highly competitive nature of the industry and the small net
> return to the producer (historically less than a nickel per pound), economic
> profitability cannot be achieved without careful attention to the welfare of
> the broiler chicken. . . . [Modern] poultry production methods employ
> better nutrition, better control of diseases and parasites, and better protection
> against predators, extreme temperatures, and storms than did earlier
> methods. As indicated by the traditional production and clinical criteria,
> modern production methods have greatly enhanced the welfare of poultry.[36]

Despite activists' campaign, chicken and egg consumption has been
rising. In fact, per capita chicken consumption has increased from 28
pounds annually in 1960 to 73 pounds today—a 160 percent increase.[37]

Veal Calves
Animal rights groups have also targeted veal farming as an example of
allegedly cruel animal agriculture. According to one survey, activists
themselves believe that veal calves are the most poorly treated of all farm
animals.[38]
Since 1982, the Farm Animal Reform Movement has organized
"National Veal Ban Action Day," distributing anti-veal literature in public
and picketing restaurants that serve veal. These and similar efforts may be
having some effect: per capita veal consumption has dropped 70 percent
since the mid-1970s, although much of this decline may be due to lower
beef consumption in general.
Most veal calves are the male offspring of dairy cows. Before veal
farming became common in the mid-1960s, male calves were of little value
to farmers, and most were slaughtered just after birth. Today, veal farmers
buy surplus dairy calves and raise them for 18 to 20 weeks, usually on a
diet of specially formulated milk, although some calves are raised on
grains, hay, and processed feeds. Veal calves are usually raised in single
stalls, although some are raised in small groups. The system used depends
on the type of calf, the region and climate, and the facilities of individual
farms.[39]
The American Society for the Prevention of Cruelty to Animals contends that "many veal calves . . . spend their entire lives on factory farms,
confined in darkened stalls just a few inches wider than their bodies."[40]
The Humane Farming Association says that a veal calf

> is locked in a tiny 22-inch-wide 'veal crate' for his entire life. Chained at
> the neck, he can't walk . . . or even turn around. . . . Excrement covers his
> rear and collects under the slats of his crate. He chokes on the ammonia
> gasses of his own waste. . . . He's confined to a building with hundreds of

other baby calves meeting the same gruesome fate. Their resistance to disease is nil. The cramped rows of tiny pens may maximize profits for agribusiness, but they are perfect breeding grounds for disease. [41]

But according to the Beef Industry Council / Veal Committee of the National Live Stock and Meat Board, the stalls in which veal calves are raised are sufficiently large for calves to stand, stretch, lie down, groom themselves, and step forward, backward, and from side to side. Slotted floors allow for efficient removal of waste. Moreover, the stalls only partition the calves up the shoulder, ensuring visual and physical interaction with adjoining calves. Stalls are used to control the calves' strong sucking instinct. When raised in groups, they often suck the mouths, ears, and scrota of other calves, which can spread disease. The age-old practice of tethering (roping an animal to its pen) is used because calves do not distinguish between a place to feed and a place to defecate. Without tethering, they will defecate in their food.[42]

The Humane Farming Association also says that veal calves "get an iron-deficient, drug-laced [milk] formula that makes them anemic—and their meat look pale. . . . For the sake of profits, agribusiness has adopted the most bizarre farming practice in history—the deliberate raising of sick, anemic animals."[43]

But according to the Beef Industry Council, when the special-fed diet is used

> the calves receive carefully controlled amounts of iron to meet their normal needs, but not so much iron that the meat would become red. . . . The diets contain iron and 40 other essential nutrients including amino acids, carbohydrates, fats, minerals and vitamins. . . . An early clinical symptom of anemia is poor appetite—a calf that will not eat will not grow. . . . The best evidence that veal calves are healthy is their excellent growth rate and very low mortality figures. The typical veal calf gains an average of 25 pounds a day. A report issued by the Council for Agricultural Science and Technology suggest that the calf mortality rate on special-fed veal farms is one of the lowest . . . in animal agriculture.[44]

Mink and Fox

Some 3.6 million mink and fox are raised annually on 700 fur farms in the United States, located mostly in Wisconsin, Utah, Minnesota, Oregon, and Idaho. Roughly 80 percent of the mink and fox pelts produced in the U.S. come from these farms (the rest are obtained through hunting and trapping). While raised primarily for fur, mink and fox carcasses are also processed into protein meal for animal feed. Mink oil is used as a lubricant for leather and as an ingredient in hypoallergenic soaps, cosmetics, and hair products. Mink manure is also applied to crops as a non-chemical fertilizer.

32

The successful domestication of fur-bearing animals in the late 19th century offers strong evidence that profitable animal agriculture can only be achieved through humane treatment. As animal rights critic Russ Carman notes,

> For many years it was considered impossible to raise wild mink and fox in captivity; both animals were thought to be too high strung and nervous to be raised successfully. . . or profitably [and both] are prone to a number of fatal diseases. . . . But through the dedicated efforts of a small handful of people . . . who were highly skilled in the science of animal husbandry, the problems were slowly solved, and a new industry was born.[45]

Nonetheless, the Humane Society of the United States contends that fur-bearers "imprisoned" on fur farms suffer "stress and pain" from living in "tiny mesh wire cages" where they "often can barely turn around."[46] People for the Ethical Treatment of Animals likewise claims that fur-farm animals live "crowded into tiny, filthy, wire mesh cages, where they suffer from poor diets, inadequate water, contagious diseases, parasites, and severe stress."[47]

But as Carman notes,

> One key to successful fur farming is cleanliness. . . . It is only through rigid sanitation efforts, and almost constant testing, that a farmer can be sure of the survival of his animals, and ultimately his business. Mink must be fed a well-balanced diet of perfectly fresh food. Because mink will quickly die after eating even slightly tainted food, great care is taken in food handling.[48]

Likewise, Gunnar Jorgenson, head of research at the State Animal Husbandry Station in Hilleroed, Denmark, notes that

> mink and fox are for the most part beasts of prey. . . . It is characteristic of [predators] that they cannot develop or reproduce normally if conditions are not optimum with regard to cages, food and care. . . . As far as nourishment is concerned, fur-bearing animals have a very low level of tolerance. Consequently, modern fur animal production is based not only on optimum supply of specific foodstuffs, but also on the fact that the foodstuffs comprise a combination of high quality ingredients and low contamination level.[49]

Steven Wahlberg, general secretary of the World Wildlife Fund (Sweden) and Gunnar Krantz, chairman of the Swedish Federation of Animal Protection Societies, add that

> only a person who is interested in animals and who likes them becomes a fur farmer. These criteria are essential for two reasons: working with furbearing animals is no easy job; it is both hard work and time-consuming.

They are live animals and must be cared for every day—weekday, weekend or public holiday. It takes a real interest in animals to work up the best material. The farmer who has no real interest in his animals or feeling for their welfare soon suffers himself, in the form of poor financial return. . . . [50]

Regarding the claim that fur-farm animals live in "tiny" cages, tests with mink have shown that neither a 400 percent increase nor a 50 percent decrease in cage size cause any changes in behavior. "Cage design, including access to nesting boxes, appears to be far more important. . . ."[51]

The Humane Society of the U.S. contends that fur-farm animals are killed by "electrocution, neck breaking and drowning."[52] In fact, mink are usually killed in the same way that dogs and cats are killed in shelters. A mobile unit with a container of carbon monoxide or dioxide gas is brought to the cages. The animals are placed inside, rendered unconscious, and die without pain.[53] For fox, lethal injection that causes immediate cardiac arrest is typically used.

Despite the anti-fur campaign, annual fur sales in the U.S. have remained relatively constant since 1990, peaking at $1.27 billion in 1997. And over 100 designers are currently working with fur, compared to 42 in 1985.

Horses

In the mid-1990s, activists began a campaign against horse farming—specifically, the use of mares to produce Permarin, an estrogen replacement therapy made from pregnant mares' urine (PMU). Manufactured since 1942, Permarin is America's most widely prescribed drug. It is taken by nine million women to ease the symptoms of menopause and is also used to help prevent and treat osteoporosis and heart disease. Some 50,000 mares are involved in Premarin production in North America.

PETA has spearheaded the anti-Premarin campaign, enlisting the support of such celebrities as Brigitte Bardot, Mary Tyler Moore, and Sally Struthers to urge women to "throw your Premarin away."[54] It contends that thousands of pregnant mares are confined to "tiny stalls for six months at a stretch."[55] The stalls are "so small" that the mares "cannot turn around or lie down comfortably.[56] Cumbersome rubber urine-collection bags," which cause chafing, are placed around the mares' legs. "Mares are given limited drinking water so that their urine will yield more concentrated estrogens."[57] Moreover, the mares' offspring are "considered unwanted throwaways" that are sold to feedlots and eventually slaughtered to produce horse meat for European and Japanese markets.[58]

In 1995 and 1996, Wyeth-Ayerst Laboratories, the sole manufacturer of Premarin, conducted inspections of PMU ranches, which work under contract for the company. Representatives from several government agencies and humane organizations, including the Alberta, Manitoba, and

Saskatchewan Ministries of Agriculture, the U.S. Department of Agriculture, the Canadian Farm Care Trust (CANFACT), and the American Association of Equine Practitioners (AAEP) visited many of the approximately 500 PMU farms located in Alberta, Manitoba, Saskatchewan, and North Dakotta. While some isolated deficiencies in care were noted, no widespread problems adversely affecting the health or well-being of mares were found. The Alberta Minister of Agriculture concluded that "in general, we found the horses were receiving good to excellent care. Some farms were better than others, but none of them was a poor quality operation."[59]

In facts of Premarin production sharply contradict PETA's allegations. The mares' urine is collected from October to March, during the harsh winter months in the Northern Great Plains. (One rancher notes that when his mares are let out for exercise this time of the year, "very often all they want is back in.")[60] The collection pouches are suspended on pulleys hung from the ceiling and are made of light-weight rubber that is loose-fitting, flexible, and non-irritating. Mares can easily move about and lie down, although they usually sleep standing up.

Approximately two-thirds of the foals remain on the PMU ranches or are sold for riding, showing, drafting, and breeding. The remaining foals are eventually sold on the international meat market after reaching maturity on feedlots. The lots, which have been inspected by CANFACT, have received favorable reports. Regarding PETA's disparagement of other countries' fondness for horse meat, one critic remarks, "Are we to assume the role of meddlesome instructor and know-it-all mentor to these other nations and cultures?"[61] In Canada, inspectors enforce the Health of Animals Act and the Meat Inspection Act to guarantee humane transport and handling at slaughter. USDA inspectors enforce the Humane Slaughter Act in the United States.

Unlike PETA, several humane organizations are working with Wyeth-Ayerst to create an optimal environment for the mares. After careful study, a team of equine experts from the International League for the Protection of Horses (ILPH), the Royal Society for the Prevention of Cruelty to Animals (WSPA), and CANFACT recommended ways to improve the mares' welfare and proposed further research on feeding, watering, and excise. In response, Wyeth-Ayerst has created a special PMU research farm in Canada. (Note: WSPA is an animal rights organization that no longer works with Wyeth-Ayerst.)

As the only manufacturer of Premarin, Wyeth-Ayerst requires ranchers to sign contracts legally obligating them to abide by a Code of Practice. Developed by a team of veterinarians, ranchers, a company representative, and the Manitoba Minister of Agriculture, it requires that: an independent veterinarian inspect the mares three times during the six-month collection cycle; farms be inspected monthly by field inspectors and mares receive adequate bedding, regular exercise, and water at intervals throughout the

CHAPTER III

day according to guidelines set by the National Research Council (NRC), a division of the National Academy of Sciences (NAS). The mares' diet is also set by NRC guidelines.

Contrary to PETA's claims, the mares' water is not restricted to produce more concentrated urine. Concentration is irrelevant because ranchers are paid per gram of estrogen in the urine. Moverover, restricting water would increase the risk of colic and other health problems for mares and unborn foals, driving up ranchers' costs.

PETA urges women to boycott Premarin and switch to synthetic and plant-based estrogen-replacement therapies, such as Estradiol, Estropipate, or Estrone. But many gynecologists warn that alternatives are not effective for all women and may even be harmful.

Regulatory Costs

Currently, no federal law prescribes standards for on-farm handling and care of animals, although two statutes address the humane transport and slaughter of livestock. While many states also regulate the transport and slaughter of farm animals, few address on-farm activities. All states have anti-cruelty laws which usually cover farm animals. There has been no new federal legislation affecting farm animal treatment since 1978 when amendments were made to the Humane Slaughter Act of 1958.

Activists' first campaign to broadly regulate animal farming occurred in Massachusetts in 1987 when the Massachusetts Society for the Prevention of Cruelty to Animals sponsored a bill to ban the raising of veal calves in stalls. Although the measure failed, a group of animal rights groups led by the Coalition to End Animal Suffering and Exploitation drafted a broader initiative, "Question 3," to broadly redefine cruel and inhumane methods of raising, handling, and transporting livestock. A petition drive was launched to place the initiative on the November 1988 ballot. It was defeated by a three-to-one margin after farmers and the Massachusetts Farm Bureau mounted a public-relations campaign that claimed the measure was "expensive, unworkable and unnecessary" and would "put thousands of farmers out of business."[62]

If activists' are successful in enacting legislation, two effects are likely:

• *Smaller farmers will be driven out of business.* Because of economies of scale, larger farms can more easily absorb the costs of regulation. According to the American Farm Bureau Federation, "there would be fewer farmers and ranchers as production shifted into the hands of larger, financially stronger units able to absorb the higher capital and management costs."[63] Such a result would obviously run counter to many activists' purported goal of ending "huge agribuinesses" and restoring small family farms.

• *Food prices will increase.* The rising productivity of farm animals has given consumers a wider choice of meat, poulty, and dairy products at

36

prices lower than at any time in our nation's history. Much of the cost of new regulation would be passed onto consumers, affecting lower income persons most adversely. As critic Russ Carman notes, "Animal rights leaders are constantly comparing their movement to the civil rights movements, and the struggle for women's equality, in an obvious effort to draw the support [of these groups]. . . . But 'animal liberation' is a call to place even greater burdens on the [less fortunate]."[64]

Many activists have proposed that egg-laying hens be raised outdoors on "free ranges" as a compromise toward the goal of fully "liberating" chickens. However, United Egg Producers estimates that egg prices would double or triple if such a requirement were imposed. Further, eggs produced on free rances have much higher rates of contamination from such diseases as coccidiosis, caused by the birds coming into contact with fecal matter.[65]

Whether other proposed changes would be best for animals themselves is questionable. Activists have strongly supported the federal Veal Calf Protection Act. It would ban the raising of veal calves in separate stalls. However, according to the Beef Industry Council / Veal Committee of the National Live Stock and Meat Board, "studies show that veal calves raised in groups have from two to 14 times the disease rate of individually penned calves. Further, farmers [using this method have] confronted a number of problems such as urine drinking and bullying of smaller calves by larger ones."[66]

In Europe, activists have been somewhat successful in enacting preferred legislation, including restrictions on indoor housing, mandated access to the outdoors, and limited or no use of antibiotics. In England, a ban on raising veal calves in stalls took effect in 1990. In Switzerland, bedding and exercise for pigs is required, and cages for egg-laying hens are outlawed. In Sweden, a 1988 law requires cows to be taken outside to graze and both cows and pigs to receive bedding. Sows may not be tethered and cages for layer hens must be phased out by 1998.[67] Germany and the Netherlands have enacted similar laws.

One critic says that "in Europe, the industry sat back and said, 'These people (animal rights activits) are kooks. They're not going to have any influence.' But they did. . . . You tend to have people developing the policies who don't understand the industry."[68] These laws already have resulted in higher production costs for farmers and higher prices for consumers.[69] The American Farm Bureau Federation notes that "the 'animal welfare' production practices required by European governments are made possible by the high government price guarantees given to farmers. These subsidies are borne largely by taxpayers in the form of higher retail prices . . . . In the U.S., producers do not have this economic shock absorber."[70]

A Congressional Research Service report notes that the "98 percent of the population no longer residing on farms holds an extremely wide range of moral and religious beliefs about man's relationship with other animals—

which ultimately could carry more weight in future policy decisions than traditional economic and scientific arguments." How successful animal rights groups will be in their campaign to "liberate" farm animals will largely depend on whether the public understands that the goal of the animal rights movement is not improved treatment for animals but an end to all animal uses, including raising animals for food.

Notes

1. John B. Harrison and Richard E. Sullivan, *A Short History of Western Civilization,* (New York: Alfred A. Knopf, 1980), p.8.

2. Animal Industry Foundation, "Animal Agriculture: Myths & Facts," undated brochure, and National Pork Producers Council, "Pork Industry Progress," undated brochure.

3. FARM, "Animal Agriculture Claims Another Record Number of Victims," *Farm Report*, Fall 1996.

4. PETA, fundraising letter dated June 1998 and signed by president Ingrid Newkirk.

5. Russ Carman, *The Illusions of Animal Rights* (Krause Publications: St. Iola, Wisconsin, 1990), p. 137.

6. Henry Spira, "Can a Perdue Campaign Put Factory Farming on the National Agenda?" *Animals' Agenda*, March 1992, p. 39.

7. Peter Singer, *Animal Liberation: A New Ethics for Our Treatment of Animals* (New York: Avon Books, 1977), cited in David Henshaw, *Animal Warfare: The Story of the Animal Liberation Front* (London: Fontana Paperbacks, 1989) pp. 27-28.

8. People for the Ethical Treatment of Animals, fundraising letter dated June 1998 and signed by president Ingrid Newkirk.

9. American Farm Bureau Federation, "Farm Bureau Policies for 1992," January 1992, p. 46.

10. John F. Kullberg, "America's Shameful Abuse of Animals," *Wall Street Journal*, November 28, 1988.

11. Beef Industry Council / Veal Committee of the National Live Stock and Meat Board, "Shedding Some Light on Veal," booklet dated 1991, p. 9.

12. Humane Farming Association, 1985 brochure.

13. United Egg Producers, "Healthy, Productive Management Practices of the Egg Industry," undated brochure.

14. American Farm Bureau Federation, "Meeting the Animal Rights Challenge," 1991 handbook, p. 5, and 1989 policy book, cited in Ann Japenga, "Livestock Liberation," *Harrowsmith*, November / December 1989, p. 36.

15. National Cattlemen's Association, "Myths & Facts about Beef Production," undated report, p. 9.

16. ASPCA, undated fundraising letter signed by former president John F. Kullberg.

17. Farm Animal Reform Movement, undated fundraising brochure, and Alex Hershaft, president of FARM, quoted in "He's Seeking Rights for Farm Animals,"

Washington Times, March 9, 1983.

18. "Frank, Are You Telling the Truth about Your Chickens," *New York Times*, fundraising ad, October 20,1989, p. A17.

19. Michael W. Fox, *Inhumane Society: The American Way of Exploiting Animals* (New York: St. Martin's Press, 1990), pp. 24, 28, 46.

20. American Farm Bureau Federation, "Meeting the Animal Rights Challenge," p. 22.

21. Carman, pp. 38, 39.

22. Fur Farm Animal Welfare Coalition, "Fur Farming in North America," undated brochure.

23. For example, the Humane Farming Association says that "the victims of factory farming suffer a relentless state of distress." Humane Farming Association, undated fundraising letter. Christine Stevens, president of the Animal Welfare Institute, says that "factory farming has taken the joy out of the lives of millions of calves and pigs . . . and billions of hens." Animal Welfare Institute, "Aims and Programs," undated brochure.

24. Council for Agricultural Science and Technology (CAST) report, 1981, cited in Geoffrey S. Becker, "Humane Treatment of Farm Animals: Overview and Selected Issues," Congressional Research Service report dated May 1, 1992, p. 20.

25. Becker, p. 20.

26. Council for Agricultural Science and Technology (CAST) report, cited in Becker, p. 19.

27. USDA, National Agricultural Statistics, "U.S. Egg Production, 1940-1997."

28. "Violence, Multilation, Electrocution, Greed . . . ," *Village Voice*, Animal Rights International fundraising ad, November 21, 1989.

29. Henry Spira, letter to colleagues dated Summer 1992.

30. Stephen Zawistowski, "ASPCA Cries Foul at Poultry Raisers," *Wall Street Journal*, November 23, 1987.

31. Singer, p. 100.

32. Farm Animal Reform Movement, undated fundraising brochure.

33. Coalition for Nonviolent Food, "A Leader among Liars . . . a Guru of Greed," undated flyer.

34. ASPCA, reply form attached to undated fundraising letter signed by former president John F. Kulberg.

35. National Broiler Council, "Physical Well-Being of Chicken Is Essential Concern of Modern Broiler Industry," undated information sheet.

36. National Broiler Council, "Broiler Industry Reference Guide," p. 7, and National Broiler Council, "Physical Well-Being of Chicken Is Essential Concern of Modern Broiler Industry."

37. National Broiler Council, "Talking Chicken," website, www.eatchicken.com.

38. Wesley V. Jamison and William M. Lunch, *A Preliminary Report: Results from Demographic, Attitudinal, and Behavioral Analysis of the Animal Rights Movement*, undated and unpublished manuscript.

39. Animal Industry Foundation.

40. ASPCA, undated fundraising letter signed by former president

CHAPTER III

John F. Kullberg.

41. Humane Farming Association, undated newsletter signed by president Bradley Miller; emphasis eliminated.

42. Beef Industry Council / Veal Committee of the National Live Stock and Meat Board, "The Truth about Veal," brochure dated 1991, and "Shedding Some Light on Veal," pp. 4, 11, 12.

43. Humane Farming Association, *ibid.*, and undated fundraising letter; emphasis eliminated.

44. Beef Industry Council / Veal Committee of the National Live Stock and Meat Board, "The Truth about Veal" and "Shedding Some Light on Veal," p. 4.

45. Carman, p. 112.

46. HSUS, "Fur Is Out, Compassion Is In," October 1989.

47. People for the Ethical Treatment of Animals, quoted in Putting People First, 1990 information sheet on fur.

48. Carman, pp. 112-113.

49. Gunnar Jorgenson, head of research, State Animal Husbandry Station, quoted in Fur Farm Animal Welfare Coalition, "Fur Farming in North America."

50. Sven Wahlberg, general secretary, World Wildlife Fund (Sweden) and Gunnar Krantz, chairman, Swedish Federation of Animal Protection Societies, quoted in Fur Farm Animal Welfare Coalition, "Fur Farming in North America."

51. National Trappers Association, "Facts about Furs!" booklet dated 1988, pp. 17.

52. HSUS, *ibid.*

53. Fur Farm Animal Welfare Coalition, "Fur Farming in North America."

54. PETA, "Time Is Running Out for these Horses," *Animal Times*, Spring 1997, p. 3.

55. Paula Moore, PETA correspondent, "75,000 Mares in Tiny Stalls," *Washington Post*, May 8, 1997.

56. Brigitte Bardot, PETA spokesman, "Time Is Running Out for these Horses," p. 3.

57. PETA, "Premarin: A Prescription for Cruelty," Internet website: www.peta-online.org.

58. PETA, "Animal Advocates Dump on Wyeth-Ayerst," Internet site.

59. Alberta Minister of Agriculture and USDA, quoted in Wyeth-Ayerst Laboratories, "Wyeth-Ayerst Committed to High Standards in Care."

60. Curt Paton, paraphrased in "Canadian PMU Farms." *Western Horseman*, Part I, April 1995, p. 47.

61. Maurice Telleen, "Canadian PMU Farms," *Western Horseman*, Part II, May 1995, p. 23.

62. Japenga, p. 36.

63. American Farm Bureau Federation, "Meeting the Animal Rights Challenge," p. 8. Similarly, "the imposition of more government standards for the care and handling of animals will be costly to the industry, and will drive many smaller, financially struggling producers out of business." Becker, p. 13.

64. Carman, p. 53.

65. United Egg Producers, "Recommended Guidelines of Husbandry Practices for Laying Chickens."

66. Beef Industry Council / Veal Committee of the National Live Stock and Meat Board, "Shedding Some Light on Veal," p. 13.

67. Becker, p. 2.

68. Joy Ripley, president, Society for the Prevention of Cruelty to Animals (Alberta, Canada), quoted in "Cattle Industry Adopts Code to Counter Anti-Meat Lobby," *Ottawa Citizen,* July 16, 1991.

69. F.J. Grommers, "The Animal Welfare Movement—European Prespective," *Animal & Human Health,* Vol.1, No. 1, 1988, and Harold D. Guither and Stanley E. Curtis, "Animal Welfare Developments in Europe—A Perpective for the U.S.," October 1983, cited in American Farm Bureau Federation, "Meeting the Animal Rights Challenge," p. 7.

70. American Farm Bureau Federation, "Meeting the Animal Rights Challenge," p. 8.

71. Becker, summary.

CHAPTER IV
Wildlife

In most of human history, man has been a hunter and gatherer. With the rise of agrarian societies and the domestication of animals 10,000 years ago, humans began to depend less on wild animals for food and clothing. However, hunting and trapping continued to be important. As ecologist Walter E. Howard notes, "the first European settlers [in America] quickly learned that [profitable] ranching was impossible without wolf control and that all forms of agricultural production required protection from many species of wildlife."[1]

With increasing industrialization and rising world population during the last two hundred years, hunting and trapping have continued to play a primary role in reducing threats to human life, property, agriculture, and other activities. At the same time, the loss of wildlife habitat in many areas and the extinction of some species have generated a growing interest in protecting threatened and endangered wildlife. The greater affluence of more fully industrialized societies, in contrast to agrarian societies and societies in the early stages of industrialization, has made this conservation possible.

Animal rights activists generally argue that it is wrong to kill animals because their "interests"—such as their desire to avoid pain or escape death—deserve equal consideration with human concerns. But if this is true, it is unclear how a person facing a hungry, wild carnivorous animal should act, or whether someone would be justified in cutting down trees and destroying other wildlife habitat to build a house. Moreover, the number of wild animals killed by hunters and trappers—slightly more than 100 million annually, according to the Humane Society of the United States[2]—is relatively low compared to those killed through other human activities such as housing and road construction, crop production, and driving motor vehicles. According to what is perhaps the most methodologically sound study, roadkills alone killed 187 million wild animals in 1993 and 137 million in 1994.[3] In addition, pesticides used on crops kill billions if not trillions of insects annually.

Some activists are candid about the implications of animal rights. Animal Liberation Front founder Ronnie Lee calls for "driving back the human species to pre-invasion boundaries" and ending "industrial society, the private car, large-scale farming and cities and a drastic cut in human numbers on the planet to about 50 million" (a 99 percent reduction).[4] Sherri Tippie, president of Wildlife 2000, a Denver-based group, says that "what we have is too many people. I'd like to do fertility controls on them."[5]

CHAPTER IV

Building Opposition to Hunting and Trapping

When moral arguments against hunting and trapping fail, activists often resort to *ad hominen* attacks. They say that hunters and trappers are "vicious, sadistic monsters . . . who revel in the killing of animals."[6] Recently deceased Fund for Animals president Cleveland Amory once said that "hunting is an antiquated expression of macho self-aggrandizement, with no place in a civilized society."[7] Luke Dommer, late president of the Committee to Abolish Sport Hunting, similarly remarked that "many hunters are sick people. . . . They kill beautiful animals. . . . They see beauty in death, not in life. They can invent all the excuses they want, but when you boil it all down, they want to kill something."[8]

These attacks avoid the issue of whether hunting and trapping are needed in modern society. As Walter E. Howard says, "'hunting' is not equivalent to 'hunters.' The motives of hunters vary widely but none explains what hunting is anymore than the motives of . . . doctors describe medical sciences, or the motives of . . . lawyers describe the judicial systems."[9] One of the few academic studies on the motivations of hunters found that 45 percent of them hunt primarily for food. Thirty-eight percent hunt mainly for sport while the remaining 17 percent hunt out of an "affection, respect, and reverence" for nature.[10]

Trapper Russ Carman offers his view on why many sportsmen trap:

> The trapper draws great satisfaction from being a part of nature [and from understanding] the workings of that force. He learns to predict the weather by observing the movement of animals. He learns to love the smells of nature that are offensive to modern man. The pungent 'skunk-like' odor of fox, the sharp acrid odor of mink, the sweet musky odor of deer, are like fine perfume to the trapper . . . when carried by the pure air of the woods and fields. . . . Because of the hardships he must endure, . . . the hard work and long hours, he better understands the hardships animals must endure, and he stands in awe.[11]

Activists also argue that hunting and trapping are merely, or mostly, for "sport" or "recreation." The Humane Society of the United States contends that "the characterization of wild animals as 'game' denies their intrinsic value," while the American Humane Association "considers sport hunting a violation of the inherent integrity of animals. . . ."[12]

This view likewise does not address the question of whether hunting and trapping are needed, but suggests that they are unjustified because hunters and trappers enjoy them—possibly implying that hunting and trapping might be justified if sportsmen did *not* enjoy them. It also highlights the difference between wildlife conservation, which seeks abundant, healthy populations of plants and animals, and animal rights, which professes a concern with the welfare of each member of an animal species.

Sport hunting has long been integral to wildlife conservation. Since the early-20th century, hunters, trappers, and fishermen have contributed $20 billion to restore wildlife habitat and replenish depleted or declining fisheries. Today, 14 million hunters and 29 million fishermen generate $950 million annually by purchasing hunting licenses. Another $440 million for wildlife conservation comes from excise taxes on sporting arms, handguns, archery and fishing equipment, and ammunition. Each waterfowler must also purchase a federal duck stamp, which generates revenue to buy or lease wetlands for waterfowl. In addition, hunters spend an estimated $250 million annually to develop wildlife habitat on private lands.[13]

Endangered or threatened species that have been restored to abundant numbers in the U.S. through conservation programs include the Canada goose (from 1.1 million in the late 1940s to more than 2.5 million today), the white-tailed deer (from 500,000 in 1900 to 18 million), the trumpeter swan (from 73 in 1935 to 17,000), the Rocky Mountain elk (from 41,000 in 1907 to 800,000), the wild turkey (from 97,000 in 1952 to four million), and the pronghorn antelope (from 12,000 in the 1940s to over one million). Such conservation efforts have also benefited hundreds of unendangered species such as chipmunks and songbirds.[14]

Wildlife conservationists recognize that the price of restoring, or even maintaining, an animal species is that many—in fact, most—of these animals will die painful natural deaths. To restore the Rocky Mountain elk to a population of 775,000, millions more had to die of starvation, disease, and predation because all species reproduce in greater abundance than their environments can support. Conservationists further argue that by following regulations to open and close seasons, set quotas, and specify the means used to take game, sport hunting and trapping reduce the suffering that occurs when animals are simply left to die natural deaths.

Necessity of Hunting and Trapping

Because man has significantly altered the environment, wildlife must be managed to reduce threats to human activity. For example, nearly half a million deer are killed by motor vehicles each year in the U.S., and some of these collisions result in serious injuries and fatalities. The U.S. Department of Transportation reports 139 fatal collisions in 1996 caused by animals.[15] The National Trappers Association, a 15,000-member conservation organization founded in 1959 to promote "sound furbearer management programs [while] protecting wildlife habitat,"[16] highlights the problems that arise when fur-bearing animals are not controlled through regulated trapping:

• Beavers build dams that flood lowlands, roads, and suburban homes. Dam building can also destroy large amounts of valuable and rare timber.

• Coyotes cause major livestock loses in western and southern states. In fact, in western states the cost of livestock predation—even with hunting and trapping—approaches $100 million a year.[17]

CHAPTER IV

• Muskrats dig holes that damage earthen dams, dikes, irrigation canals, and farm ponds. Large populations can also cause "eat-outs," striping large areas of vegetation and making them less productive for other species, some of which may be threatened or endangered.

• Raccoons can raid farmyards for chickens and other fowl and can heavily damage cornfields. They are also the main carrier of rabies in some eastern and southeastern states.

• Red fox also kill domestic poultry and sometimes carry rabies.

• Spotted skunks kill poultry and striped skunks are a major carrier of rabies.

All wild animals reproduce beyond the carrying capacity of their environments. With denser populations, disease transmission can increase and starvation and predation increasingly become ways in which populations are reduced. As Russ Carman notes,

> life in nature is seldom easy. Wild animals often become old very quickly. Compared to the pampered life of people's pets, wild animals often spend long hours of hunting to find a meal. They often have to endure extreme weather conditions [and] competition from other animals. Any accident that causes a broken bone [or] severe laceration must be endured until it heals or until the animal dies. As the animals get older, their reflexes slow, and their teeth become dull. If they survive long enough, they will slowly die of starvation.[18]

Disease is the major killer of wildlife. Fatal diseases include distemper in fox, bobcats, and raccoons, which causes inflammation of the mucous membranes and fever; Aleutian disease in mink, which causes loss of appetite and weight loss; tularemia in muskrats and beaver, which can spread to humans and cause fever and inflammation of the lymph glands; Parvo virus in canines, which causes intense abdominal pain and dehydration; and rabies in all animals, which can be transmitted to humans and cause choking, inability to swallow, and convulsions.[19] Millions of fox die annually of mange, caused by parasitic mites that burrow into the skin and cause severe itching and hair loss. The disease usually takes about two months to run its course. Carman describes his boyhood experience of capturing a fox in the advanced stages of mange:

> One early fall morning, as I entered a small pasture field, I saw something caught in my trap close to a hundred yards away. I didn't recognize it . . . and as I approached closer I began to wonder what kind of creature I had caught. As I approached to within twenty-five yards, the wind assaulted my nostrils with a terrible stench of rotted flesh that was obviously coming from the animal in my trap. As I walked up to the animal, I was shocked to realize that it was a fox. . . . He stood there with his head hung down, and his body shivered from the early morning chill. . . . All that remained of

his beautiful fur was a small strip down his back bone that he had been unable to reach. The rest of his body was covered with dry crusted scabs and weeping sores. His muzzle and legs were swollen to double their normal size, and his eyes were swollen to mere slits. . . . I quickly put the poor animal out of his misery. . . .[20]

As a boy, Carman often questioned whether he should trap. After capturing the mange-infested fox, however, "I suddenly understood that . . . if I quit trapping fox this is what I would be saving them for. Hours, days and months of intense suffering far greater than they could ever experience in a trap."[21]

Over half of all trapped animals are killed almost instantly in killer traps or are drowned in traps set near water. Compared to most natural deaths, these killings are relatively humane. The rest are captured in steel-jaw leghold traps that hold an animal by the foot or paw, usually for a few hours. Trappers generally kill the animals by shooting them in the head, causing instant death.[22]

Leghold Traps

Animal rights groups have raised large sums of money in efforts to outlaw the steel-jaw leghold trap, a device the American Humane Association (AHA) calls "the most inhumane weapon in the fur trapper's arsenal."[23] The Humane Society of the United States (HSUS) says the traps are "torturous."[24] The Animal Protection Institute of America (API) calls them "bone-crushing" and "spirit-mangling."[25] According to the AHA, the trap is "like a land mine, . . . concealed and deadly. Once stepped on, its 'jaws' instantly clamp shut, relentlessly clenching its startled victim's foot or paw."[26]

Not to be confused with steel-toothed traps, which are illegal in all 50 states, leghold traps have smooth jaws. They apply pressure to two sides of an animal's limb, causing numbness. The National Trappers Association notes that researchers have monitored many trapped animals with radio sending units. While heart rates and body temperature elevate quickly after the capture, they soon settle down to near normal. Video taped observation shows that trapped animals initially try to escape until they realize they are securely held. Usually they relax until daylight, at which time they test the trap again since they often retire to dens and other safe places during the day. If not disturbed by the approaching trapper or other threats, most trapped animals simply rest during the day.[27]

HSUS claims that "animals frequently bite off their own trapped limbs" in efforts to escape.[28] The American Society for the Prevention of Cruelty to Animals (ASPCA) likewise says that animals "frequently" chew off their trapped limbs.[29] But if this "frequently" happened, most animals would get away, making the traps useless. While it occasionally happens, most animals recognize their trapped foot or paw and will not bite it.

HSUS also claims that "animals may remain trapped for long periods, during which they are likely to suffer and die from exhaustion, dehydration, predation, freezing, or starvation. . . . Many animals have been found alive after suffering in traps for as long as two weeks."[30] In fact, research shows that most trapped animals are held for less than eight hours.[31] Many states also require that leghold traps be inspected every 24 hours. Even so, it is in a trapper's interest to frequently check his traps since poachers may take captured animals. Since most fur-bearing animals are nocturnal, they are usually captured at night and traps are checked the following morning.

Activists also say that many "nontarget" animals, including threatened and endangered species, are accidentally caught in leghold traps. According to HSUS, "5 million nontarget animals . . . are accidentally caught in traps . . . each year;"[32] and "small children" and pets are also at risk.[33] The American Humane Association says that "your pet may not be safe in a wooded area. . . . [P]ets have been maimed or crippled by the trap."[34] The ASPCA likewise says that "often family pets, cats and dogs, are the victims of steel jaw leghold traps." Moreover, the traps "can be a hazard to humans, especially children."[35]

Many animals "accidentally" caught in leghold traps are actually secondary target species such as skunks which threaten waterfowl or livestock. Trappers minimize the possibility of accidental captures by using appropriately sized traps and selective baits and by placing traps in favorable locations such as just outside a muskrat burrow. Leghold traps also offer advantages over other alternatives: since killer (body-gripping or conibear) traps usually cause almost instant death, they cannot be used around pets or livestock. Many target species are also wary of cage traps and will not enter them. With leghold traps, nontarget catches can usually be released without harm. In fact, wildlife biologists often use leghold traps to safely capture animals such as fox and coyote for "catch-and-release" scientific research.

Commonly used leghold traps spring harmlessly under human feet. There is no documented case of a child being seriously injured in a leghold trap.[36] While some pets have been injured in leghold traps, *supervised* pets can usually be easily released by compressing the trap springs. Russ Carman notes that "the biggest problem trappers face is the irresponsibility of pet owners. [Occasionally], stray or unsupervised dogs wander into areas where they do not belong and become caught in traps. . . . [However], tens of thousands more of these unsupervised dogs end up under the wheels of cars and eighteen wheelers. . . ."[37]

HSUS also says that trapping "threatens the survival of entire species."[38] As noted, hunters and trappers have helped many animal species to recover and thrive. No species of animal in the United States today is threatened or endangered because of hunting or trapping.

Finally, trapping is heavily regulated in all 50 states. For example, Ohio's laws, which are fairly typical, read in part:

> All first-time trappers and hunters must successfully complete an education course offered through the Division of Wildlife. . . . All traps . . . must be tagged with the name and address of the trapper in legible English. . . . All traps must be checked every 24 hours. . . . Traps with teeth in the jaws are prohibited. . . . It is unlawful [to] set, maintain, or use a trap . . . in or upon any cart or wagon road, or in or upon any path ordinarily used by domestic animals or human beings."[39]

Alleged Alternatives to Hunting and Trapping

Just as animal rights organizations claim there are alternative to animal research, they say there are alternatives to hunting and trapping that can be used to control wildlife. While all of these are used on occasion, they are generally too costly or have limited effectiveness. They include:

• *Trapping and transferring animals to other locations.* This can be costly and can lead to the spread of disease. Moreover, relocated animals are likely to die. Florida state wildlife biologist David Maehr says that "you don't take an animal out of the place it has been born and raised . . . without totally impacting the animal and the environment where you have moved it to. [Because of limited habitat, food, etc.], animals are going to die, either the ones you moved or the ones that were already there."[40]

Often the animals that activists wish to move are "pests." In the early 1990s, beavers in several northern Chicago suburbs were destroying hundreds of trees and building dams that clogged drainage ditches and flooded homes. Mary Beth Sweetland, a spokesman for People for the Ethical Treatment of Animals, called the situation "a perceived problem" and suggested relocating the beavers.[41] Illinois Department of Conservation biologist Bob Bluett responded, "It's like asking somebody to take termites out of your house and letting them go outside. That's essentially dumping them on your neighbor."[42] In 1998, PETA asked its members to write Disneyland to protest its use of sticky glue traps to catch mice and rats. It suggested using traps that would allow the rodents to be released "in another place."[43]

• *Using fertility controls.* Major problems: cost and effectiveness. Some field studies are underway that use baits to sterilize deer and other forms of nuisance wildlife, but they are largely experimental and not of a sufficient scale to adequately control large roaming animal populations. Baits may also cause sterility in non-targeted animals including threatened and endangered species. Moreover, as philosopher Loren Lomasky notes, if animals have rights similar to those of humans, such measures "would partake of the same moral odiousness that stains the 'eugenic' sterilizations perpetrated on blacks and the feebleminded earlier in this century."[44]

• *Reintroducing predators.* Major problems: increased threat to human lives and property. Moreover, in some areas predator reintroduction could create the need to manage the predator through hunting and trapping. Says one critic, "there is little sense in reintroducing . . . large carnivores into their former range unless there is a good chance that they will reproduce, which means it is inevitable that they will multiply beyond the carrying capacity of the habitat. . . ."[45] In other areas, predators may not reproduce in sufficient numbers to effectively control a "pest" species. In still other areas, predators may kill threatened or endangered species since most of them are not species-specific in their eating habits—they will eat whatever they can catch.

• *Using fencing and other methods to confine a species in an area.* Major problems: cost and effectiveness. In Yellowstone National Park in the early and mid-1980s, several consecutive years of unseasonably mild winters and wet summers increased the bison population to record numbers. In 1988, however, severe drought, fires, and a return to normally cold and snowy winters reduced food supplies. Many bison began wandering out of the park to find food, raising fears that brucellosis—a bacterial disease often carried by bison that can cause cows to abort their calves—would be spread to local cattle ranches.

Consequently, the National Park Service authorized a hunt to kill 20 percent of Yellowstone's 2,700 bison herd. The Animal Protection Institute of America said that "nearly all wildlife experts . . . agree [that] Yellowstone [can] maintain a balance of bison forever without resorting to control by gunfire."[46] Wayne Pacelle, former executive director of the Fund for Animals, called the killings a "preventable tragedy,"[47] saying the bison could have been pushed back into the park. However, the Park Service's earlier efforts to herd the bison had failed. "They . . . walked through fences and cattle guards, ignored helicopter sorties and proved largely indifferent to cracker shells, tin-can rattles, vehicle sirens, flashing lights, bird shot, rubber bullets and recorded wolf sounds."[48]

The experience of Fairfax County, Virginia, located just outside Washington, D.C., is typical of other counties that border many large eastern cities. The deer population has swelled to 25,000, which officials say is five times the number that can be properly sustained. Autopsies show that the deer are often underweight and in poor physical health. The number of people with Lyme disease, which is often carried by ticks on the deer, increased from 14 in 1996 to 31 in 1997. County supervisors authorized two deer hunts in 1997 after a librarian was killed when a deer dashed into traffic, bounced off the fender of an oncoming car, and was propelled through her car's windshield. In 1997, 20 other people were injured in deer-car collisions in the county, although the total number of accidents was probably 1,438—the number of deer carcasses picked up by road crews. John W. Grandy of the Humane Society of the United States called the hunts "cruel, inhumane, and unnecessary," saying that fences and road reflectors could keep the deer away from roads. But he gave no estimate of the cost or effectiveness of these approaches.[49]

Canada geese are also becoming an increasing problem in many parts of the country. In recent decades, their numbers have doubled to over 2.5 million. The geese's droppings litter many golf courses, picnic areas, lawns, and other grassy areas. Moreover, geese and other birds pose a significant hazard at airports. The Federal Aviation Administration reports 759 bird-airplane collisions between 1988 and 1994, more than a third resulting in malfunctions or defects likely to cause an accident. The most common problem is birds smashing into jet engines, causing engine shutdowns, explosions, and fluid loss. The 759 collisions resulted in 53 shutdowns, 45 aborted takeoffs, and 155 unscheduled landings.[50]

In 1996, the ASPCA joined the Coalition to Prevent the Destruction of Canada Geese in a lawsuit against the city of Clarkstown, New York, which that summer killed 271 geese. Despite the city's earlier failed effort to move the geese, the ASPCA believes the birds can be deterred by constructing fences, detonating loud explosives, and playing recordings of the birds' distress call. However, it gives no estimate of the cost of these alternatives, some of which might be more annoying than the geese. It notes that the neighboring town of Mamaroneck has used border collies to chase the geese away. But Salvatore DeSantis, a county commissioner, concedes that the geese "do return. It's not a permanent solution, but . . . an ongoing way to address the problem."[51]

In recent years, more people have expressed concern about managing wildlife in ways that minimize suffering. The Fur Institute of Canada has provided millions of dollars to several U.S. and Canadian universities to study more effective and humane trapping methods for fur-bearing species.[52] Many newer leghold traps, which offer shock-absorbing springs, padded jaws, and reduced spring pressure, have been suggested or developed by trappers themselves.[53] But while some animal rights organizations have spent nominal amounts to research humane methods of controlling wildlife, most have simply promoted outright bans on hunting and trapping.

Ending Fishing
While many may find it hard to believe, People for the Ethical Treatment of Animals recently launched a campaign to convince America's 60 million fishermen to stop fishing. As in its other campaigns, it has heavily targeted youth, who seem most susceptible to animal rights ideas and who, after all, are the next generation of fishermen. In 1995, PETA distributed 65,000 teacher information packets to every public and private school in the country, reaching an estimated nine million children. Its anti-fishing leaflets are often distributed outside schools with the assistance of a six-foot costumed fish named "Gill."

PETA contends that fish "can feel pain just like cats, dogs, and humans."[54] In a recent letter pleading for an end to fishing at historic Walden Pond outside of Boston, PETA told Massachusetts wildlife officials, "fish have a neurochemical system like ours, the brain capacity to experience fear and pain." (It added: fish have "individual personalities" and "develop special relationships with each other.")[55] The only evidence it cites to support this claim is a 1976-1979 British report that says, "the evidence *suggests* that all vertebrates (including fish) . . . experience *similar sensations to a greater or lesser degree* in response to noxious stimuli" (emphasis added).[56]

In fact, the overwhelming majority of biologists do not believe fish can feel pain. Based on extensive studies at the Seattle National Fishery Research Center and the Oregon Cooperative Fishery Research Unit, John G. Nickum, a fishery biologist with the U.S. Fish & Wildlife Service, notes that "no 'pain' receptors, nor 'pain' recognition systems, have been identified in fish. . . . There is evidence that the struggle that fish carry out when hooked, or captured in other ways, is a behavioral characteristic. . . . If the response is behavioral, it would have considerable survival value (i.e., those fish with well-developed escape behavior survive to produce the next generation.")[57] The American Society of Ichthyologists and Herpetologists likewise notes that "an increasing body of knowledge indicates that pain perception of the many species of vertebrates is not uniform over the various homologous portions of their bodies [e.g., the wing of a bat and the foreleg of a mouse]. Therefore, broad extrapolation of pain perception across taxonomic lines must be avoided. For example, what causes pain and distress to a mammal does not cause an equivalent reaction in a fish."[58]

PETA also notes that introducing such valued fish as trout in certain lakes has altered the food chain, sometimes with negative results. But rather than advocate better fisheries management, it calls for an end to fishing. Other arguments are merely *ad hominen* attacks that accuse fishermen of leaving a trail of "empty worm containers, crushed beer cans and wads of old fishing line" wherever they go.[59]

To draw attention to its campaign, PETA recently tried to convince the residents of Fishkill, New York, a village of 2,000 about 60 miles north of New York City, to change their town's name to "Fishsave." The village traces its name to the area's original Dutch settlers. "Kill" means "stream" in Dutch. Said Mayor George Carter, "Oh, my goodness. Fishsave Elementary School. Good Lord! I think if they would look the word up, they would find out what it means. . . . We are not going to change the name."[60]

Thus far, PETA has held a handful of anti-fishing demonstrations at fishing tournaments around the country, which have caused some concern. Pennsylvania and Virginia were among the first states to pass legislation making it illegal to harass fishermen, and other states are following.

Anti-Hunting and Anti-Trapping Campaigns

Activists' efforts to end hunting and trapping have included demonstrations, letter-writing campaigns, interruptions of hunts, temporary restraining orders to stop hunts, lawsuits, the introduction of statewide ballot initiatives, and legislation at all levels of government. Some of these, such as the "Save the Seals" and "Save the Whales" campaigns, have achieved some success. (See Chapter VII for a discussion of these two campaigns. Also see profiles on: the American Society for the Prevention of Cruelty to Animals, Appendix II; the Animal Legal Defense Fund, Appendix III; the Animal Protection Institute, Appendix V; Friends of Animals, Appendix IX; the Fund for Animals, Appendix X; and the Humane Society of the United States, Appendix XI.)

In recent years, dozens of pieces of legislation have been introduced annually at the municipal, township, county, state, and federal levels to restrict or ban hunting and trapping. As of 1998, there was only one major congressional bill to affect hunting and trapping that animal rights groups supported—the Steel Jaw Leghold Trap Prohibition Act (H.R. 1176 and S. 1557). Introduced by Rep. Nita Lowey (D-NY) and Sen. Robert Torricelli (D-NJ), it would prohibit the import, export, or shipment in interstate commerce of leghold traps and furs derived from animals caught in those traps. As of late 1998, it has 85 co-sponsors in the House and three in the Senate.

Animal rights groups have had more success in convincing state legislators and voters to restrict or ban hunting and trapping at the state level. Many animal rights groups, including the American Society for the Prevention of Cruelty to Animals, the Animal Legal Defense Fund, Friends of Animals, the Fund for Animals, and the Humane Society of the United States, maintain regional or field offices to help initiate legislation. Since 1977, they have used statewide ballot initiatives 18 times, winning nine of these.[61]

Activists' first campaigns to outlaw trapping through ballot initiatives occurred in Ohio in 1977 and Oregon in 1980. Voters defeated the measures by 2-to-1 margins.[62] In Arizona in 1992, an animal rights group called Arizonians for Safety and Humanity on Public Lands launched "Proposition 200," an initiative calling for the "non-lethal" management of all wildlife on state-owned land. It would have banned all hunting, trapping, and fishing on public lands. After a coalition of over 90 groups, including the Archery Manufacturers Association, Putting People First, and the Wildlife Legislative Fund of America mounted a massive campaign, the initiative was defeated by a 60-to-40 margin. However, a modified anti-trapping initiative passed in Arizona in 1994. In 1996, voters in Colorado and Massachusetts approved initiatives that ban steel-jaw leghold traps. Oregon voters upheld a 1994 ban on black bear baiting (i.e., using food to attract bears) and the use of hounds to hunt bears. And Washington voters approved a ban on baiting and hound hunting of bears, cougars, and bobcats.

CHAPTER IV

In 1998, activists promoted ballot initiatives to restrict hunting and trapping in three states. In California, seven animal rights groups—the American Society for the Prevention of Cruelty to Animals, the Animal Protection Institute, the Ark Trust, the Doris Day Animal League, the Fund for Animals, the Humane Society of the United States, and the International Fund for Animal Welfare—formed a coalition called ProPAW (Protect Pets and Wildlife) to ban leghold, snare, and conibear (body-gripping) traps and to prohibit the sale of pelts from animals caught in these traps. The initiative, which passed, also bans two poisons used to kill nuisance wildlife. In Ohio, however, activists failed to pass an initiative to ban dove hunting. They also failed to end the use of snare traps to catch wolves in Alaska.

Pro-hunting groups have helped to defeat half these initiatives. In 1996, Idaho voters rejected a proposed ban on the springtime hunting of black bears and the use of baits and hounds, and Michigan voters defeated a proposed ban on baiting and hounding of black bears. Moreover, all states now have laws that prohibit animal rights activists from harassing hunters or otherwise interfering with lawful hunts. Rhode Island's law, which is fairly typical, reads in part,

> no person shall obstruct or interfere with the lawful taking of wildlife by another person. . . . A person violates this section when he or she intentionally or knowingly drives or disturbs wildlife . . . uses natural or artificial visual, aural, olfactory or physical stimuli to affect wildlife behavior . . . erects barriers with the intent to deny ingress or egress to areas where the lawful taking of wildlife may occur . . . interjects himself into the line of fire.

Violation of the law is a civil crime carrying a $100 to $500 penalty. A hunter, trapper, or fisherman may also receive punitive damages for license and permit fees, travel guides, special equipment, and supplies "to the extent that such expenditures were rendered futile by prevention of taking of a wild animal."[63]

In 1993, Congress also passed the Recreational Hunting Safety and Preservation Act, making it illegal to disrupt hunts on federal lands, national forests and parks, and federal wildlife refuges. Violations carry a $500 to $5,000 fine and a $1,000 to $10,000 fine if violence is involved.

Costs of Hunting and Trapping Bans

Because hunting and trapping are integral to wildlife conservation and are needed for predator and pest control, widespread hunting and trapping bans would impose significant costs on both humans and animals. These include:

54

• *Species extinction.* In the millions of acres of estuaries and marshes in coastal Louisiana, a trapping ban could have devastating results on wildlife. The region is home to muskrat, nutria (an aquatic rodent with short brown hair), and over 400 species of birds. More ducks and geese spend their winters in Louisiana than any other part of the country.

However, muskrat and nutria are extremely prolific. Left unchecked, they could consume much of the vegetation of coastal Louisiana. Already, some former marshes have become open water due to natural and man-made erosion, and many conservationists fear that these areas may not recover. Louisiana Department of Wildlife and Fisheries biologist Greg Linscombe says that "if we could not trap in these marshlands, a large portion of coastal Louisiana would be affected. The total loss of marsh vegetation would be phenomenal. This would mean . . . a loss of habitat essential to migratory waterfowl and to hundreds of other species of birds and mammals dependent on these wetlands."[64]

Due in part to predation by the non-native red fox, the California clapper rail, a ground-nesting bird that inhabits the San Francisco Bay area, has become endangered. When the U.S. Fish & Wildlife Service announced plans in 1990 to trap and kill some of the fox in the San Francisco Bay National Wildlife Refuge, the Humane Society of Santa Clara County threatened to file suit. Said refuge manager Rick Coleman, "the challenge we face is that the red fox is always portrayed as a warm fuzzy [animal] with a smile on his face. We're taking on the cover girl of the *nouveau* wildlife set."[65] Similarly, in 1986, a group called the Animal Lovers Volunteer Association tried to stop a program to trap red fox that were eating least terns and light-footed clapper rails, two endangered birds of Southern California.

• *Increased animal suffering.* Without hunting and trapping, the number of animal species would increase in many areas, and roadkills, disease, and starvation would become more important in reducing populations. Moreover, some of these diseases would likely be spread to humans and pets. When the Ohio Wildlife Council announced in 1994 that trappers must kill all raccoons, skunks, opossums, and other nuisance animals in counties where rabies and distemper had been identified, John W. Grandy of the Humane Society of the United States called the policy a "doomed attempt to prevent the spread" of disease.[66] But according to Charles Pils, a biologist with the Wisconsin Department of Natural Resources, trapping "can reduce threats to the health of humans and domestic animals. . . . By removing population excesses which promote diseases such as canine distemper . . . in a localized situation, trapping can reduce and even stop the spread of a disease outbreak."[67]

Activists' successful effort to end the commercial hunting of baby Canadian harp seals in 1987 (see Chapter VII) resulted in a population increase from 1.8 million in 1983 to four million in 1993. Janice Henke, author of a book on the hunt, describes the results of this increase:

In times of dense population, fighting wounds on sexually mature males [seeking female mates] are very common, and quite often debilitating. Infections and pain from repeated bite and slash wounds hamper the [males] in obtaining enough fish to eat, and the healing process is slowed by [their] weakness and deteriorating condition. . . . Both males and females are affected by relatively poorer nutritional status in times when the herds are not depleted by human predation. . . . The net result, after a long period of greatly increased stress on each animal in the herd, is that fewer seals are born alive, fewer newborn seals reach one year of age, and fewer females reach sexual maturity. . . . Through chronic hunger, fertility of the herd is lessened and growth in numbers stops, then numbers decline. An environmental adjustment has been made, at a cost of discomfort and suffering for millions of the animals.[68]

Moreover, North Atlantic sea birds and whales, which compete with the seals for fish that are now in dwindling supply in part because of the seal population increase, "are suffering due to the . . . lack of harvest of a species that never was endangered by the hunt. . . . The lack of harvest . . . has resulted in total ecological disaster in a system which had remained rich in abundance and diversity for centuries without any threat to harp seals or their fellows in the Atlantic food chain."[69]

• *Increased property damage, including loss of crops and livestock and damage to scenic areas.* As Russ Carman notes, "beaver populations [would] increase dramatically, causing great damage by flooding valuable woodlands, flooding roads and plugging drain pipes. . . . Raccoons can also increase to dramatic numbers, and as long as there are farmers' crops in the fields for them to feed on, their populations will grow."[70] In the U.S., increased loss of livestock due to predation and competition from wild animals for food would result in higher costs for meat, affecting low-income consumers most adversely.

Since the 1960s, the Canada snow goose population has increased from a half million to more than three million. The geese, which spend the summer feeding on the Canadian tundra in northern Quebec, Ontario, Manitoba, and parts of the Northwest Territories, have stripped much of the area's vegetation, driving out other species and turning the land into mud flats and virtual desert. When the U.S. Fish & Wildlife Service and its Canadian counterpart announced they were considering culling half the population over a period of years through year-round unlimited hunting, Susan Hagood of the Humane Society of the United States said that a population crash would be preferable: "Let nature takes its course. The population will continue to increase. It will probably then crash at some point, and that will give the tundra the break it needs."[71] Of course, a crash would occur through mass starvation or disease.

• *Increased control of wildlife at taxpayer expense.* Historically, hunters and trappers in the United States have hunted and trapped largely at their own expense. But if hunting and trapping were banned, the government would still need to continue them. In Holland and Switzerland, which have banned leghold traps, government employees must now be paid to trap and shoot muskrat that are seriously damaging dikes, canals, and river beds.[72]

• *Loss of jobs and the deterioration of traditional local economies.* When activists pressured the European Community in 1983 to ban imports of Canadian baby harp sealskin products to EC countries, 75 percent of the seal product market was eliminated, and the ability of the Inuit (Eskimos) of northern Canada to make a living was greatly diminished. As one of them explained,

> The money that we earn from [seal hunting] is absolutely critical for us to continue the rest of the year's fishery. About the same time that the seal fishery ends [mid-April] we bring our boats on dry dock for their annual refit. If there is a poor seal fishery we will not have the funds necessary to repair our boats properly, to invest in new equipment, to buy new nets, and to make payments on our loans. Without the seal fishery, we cannot get the rest of the year's fishery off to a good start. . . .
>
> On average, our incomes are well below the poverty line. . . . [For families in poverty], a few hundred dollars [from sealing] means a lot. Without that money we can't continue to make money, because we need it to reinvest in the rest of the year's fishery. . . . The fishermen are losing their cash flow and their line of credit. We are all technically bankrupt. . . . Sealing by itself is a small industry, but it is an absolutely integral part of our community fishery and subsistence living. . . . Take one element out, . . . and you will see economic and social collapse. Already I see it in my own community.[73]

In 1987, Canada ended the hunting of baby harp seals. According to Canadian historian Pierre Berton, the Inuits' lives "have been ruined, and the result has been suicide, drugs, alcohol, and murder."[74] (Recently, the hunting of adult harp seals has resumed. See Chapter VII.)

In 1985, activists pressured Congress to ban seal hunting off the Pribilof Islands of Alaska, where Aleutians had hunted seals for centuries. Larry Merculieff, an Aleutian leader and commissioner of the Alaska Department of Commerce and Economic Development, says, "literally overnight, we had human suffering, suicides, more than 100 documented attempted suicides, massive anxiety."[75] Pat Ragan, program director of wildlife for the Humane Society of the United States (which supported the ban), remarked, "we don't have an official position on that. Our job is protecting animals."[76] Priscilla Feral, president of Friends of Animals, said flatly, "the goddamn Aleuts . . . don't need to eat those seals."⁷⁷

As the United States becomes increasingly urban, fewer Americans are likely to have direct contact with wildlife or to understand the need for wildlife management. Indeed, the experience with anti-hunting and trapping ballot initiatives suggests that many Americans do not support all types of hunting and trapping. Having succeeded in restricting some forms of wildlife management, animal rights groups will no doubt seek further restrictions. How successful they will be in their ultimate campaign to end all hunting and trapping will largely depend on how well hunters, trappers, wildlife biologists, and conservationists educate an increasingly urban public about the need to humanely manage wildlife.

Notes

1. Walter E. Howard, *Animal Rights vs. Nature* (Walter E. Howard: Davis, California: 1990), p. 120.

2. HSUS study cited by the Animal Protection Institute, "The Fallacy of Sport Hunting," API website, www.api4animals.org.

3. The study, ironically, is called Dr. Splatt's Roadkill Project, cited in the September 1994 issue of *Animal People*.

4. Ronnie Lee, founder, Animal Liberation Front, quoted in Putting People First, facsimile transmission dated March 10, 1993, p. 3.

5. Sherri Tippie, president, Wildlife 2000, quoted in "Denver's Vets Offer Services to Sterilize City's Busy Beavers," *Wall Street Journal,* March 20, 1989.

6. Russ Carman, *The Illusions of Animal Rights* (Krause Publications: St. Iola, Wisconsin, 1990), p. 126.

7. Cleveland Amory, president, Fund for Animals, quoted in "The American Hunter Under Fire," *U.S. News & World Report* , February 5, 1990, p. 35.

8. Luke Dommer, former president, Committee to Abolish Sport Hunting, *Animals' Agenda*, January 1989, cited in "Hunting," information sheet published by Putting People First, 1990.

9. R. Henning, "Was ist Jagd?" ["What is Hunting?"] *Die Pirsch*, 5:3-6, 1988, paraphrased in Howard, p. 133; emphasis eliminated.

10. Stephen Kellert, "Attitudes and Characteristics of Hunters and Anti-Hunters," Forty-Third North American Wildlife and Natural Resources Conference, 1978.

11. Carman, pp. 6-7.

12. Statements of the Humane Society of the United States and American Humane Association, cited in National Shooting Sports Foundation, "What They Say about Hunting: Position Statements on Hunting of Major Conservation or Preservation Organizations," undated booklet.

13. National Shooting Sports Foundation, "Money for Conservation," "Dollars for Ducks," "Organized Outdoor Enthusiasts," website, www.nssf.com.

14. National Shooting Sports Foundation, "The Un-Endangered Species, It Didn't Just Happen," brochure dated September 1992.

15. U.S. Department of Transportation, "Fatal Crashes by First Harmful Event and State," 1996.

16. National Trappers Association, "Facts About Furs!" booklet dated 1988, p. 45.

17. National Trappers Association, "Furbearer Management: Myths and Facts," undated brochure.

18. Carman, p. 129.

19. *Ibid.*, p. 131.

20. *Ibid.*, pp. 130-131.

21. *Ibid.*, p. 131.

22. *Ibid.*, p. 126.

23. American Humane Association, undated fundraising letter.

24. Humane Society of the United States, "Fight Fur Now!" *Close-Up Report*, October 1992.

25. Animal Protection Institute of America, undated fundraising letter.

26. American Humane Association, undated fundraising letter.

27. National Trappers Association, "Traps Today: Myths and Facts."

28. HSUS, "Fight Fur Now!"

29. ASPCA, "Bill to Regulate Use of Steel Jaw Leghold Traps and Bear Hunting with Dogs Pending in Wisconsin Legislature—Help Needed," website: www.aspca.org.

30. Humane Society of the United States, "Fight Fur Now!"

31. National Trappers Association, "Traps Today: Myths and Facts."

32. Humane Society of the United States, "Fight Fur Now!"

33. Humane Society of the United States, "Trapping in the Nineties: Who Pays the Price?" *HSUS News*, Fall 1992, p. 9.

34. American Humane Association, undated fundraising letter.

35. ASPCA.

36. Carman, p. 127.

37. *Ibid.*, p. 128.

38. Humane Society of the United States, "Fight Fur Now!"

39. Ohio Department of Natural Resources, website: www.dnr.ohio.gov.

40. David Maehr, Florida state wildlife biologist, quoted in "Unlikely Foes Clash Over Animal Rights," *Los Angeles Times*, December 12, 1990.

41. Mary Beth Sweetland, spokesman, People for the Ethical Treatment of Animals, quoted in "Busy Beavers Take Heat for Property Damage," *Peoria Journal Star*, January 1, 1991.

42. Bob Bluett, biologist, Illinois Department of Conservation, quoted in *ibid*.

43. PETA, "Disneyland Dismal for Mice," website posting, May 1998, www.peta-online.org.

44. Loren E. Lomasky, *Persons, Rights, and the Moral Community* (New York: Oxford University Press, 1987), p. 227.

45. Howard, p. 120.

46. Animal Protection Institute of America, "The Buffalo Kills: We're Only Half Way," *Emergency Update,* Summer 1991.

47. Wayne Pacelle, former executive director, Fund for Animals, quoted in

CHAPTER IV

"Hunters Kill 20% of Buffalo in Yellowstone," *New York Times*, March 9, 1989.

48. *Ibid.*

49. John W. Grandy, quoted in "Deer Hunts Approved in 2 Great Falls Parks," *Washington Post*, December 9, 1998.

50. "Birds Linked to 759 Reports of Flight Trouble Since '88," *Boston Globe*, September 12, 1994.

51. Salvatore DeSantis, quoted in "Flying Circus," *ASPCA Animal Watch*, Fall 1996.

52. National Trappers Association, "Facts About Furs!"

53. National Trappers Association, "Traps Today: Myths and Facts."

54. PETA, "For Cod's Sake," *Animal Times*, Spring 1997, p. 16.

55. PETA letter, quoted in "Animal Activists Angle for a Fishing Ban at Walden Pond," *Boston Herald*, January 6, 1997.

56. "RSPCA Panel of Inquiry into Shooting and Angling," *Medway Report*, 1976-1979, para. 57, cited in PETA, "Fishing: Aquatic Agony," wildlife fact-sheet #4.

57. John G. Nickum, Ph.D., letter to Charles E. Brackett, M.D., dated April 11, 1988, on file with author.

58. American Society of Ichthyologists and Herpetologists, "Guidelines for the Use of Fishes in Field Research," undated.

59. PETA, "Anglers . . . Environmentally Friendly? That's Just Another Fish Story," Internet site.

60. George Carter, quoted in "Fishkill, New York, Will Not Become Fishsave," CNN, transcript number 1617-5, September 6, 1996, and "PETA Can't Be Serious, Fishkill Mayor Says," *Washington Times*, September 7, 1996.

61. Wildlife Legislative Fund of America, "Anti-Hunting / Management Ballot Issues," 1977 - 1996.

62. *Ibid.*

63. Rhode Island Gen. Laws @ 20-13-16 (1996).

64. Greg Linscombe, wildlife biologist, Louisiana Department of Wildlife and Fisheries, quoted in National Trappers Association, "Facts About Furs!"

65. Rick Coleman, refuge manager, San Francisco Bay National Wildlife Refuge, quoted in "Unlikely Foes Clash Over Animal Rights."

66. John W. Grandy, quoted in "The Humane Society of the United States Denounces New Wildlife Killing Rules," *PR News*, April 19, 1994.

67. Charles Pils, quoted in the National Trappers Association, website, www.nationaltrappers.com.

68. Janice Henke, *Seal Wars* (St. John's, Newfoundland: Breakwater Books, Ldt., 1985), pp. 77-78.

69. Henke, letter dated June 2, 1993, on file with author.

70. Carman, pp. 24-25.

71. Susan Hagood, quoted in "Trouble on the Tundra," *Washington Post*, August 20, 1997.

72. National Trappers Association, "Facts About Furs!"

73. Mark Small, president, Canadian Sealers Association, quoted in Henke, pp. 199-201.

74. Pierre Berton, Canadian historian, quoted in "Canada's Fur Trade Feels Chill," *Los Angeles Times*, November 11, 1990.

75. Larry Merculieff, commissioner, Alaska Department of Commerce and Economic Development, quoted in Associated Press, "Natives to Take on Anti-Fur Movement," July 3, 1990.

76. Pat Ragan, program director of wildlife, Humane Society of the United States, quoted in *ibid.*

77. *Newsday* (Garden City, New York), February 21, 1988.

CHAPTER V

Animals in Education and Entertainment

Archaeologists believe the first zoo was created in the Sumerian city of Ur around 2300 B.C. Assyrian rulers often traded animals, including crocodiles and monkeys, for their private zoos. In ancient China, the emperor Wu Wang of the Chou dynasty built a zoological garden called the Park of Intelligence. Around 1490 B.C., Queen Hatshepsut of Egypt ordered what was probably the first animal-collecting expedition. In the fourth century B.C., Aristotle created a zoo for his own observation. Alexander the Great, a student of Aristotle, built what was probably the first public zoo in Alexandria, Egypt.

In ancient times—and well into the 18th century—zoos were usually created by political rulers and the wealthy to display power and affluence or to provide animals for hunting and entertainment, not for educational purposes. After the fall of Rome, monasteries preserved the tradition of menageries and game parks. With the discovery of the New World, Ferdinand and Isabella of Spain filled their palace gardens with monkeys and parrots. King Manuel the Great of Portugal also displayed monkeys and macaws. In the 17th and 18th centuries, private zoos flourished among the aristocracy in Augsburg, Paris, Vienna, and other European cities.

Circuses were common in the Roman Empire and often featured animals and humans fighting to the death. Throughout the Middle Ages, groups of touring performers appeared at marketplaces with trained animals that performed tricks and other feats. In the 19th century, traveling shows that pitched their tents on village greens generally replaced permanent equestrian shows. In frontier America, traveling menageries that combined animal and human performances brought entertainment to remote areas.

With industrialization and growing wealth in Western societies in the early-19th century, zoos began to be seen as repositories of exotic life that could be studied to better understand flora and fauna. Paralleling the rise of the humane movement, the Zoological Society of London founded what is generally considered the first modern zoo at Regent's Park in 1826. As one writer explains, "the purpose was expressly the study of living animals to better understand the natural history of their wild counterparts in the far-flung realms of the British Empire. Veterinary care and post mortems were the norm, and once a zoo animal died, it could be given to the British Museum . . . for further study. Zoos had . . . become part of the quest for knowledge."[1]

In the United States, zoos were built in the late-19th and early-20th centuries in Atlanta, Chicago, Denver, New Orleans, New York, Philadelphia, San Diego, Toledo, and Washington, D.C. In 1907, Carl Hagenbeck, a European animal dealer, built a private zoo near Hamburg that incorporated "naturalistic" settings for animals. Instead of barred cages, animals were exhibited in landscaped enclosures that included artificial rocks, plants, and ponds. In the last few decades, leading zoos have built upon this idea. Research done on captive and wild animals has led to improvements in the quality of these enclosures, including the provision of areas to rest and withdraw from public observation and the housing of social species in groups.

Building Opposition to Animals in Education and Entertainment

Most animal rights leaders believe it is wrong to confine animals or train them to perform. According to activist Merritt Clifton, the "cruelty of holding wild animals hostage in foreign, artificial environments [is] self-evident."[2] Echoing activist Gary Francione, who believes that "you can't make farming morally acceptable by just providing more space for animals. . . . We have to have *total liberation* from this system,"[3] John Grandy of the Humane Society of the United States says that "it is not just zoo cages that are inadequate; it is the reality of today's zoos as places where we permit animals to be incarcerated for our recreation and enjoyment."[4] Writer Peter Hamilton believes that "we must stop [the] expansion [of zoos and aquariums]. . . . The existing prisons should be shut down and rehabilitation centers created in order to release the prisoners back into the reserves—to give them back their freedom."[5]

Zoos, Aquariums, and Circuses

Insofar as animal rights groups have been unable to convince the public that it is inherently wrong to confine animals or train them, they have used other arguments to build opposition. One of these is to say that zoos, circuses, and the like are dangerous. Animal rights publications often carry stories of freak accidents at zoos and circuses where a person or animal is injured or killed. People for the Ethical Treatment of Animals says that "in February 1992, Janet, an Indian elephant, ran amok while being used to give rides at a Florida circus. On her back were five children and a woman. Janet stomped on a security guard who tried to stop her and went on to injure five other people. Police fired 43 rounds of ammunition at Janet before killing her."[6] One critic notes that while children are sometimes injured on playgrounds, no one argues that playgrounds should be abolished for this reason.[7]

Another approach is to say that zoos, aquariums, and circuses do not educate the public. The Humane Society of the United States says that "people don't attend zoos because of the educational experience they provide. Zoos are cheap recreation, particularly for families with children. We should not confuse the enjoyment of snowcones and popcorn with an enlightening educational experience for either children or adults. . . ."[8] Activist Michael Fox says that "there can be no communion with our animal kin when they are held captive, . . . only amusement, curiosity, amazement, and perhaps sympathy."[9]

According to the American Zoo and Aquarium Association, over 100 million people visit zoos and aquariums in North America each year. Over eight million students attend as part of classroom and summer camp activities, and nearly 2.2 million receive formal instruction through classes, tours, and lectures sponsored by zoos and aquariums. Over 25,000 teachers also participate in training courses offered by zoos and aquariums on such topics as endangered species and declining habitat. And zoo personnel regularly conduct educational programs at hospitals, retirement homes, community centers, pre-school and day-care facilities, and public and private schools.[10] Moreover, the AZA contends that

> public education in zoos and aquariums increases interest, knowledge and concern for wildlife and their diminishing habitat. . . . For some people, a visit to their local institution may be their only experience with animals outside their neighborhood. . . . Because of their commitment to captive propagation of endangered species, zoos and aquariums . . . are the last refuge many animals have against extinction. . . . Zoological research and breeding efforts . . . have generated a wealth of genetic, reproductive, nutritional, behavioral, and veterinary information. It is anticipated that this knowledge will prove to be invaluable in the management of animal populations in the wild, as well as in zoological facilities.[11]

Similarly, Circus Vargas notes that "circuses give many people [who] never have a chance to go to a zoo the opportunity to see exotic animals. . . . Circus acts that feature [animals'] natural beauty, grace and athletic ability inspire public interest in animals and, consequently, in their well-being and preservation."[12] Dr. Marthe Kiley-Worthington, a well-known animal behavior scientist, notes that circuses can "[raise] public interest [concerning] the plight of species by demonstrating their special cognitive abilities. . . . Circuses are perfectly placed to do research on cognition: how and what different species can learn; how and what they think, and how they perceive the world. . . ."[13]

Another argument is that zoos, aquariums, and circuses fail to teach important lessons or even teach disrespect for animals. Michael Fox contends that "even the best zoos cannot justify their existence if they do not sufficiently inform and even shock the public into compassionate concern and political action. . . . For example, the high-tech Baltimore Aquarium should be abolished as it makes no attempt to engender public outrage at what is happening to the oceans and all that live therein."[14] But in fact, all major zoos and aquariums seek to educate the public about the problems of over-fishing, pollution, and dwindling wildlife habitat.

Similarly, Friends of Animals says that "when we take children to the circus, we are showing them that it is socially acceptable to force wild and endangered animals to bend to our will. . . . We are showing them [that] we find it acceptable to reduce and degrade animals to the level of mere puppets that will do silly or amazing tricks for our amusement. . . ."[15] However, as Circus Vargas notes, "circuses require the animals to 'think' or use their intelligence. . . . Circus animals, like people, tend to be healthier and happier when they [engage in productive activities]."[16] Similarly, the Circus Fans Association of America, a 2,500-member organization that seeks to "create an enthusiasm for the circus . . . and preserve it for future generations,"[17] says that circus animals, "because of the exercise and stimulus provided, . . . are healthier psychologically because of the training they receive and their association with the humans who care for them."[18]

In the most comprehensive study of circus animals, commissioned by the Royal Society for the Prevention of Cruelty to Animals (itself an organization partial to animal rights ideas), Dr. Marthe Kiley-Worthington notes that

> elephants do not normally stand and balance on revolving spheres, yet some can be taught to do this in the circus. This takes a long time, a great deal of patience and a lot of skill on behalf of the *trainer and the elephant* and it is not every elephant that will learn to do this. It is not possible to use negative reinforcement [punishment] to teach an elephant to do this type of thing. . . . When an animal trainer, or anyone who has even a little understanding of animal education, sees such acts, what they admire is the mutual skills of animal and trainer in achieving it [and] the elephant / trainer mutual trust and understanding that has risen in order for the elephant to do this.

> The essence of circus training is that it concentrates on the *individual.* Every animal has a name, and his personality [is] known. . . . The recognition of an animal as an individual, to be related to, with the possibility of having the whole gamut of desires, emotions, likes and dislikes is I believe crucial in the development of . . . respect for other sentient beings. . . . The circus . . . can increase the quality of life for the animal and the human by allowing for the development of positive emotional relationships (affection, in other words) between species. . . . One of the most exciting and interesting findings [of the study] was this mutual respect, trust and affection I found between the animals—big cats, elephants, zebras, horses, dogs, pigs, llamas and so on—and their trainers and handlers.[19]

As with animal research and livestock and poultry farming, activists use allegations of animal abuse as their primary means to build opposition to zoos, aquariums, and circuses. According to the American Society for the Prevention of Cruelty to Animals, "animals exploited for 'entertainment'. . . often suffer lifelong pain and / or intense distress."[20] According to the Washington [D.C.] Humane Society, "it is time the public saw the other side of the circus. It is only the fear of beatings, hook punctures, paw burnings and worse that produces much of the unnatural behavior seen in circus acts. If the public could see, we think people would demand that animal acts be abolished."[21] Friends of Animals, which calls circuses "Hell on Earth," makes several allegations:

> circus animals . . . work from fear. Most circus animals have been brutalized and perform because their food, water, rest (or all three) have been withheld. . . . Elephants are routinely shackled, deprived of food and water and beaten with bullhooks until their spirits are broken, after which they'll allow someone to sit on their heads, or they'll submit to waltzing on their hind legs. . . . Elephants and primates [are] brutally beaten on a routine basis. . . . Other animals are hit, poked, prodded with electricity, jerked with choke collars, have their paws burned, their food withheld and their bodily orifices invaded.[22]

In responding to such charges, the late Clyde Beatty said that "only trainers anxious to get themselves killed would attempt such cruelties. . . ."[23] Another trainer says that the use of force would only antagonize and confuse animals and lead to poor performance. "As with children, . . . the reward system is far more effective than punishment."[24] Says another, "You can't hurt an animal and have him give you his best performance. I have five or six tigers that aren't scared of fire. They are the ones I use to jump through a (flaming) hoop, not a cat that's scared."[25] Mark Landon, a spokesman for Circus Vargas, notes that "the cost of caring for your animals and treating them humanely is much cheaper than abusing them, having them die and then having to replace them."[26] The Kiley-Worthington study concludes that "if [circus] animals lost dignity, this would be reflected in their behavior, by not wanting to do certain actions, being frightened, and showing other signs of distress. This was rarely seen to be the case."[27]

Animals in education and entertainment are protected by three federal laws—the Animal Welfare Act, the Endangered Species Act, and the Marine Mammal Protection Act—as well as by state and municipal statutes that prohibit the abuse or neglect of animals, including beating, whipping, and withholding food and water. These laws also regulate husbandry practices including feeding, watering, sanitation, housing, ventilation, transport, exercise, and veterinary care. The Animal and Plant Health Inspection Service (APHIS) of the U.S. Department of Agriculture regularly inspects animal exhibitors, and some states require their own inspections before traveling exhibits may appear. USDA officials are also empowered to make unannounced inspections, request additional information, issue citations, and revoke licenses.

Rodeos

Roughly 4,000 rodeos that use some 27,000 horses and bulls are held in the United States each year. Animal rights author Peter Singer says that "any rodeo is inherently an abuse of animals, as anyone who has watched one can see."[28]

But the Professional Rodeo Cowboys Association, a 11,000-member association of cowboys, breeders of rodeo animals, and contract performers,[29] notes that

> in terms of expense, a top-performing rodeo animal is like [a new] car.
> A good bucking horse can cost up to $15,000, while some rodeo bulls sell
> for as much as $20,000. Obviously, the owners of such animals [won't] do
> anything to jeopardize their investments. . . . It simply would be senseless
> for anyone connected with professional rodeo to give their animals
> anything but the best care. Like a well-conditioned athlete, an animal can
> perform well only if it is healthy. Any cowboy will tell you he takes home
> a paycheck only when the animal is in top form. Stock contractors, the
> ranchers who raise rodeo stock for a living, also have an obvious financial
> interest in keeping the animals healthy.[30]

Rodeos, which allow cowboys to exhibit the skills used in everyday ranching, include most of the following events: bucking (saddle bronc riding, bareback riding, and bull riding), roping (of calves and steers and team roping), steer wrestling, and cowgirls barrel racing.

In bucking, a cowboy tries to stay on a horse or bull for eight seconds. Usually, a flank or bucking strap (a quick-release belt covered with sheepskin) is placed loosely around a horse's flank area to encourage higher kicking. Animal rights groups often say the straps are pulled tight, cutting into the animals' genitals. The Humane Society of the United States calls them "painful."[31]

However, the International Professional Rodeo Association, a 4,000-member professional cowboys association, notes that rodeo horses are usually geldings (castrated males) and mares. Stallions (uncastrated males) are very rarely used. Moreover, a horse's anatomy is such that it is impossible to place a flank strap over its genitals. The IPRA also notes that if a flank strap is pulled tight, a horse will refuse to buck and may even lie down.[32] In fact, veterinarians who treat large animals often restrain them with ropes tied tightly in the same place as flank straps.

Roping events arose from the need to care for cattle on ranges. According to the IPRA, "when a calf is sick, injured or needs branding, the only method a lone cowboy can use to catch the animal on the open range is to rope and tie the calf. This action is quick, easy and keeps the calf from hurting itself or the cowboy."[33] As in other rodeo events, the rules of calf roping help protect the animals: any injury costs the contestant time, and "there is no chance of winning anything if the animal is injured."[34]

In steer wrestling, a steer weighing between 450 and 750 pounds is wrestled to the ground by a cowboy usually weighing less than half that amount. The Professional Rodeo Cowboys Association asks, "Who is more apt to be injured?"[35] Although steer wrestling may look rough, a 1988 survey conducted by the PRCA found that in 1,633 steer wrestling runs in eight cities, no steers were injured.[36] In fact, the same survey found that "the injury rate for animals at PRCA rodeos was so low as to be statistically negligible. In 6,933 outings, just 12 animals [less than two-tenths of one percent] were injured, according to data compiled by on-site veterinarians."[37] A survey of the 1,768 animals used at the ten-day, 1992 National Rodeo Finals found that only two animals were injured, and both were given a prognosis for full recovery.[38]

Animal rights groups often criticize the use of electric prods or "hot shots" at rodeos, saying these "shock" animals into performing. Prods were actually created by a veterinarian to humanely move cattle in pens. In rodeos, they are used to move animals into chutes. The IPRA notes that "although the electric prod gives the animal a minor surprise shock and untracks him, it has no after-effects and does not injure the animal."[39]

Prods are usually powered by C-size batteries. At PRCA-sanctioned rodeos, prods can only be used on an animal's hip or shoulder areas, where nerve endings are less dense and sensation is weaker. PRCA rules prohibit the use of prods in arena competition.[40]

Initial Campaigns

In the last few years, animal rights groups have organized hundreds, and possibly thousands, of demonstrations against zoos, aquariums, circuses, and rodeos. While such protests usually attract only a handful of activists, groups such as the Fund for Animals and People for the Ethical Treatment of Animals have local affiliates that can quickly mobilize to protest zoos, aquariums, and the nearly 1,500 circuses, stage shows, and other animal exhibits that travel around the country each year. These efforts appear to have had little or no effect on attendance rates. Attendance at Ringling Bros. and Barnum & Bailey Circuses has increased slightly in the 1990s.[41] Attendance at rodeos sponsored by the Professional Rodeo Cowboys Association has been constant at 22 million annually. And attendance at zoos and aquariums belonging to the American Zoo and Aquarium Association has risen in recent years.[42]

The Humane Society of the United States advises activists to "attack the problem of rodeo cruelty" by lobbying for county and municipal ordinances that prohibit the use of flank straps and prods. "The most effective" ordinance would consider "every separate act committed in violation of this section . . . a separate and distinct offense, . . . punishable by a fine not to exceed one thousand dollars ($1,000.00) and / or a term of imprisonment not to exceed thirty (30) days."[43] People for the Ethical Treatment of Animals urges activists to seek injunctions or restraining orders against traveling animal shows and other animal acts:

> Some . . . bases for [injunctions] may be state or local sanitation standards, state or local liquor licensing laws, . . . vicious or dangerous animal laws, . . . liability and insurance laws [and] transportation laws including intrastate and interstate travel and carrier requirements. Ask your attorney to explore non-statutory areas of regulation that might provide a basis for [injunctions] including private and public nuisance cases.[44]

Animal rights groups have also filed lawsuits against individuals and institutions that use animals in education and entertainment. Two of these suits—the "Berosini Case" and a lawsuit against the New England Aquarium in Boston—are noteworthy because they illustrate how animal rights organizations attract media attention and raise funds.

The Berosini Case

In July 1989, a dancer working covertly for PETA videotaped Bobby Berosini, a Las Vegas animal performer, "beating" several of his orangutans just before the animals were to perform at the Stardust Hotel / Casino. PETA and the Performing Animal Welfare Society (PAWS), another animal rights group, immediately circulated copies of the tape to the media, including the popular television show "Entertainment Tonight." Because of concerted pressure from activists, which included picketing the hotel and jamming its toll-free reservation number, Berosini's show was temporarily cancelled.

Berosini in turn filed a lawsuit against PETA and PAWS, alleging that they had falsely accused him of abusing his orangutans. The suit also charged that he was selected as the target of a multi-million dollar fundraising campaign to stop the use of animals in entertainment, and that at PETA's urging, some of the dancers backstage intentionally taunted the orangutans, upsetting them so much that they had to be physically restrained to prevent injury to themselves and the audience. Although PETA filed a counterclaim and requested confiscation of the orangutans, the claim was dismissed.

The trial revealed, among other things, that the videotapes the media received were not originals but edited copies with altered sound tracks. According to the *Las Vegas Sun*, these made "it appear the entertainer was hitting the animals harder than he was."[45] The producer of the tape admitted in court that he had altered the tape's sound and appearance.

Although PETA employed three experts to examine the orangutans, none would sign a statement saying the animals had been abused. In fact, the court fined PETA for filing and seeking to publicize the "unsigned and unsubstantiated" report. Officials from the Animal and Plant Health Inspection Service of the U.S. Department of Agriculture also conducted an on-site investigation of Berosini's facilities and the orangutans, finding no evidence of abuse. In addition, pursuant to a court order, two veterinarians from the local humane society examined the orangutans, again finding them in excellent health with no signs of abuse.

According to news accounts, on the first day of the trial, "jurors smiled, and others in the crowded courtroom laughed as Mr. Berosini ran his charges through their motions, calling each orangutan to a podium to lift his arms and show off for the panel."[46] Yet throughout the trial PETA solicited funds on the pretext that the animals had been abused.

Three other incidents in the case are noteworthy:

• PETA's lawyers were reported to the bar counsel for, among other things, manufacturing evidence, resulting in a $12,500 fine.

• PETA was fined another $10,000 for trying to organize a news conference with celebrities while the case was pending.

• Berosini's lawyer received dead birds in the mail and was subjected to death threats.

After 29 days of testimony, the jury found PETA guilty of defamation and invasion of privacy. It concluded that PETA had "knowingly, willfully, and maliciously" made false statements about Berosini's treatment of his orangutans. Berosini was awarded $3.1 million in damages, court costs, and interest. Additionally, PAWS and its president were each assessed $100,000, also for defamation and invasion of privacy. Nonetheless, PETA continued to say in fundraising letters that its "statements about Berosini's treatment of the animals were true" and that it had lost the case because of "egregious legal prejudice and vested interests."[47]

With support from the American Society for the Prevention of Cruelty to Animals and the Humane Society of the United States, PETA sought an appeal based on "new evidence" of alleged violations of the Endangered Species Act and Animal Welfare Act. It charged that Berosini had dressed the orangutans "in demeaning costumes" and allowed audiences to pet the animals, even though, in PETA's words, orangutans "are highly susceptible to many human ailments" such as "flu viruses, pneumonia, and tuberculosis." One fundraising letter asked donors to send "as generous a membership gift as possible" so that the USDA and U.S. Department of the Interior would "have the orangutans taken from Berosini and placed in a wildlife sanctuary."[48] According to one news source, PETA supporters "blanketed Capitol Hill with protest mail [and recruited] at least 13 House members to write letters to the Interior Department's Fish and Wildlife Service . . . in a successful effort to have the agency suspend Berosini's federal permit to buy and sell wildlife."[49]

Berosini later remarked that "the Animal Rights Movement was born on [so-called] exposes" that have "been skillfully manipulated and force fed to a [media] hungry for ratings, and an emotional public who generously open their purse strings, [believing] they can help."[50]

The New England Aquarium Case

In 1991, three animal rights groups—the Animal Legal Defense Fund, Citizens to End Animal Suffering and Exploitation, and the Progressive Animal Welfare Society (PAWS)—began what one critic called a campaign "to close all aquariums."[51] In fundraising letters and other materials, the groups charged that the New England Aquarium in Boston kept dolphins in containers "barely larger than their bodies;" that it overworked dolphins and trained them by withholding food; and that it "violently removed" a dolphin named Kama "from his family" off the coast of Bermuda and "put [him] into captivity at the [aquarium],"[52] where he became "a shadow of his former, magnificent self."[53] The groups filed two lawsuits against the aquarium, alleging that Kama and another dolphin named Rainbow had been illegally transferred to the U.S. Navy for use in military research.

The aquarium responded that it provides 30-by-40 foot pools for dolphins;[54] that trainers do not withhold food; that Kama was born at Sea World in San Diego; and that the agreement with the Navy limited the dolphins to doing scientific research on sonar.[55] It also filed a $5-million defamation countersuit, saying the groups had "filed their complaint knowing that their claims were completely without merit;" that "they [had] misused the legal process . . . for ulterior and illegitimate purposes;" and that the aquarium had been forced to "spend time and resources to retain counsel and defend itself in court and to counter negative publicity. . . . The lawsuit has had adverse effect on public support; by filing their suit, the groups intend to make it impossible for the Aquarium to carry out its mission."[56]

In 1993, a federal judge ruled that the animal rights organizations did not have legal standing to sue since they had not been harmed by the dolphins' transfer. Moreover, the animals had no standing to sue. A spokesman at the National Aquarium in Baltimore said that "this is the culmination of the kind of harassment we have been dealing with the last three to five years."[57] Another critic at the Point Defiance Zoo and Aquarium in Tacoma, Washington, remarked that "their agenda is for dolphins not to be on display. . . . They only want them to be out in the ocean."[58]

Legislation and Costs

Thus far, animal rights organizations have made little legislative headway in banning the use of animals in education and entertainment. A few localities, however, have banned certain kinds of animal entertainment events, including Lauderdale Lakes, Florida; Leesburg, Virginia; Pinellas County, Florida; Pittsburgh; Southampton, New York; and Washington, D.C. The state of Rhode Island bans calf roping at rodeos. In Canada, the Ontario Court of Appeals recently struck down a 1992 Toronto city council bylaw that prohibited circuses from performing in the city. Spearheaded by the Toronto-based Zoocheck Canada, the ordinance was passed after People for the Ethical Treatment of Animals helped distribute a videotape that showed circus animals allegedly being abused. Other jurisdictions where legislation to ban animal entertainment events has been blocked or changed in favorable ways include Boca Raton, Florida; Hamilton, Ontario; San Juan Capistrano, California; Toledo; and the states of California and Ohio.

While efforts to ban animal entertainment events have usually failed, animal rights activists have nonetheless imposed significant costs on individuals and organizations they target. For example, in 1997 Lisa MacGregor, owner of Horse and Chaise Carriage Rides, received a license to operate a horse and carriage in downtown Venice, Florida. But an organization called the Animal Rights Foundation of Florida issued an "action alert" to its 4,000 members, urging them to write their local council members and criticize the licensing. MacGregor responded that her business would operate in strict accordance with guidelines issued by the Carriage Operators of North America, which specify in detail how animals should be handled. MacGregor's horse would work only four hours a day, noon to 4:00 p.m., during the winter and four hours during the evening in the summer. The horse would have two days off each week.

Two animal rights activists, Diana Cao and Deurita Wieczorek, persuaded city manager George Hunt to reexamine the decision to grant the license. In the meantime, the loss of revenue forced MacGregor to remortgage her home and eventually put it up for sale. Cao also went to MacGregor's house and demanded to see her two horses. When MacGregor refused, Cao pushed her to the ground. She was found guilty of misdemeanor battery and fined $1,000 plus court costs. MacGregor had to sell one of her horses, fearing to leave it alone while activists knew she was busy working with the other horse. Some passengers also expressed fear about riding in the carriage, and others cancelled special events, not wanting to become targets of protest.[59]

In 1991, former U.S. Rep. Peter H. Kostmayer (D-PA) introduced the Exhibition Animal Protection Act, ostensibly to provide further federal protection to all vertebrates used in circuses, zoos, and rodeos. Initiated by the American Society for the Prevention of Cruelty to Animals, the bill attracted only 11 co-sponsors in 1992. The same year, Friends of Animals proposed an open-ended revision to the Animal Welfare Act space requirement for animals in captivity that would have read: "all animals must be given a proper allotment of space to enable them to exhibit the full range of their behaviors normally displayed in the wild."[60] While ostensibly intended to improve the treatment of animals, such a rule would effectively ban most if not all use of animals in education and entertainment since many animals would have to be given miles of territory in which to roam or fly. FoA conceded that the rule would regulate what it calls "the worst facilities right out of business. That, of course, is part of the plan."[61] Moreover, "circuses must be banned, and any piece of legislation that will do that should be pursued."[62]

While many traditional humane organizations have historically worked with zoos, aquariums, circuses, and rodeos to improve animal treatment, the Humane Society of the United States, like FoA, is "committed . . . to the 'eradication' of zoos" that it claims "will not or cannot improve. . . . Most zoos cannot and will not improve significantly to meet the legitimate needs of animals. . . ."[63]

If the use of animals in education and entertainment is banned, some people will never have a chance to see rare animals, efforts to breed threatened and endangered species in captivity will be undermined, and interest in preserving wild animals and their habitat will most likely decline. How successful animal rights organizations will be in their effort to "liberate" animals used in education and entertainment will largely depend on whether the public understands that the goal of the animal rights movement is not improved treatment for animals but an end to all animal use.

Notes

1. Jake Page, "The Revolutionary Zoo" (Chapter 1), *Zoo: The Modern Ark* (New York: Key Porter Books Limited, 1990), p. 17.

2. Merritt Clifton, *Animals' Agenda*, "Zoos May Entertain, But They Do Poorly at Preserving Species," *New York Times* op-ed, June 16, 1991.

3. Gary Francione, quoted in Karen A. McMillan, "Welcome Terrorists," *Dairy Today*, June / July 1990, p. 6; emphasis in original.

4. John W. Grandy, vice president, Wildlife and Habitat Protection, Humane Society of the United States, "Zoos: A Critical Reevaluation," *HSUS News*, Summer 1992, Vol. 37, No. 3, p. 12; emphasis eliminated.

5. Peter Hamilton, *Animals' Agenda*, September / October 1988.

6. People for the Ethical Treatment of Animals, "Traveling Acts: What's Wrong with this Picture?" *PETA News,* Summer 1992, p. 6.

7. Irvin C. Miller, secretary / treasurer, Circus Fans Association, telephone conversation, April 27, 1993.

8. Grandy, p. 14.

9. Michael W. Fox, *Inhumane Society: The American Way of Exploiting Animals* (New York: St. Martin's Press, 1990), p. 154.

10. American Zoo and Aquarium Association, formerly American Association of Zoological Parks and Aquariums, "Caring Today for the Future of Wildlife," 1993 brochure.

11. American Zoo and Aquarium Association, "The New Ark: The Importance

of Zoos and Aquariums in Wildlife Conservation," 1990 brochure, and *ibid.*

12. Circus Vargas, statement quoted in Circus Fans Association of America, "Animal Rights Backgrounder," sheet dated 1991, and Circus Fans Association of America, "Position Statement on Animal Welfare," undated sheet.

13. Eighteen-month study conducted by Dr. Marthe Kiley-Worthington, animal behavioral scientist at the University of Edinburgh, *Animals in Circuses and Zoos: Chiron's World* (Basildon, England: Little Eco-Farms Publishing, 1990), p. 222.

14. Fox, pp. 151, 152.

15. Friends of Animals, "The Circus: Hell on Earth," *ActionLine*, Summer 1992, p. 7.

16. Circus Vargas, statement quoted in "Animal Rights Backgrounder."

17. *Encyclopedia of Associations*, 27th ed. (Detroit: Gale Research, Inc., 1993), entry 8841.

18. Circus Fans Association of America, "Position Statement on Animal Welfare."

19. Worthington, pp. 133-135; emphasis in original.

20. ASPCA, reply form attached to undated fundraising letter signed by former president John F. Kullberg.

21. Jean Goldenberg, Washington [D.C.] Humane Society, *Animals' Agenda,* November 1989.

22. Friends of Animals, "The Circus: Hell on Earth," undated sheet, and "The Circus: Hell on Earth," *ActionLine*, Summer 1992, p. 6.

23. Clyde Beatty, paraphrased in Circus Fans Association of America, "Animal Rights Backgrounder."

24. Roman Proske, paraphrased in *ibid.*

25. Gunther Gebel-Williams, quoted in "Gunther Gebel-Williams Says He Never Mistreated Animals, But Animal Activists Disagree in Never-Ending Controversy," PR Newswire Association, August 15, 1991.

26. Mark Landon, spokesman for Circus Vargas, quoted in "Circus Barkers: Treatment of Performing Animals Called 'Cruel,'" *Los Angeles Times*, August 7, 1990.

27. Study conducted by Dr. Marthe Kiley-Worthington, published in *King Pole*, No. 86, 1990, cited in Circus Fans Association of America, "Animal Rights Backgrounder."

28. Peter Singer, *Animal Liberation: A New Ethics for Our Treatment of Animals* (New York: Avon Books, 1977), p. 231.

29. *Encyclopedia of Associations*, entry 20929.

30. Professional Rodeo Cowboys Association, "Humane Facts: The Care and Treatment of Professional Rodeo Livestock," 1992 booklet, pp. 4, 16.

31. *Ibid.*, p. 13.

32. International Professional Rodeo Association, "To Protect an American Tradition for the Next Generation: Rodeo Looks at Its Critics," pamphlet dated 1991.

33. *Ibid.*

34. Professional Rodeo Cowboys Association, p. 11.

35. *Ibid.*, p. 11.

36. *Ibid.*, p. 11. The cities were Colorado Springs, Fort Worth, Houston, Salinas, San Francisco, Prescott, and Vinita.

37. *Ibid.*, p. 7.

38. Professional Rodeo Cowboys Association, "1992 National Rodeo Finals Injury Report," undated sheet.

39. International Professional Rodeo Association.

40. Professional Rodeo Cowboys Association, "Humane Facts: The Care and Treatment of Professional Rodeo Livestock," pp. 14-15.

41. Kathryn Orth-Mabry, telephone conversation, November 20, 1998.

42. AZA, "Attendance Figures," on file with author.

43. Humane Society of the United States, "Say Whoa to Rodeo: Model Ordinances," undated sheet.

44. People for the Ethical Treatment of Animals, "Model Injunction Against Animal Acts," undated sheet.

45. "Expert Testifies Berosini Tape Altered," *Las Vegas Sun*, July 19, 1990, p. 3A.

46. "Orangutans Appear in Courtroom," *Washington Times*, July 13, 1990.

47. People for the Ethical Treatment of Animals, undated fundraising letter; emphasis eliminated.

48. *Ibid.*

49. Carol Matlack, "Animal-Rights Furor," *National Journal*, September 7, 1991, p. 2146.

50. Bobby Berosini, "Fact Sheet on Berosini's Successful Lawsuit Against PETA & PAWS," undated statement.

51. Paul Boyle, director of programs and exhibits, New England Aquarium, quoted in "Claiming Harassment, Aquarium Sues 3 Animal Rights Groups," *New York Times*, October 1, 1991.

52. *Ibid.*

53. *Boston Globe,* September 23, 1991.

54. *Ibid.*

55. "Claiming Harassment, Aquarium Sues 3 Animal Rights Groups."

56. New England Aquarium, undated news release.

57. Bob Jenkins, senior adviser for research and animal affairs at the National Aquarium in Baltimore, quoted in "Claiming Harassment, Aquarium Sues 3 Animal Rights Groups."

58. Tom Otten, director of the Point Defiance Zoo and Aquarium, quoted in "Claiming Harassment, Aquarium Sues 3 Animal Rights Groups."

59. *Venice Gondolier*, articles in December 7-10, 1996, January 4-7, February 8-11, 22-25, and July 23-25 1997 issues.

60. Friends of Animals, "Zoo Horrors: 100% USDA-Approved," *ActionLine*, Fall 1992, p. 18.

61. *Ibid.*, p. 18.

62. Friends of Animals, "The Circus: Hell on Earth," *ActionLine*, p. 8.

63. Grandy; emphasis eliminated.

CHAPTER VI
Pets

Pets were not common in Western societies until a century ago. Anthropologist Susan Sperling notes that the popularity of pets increased as cities grew:

> The British had always kept dogs, but it was during the Victorian period that the cult of the pet developed, based in part on the perception of pets as a surviving link to older rural values. Pet-keeping also reflected a trend toward [smaller families], in contrast to the extended rural family, in the pursuit of emotional satisfaction. . . . The daily rounds of agrarian life in nineteenth-century England involved riding, shearing, butchering, herding of animals, and crude veterinary surgeries. Domestic animals were used in working roles. . . . [But with] rapid urbanization, . . . animals became marginal to processes of industrial production [and] ideals of land ownership and rural ways of life were retained as important cultural values. The urban middle class took weekend trips to the countryside, developed elaborate gardening hobbies in small urban plots, and kept pets.[1]

While American households today own over 150 million pets, including 52 million dogs and 57 million cats,[2] activist Michael Fox says that

> scientists involved in genetic engineering, who create transgenic animals, such as pigs and mice that have human genes, see nothing wrong in what they do. . . . Likewise, people who create bonsais, deformed bulldogs, Persian cats, and overdependent 'doglets'—perpetual puppy 'toy' breeds— see nothing wrong in what they do. But isn't it time we asked whether it is right to treat other living beings in such ways?[3]

Friends of Animals says that on the "issue of whether any breeding of companion animals is defensible, . . . most activists [say] no."[4] A People for the Ethical Treatment of Animals "factsheet" entitled "Companion Animals: Pets or Prisoners?" likewise states that "no breeding can be considered responsible."[5] PETA's "Statement on Companion Animals" quotes John Bryant of the New Jersey Animal Rights Alliance, who says, "[pets] are like slaves, even if well-kept slaves. . . . Let us allow the dog to disappear from our brick and concrete jungles—from our firesides, from the leather nooses and chains by which we enslave it."[6] Elsewhere Bryant remarks, "the cat, like the dog, must disappear. . . . We should cut the domestic cat free from our dominance by neutering, neutering, and more neutering, until our pathetic version of the cat ceases to exist."[7]

PETA believes that "in a perfect world, all other-than-human animals would be free of human interference, and dogs and cats would be part of the ecological scheme" (i.e., wild predators).[8] PETA president Ingrid Newkirk once remarked that "pet ownership is an absolutely abysmal situation brought about by human manipulation."[9] Moreover,

> we would no longer allow breeding. People could not create different breeds. There would be no pet shops. If people had companion animals in their homes, those animals would have to be refugees from the animal shelters and the streets. . . . But as the surplus of cats and dogs . . . declined, eventually companion animals would be phased out, and we would return to a more symbiotic relationship—enjoyment at a distance.[10]

PETA "opposes horse breeding," calls pet birds "enslaved and distressed," and even claims that aquarium fish "suffer miserably when forced to spend their lives enclosed in glass."[11] But animal rights organizations have criticized the breeding and ownership of dogs more than these other "pet trades." Many seek to shut down commercial breeding kennels, which they claim are all unsanitary and inhumane. They also seek to raise the cost of breeding dogs by requiring all breeders, even small-time hobbyists, to buy costly breeding permits. In addition, they would raise the cost of owning a dog by increasing license fees, enacting mandatory spaying and neutering ordinances, and imposing heavy fees on owners who wish to keep their dogs fecund.

Building Opposition to Pet Breeding and Ownership

When animal rights groups fail to convince others that it is morally wrong to breed pets or use them for companionship, they invoke other arguments. One of these is to exaggerate the number of cats and dogs euthanized in shelters and to attribute these killings to overbreeding and inadequate spaying and neutering. The Humane Society of the United States believes there is a "raging pet-overpopulation crisis" caused by "human carelessness and irresponsible breeding."[12] It claims that 7.5 million dogs and cats are euthanized in shelters annually.[13] In Defense of Animals puts figure at ten to 12 million.[14] At a 1993 press conference, the American Humane Association claimed 12.1 million euthanasias and warned that the number is rising.[15] Citing a ten-year-old article, People for the Ethical Treatment of Animals claims an alarming 17 million.[16]

In fact, the most methodologically sound study of dog euthanasia, conducted by Gary Patronek of the Purdue University School of Veterinary Medicine and Andrew Rowan of the Tufts University School of Medicine, estimates that 2.4 million dogs are killed annually in shelters.[17] In 1993, *Animal People* magazine, which has gathered complete data from shelters in 20 states, estimated that combined dog and cat euthanasia is no more than 5.1 million.[18] In 1996, it estimated an even lower figure—4.5 million.[19]

Rates of euthanasia have in fact fallen dramatically in the last two to three decades. The Tufts Center for Animals and Public Policy estimates a decrease in shelter euthanasia of more than 60 percent from the early 1970s to the early 1990s—even though the U.S. population has increased by 50 million and the number of pets has nearly doubled.[20] In 1973, 20 percent of all dogs and cats—one animal in five—were euthanized in shelters annually. Today, the figure has fallen to less than five percent—one animal in 20.[21] Two critics note that "at the turn of the century in America, packs of wild dogs ran through the streets; people in their 40s and 50s may recall childhood memories of dogs running wild."[22] While the U.S. still has a feral (wild) cat population of unknown size, the problem of feral dogs has been virtually eliminated by humane organizations, veterinarians, breeders, and concerned citizens who have recommended or paid for pet sterilization, sponsored dog-obedience classes (behavior problems—barking, soiling, hyperactivity—are a main cause of dog abandonment), and otherwise informed the public about responsible pet ownership. Moreover, some euthanasia will always be needed because some animals are too old, sick, or vicious to be adopted. About 20 percent of owners who take their dogs to shelters want them to be euthanized.[23]

Another criticism animal rights organizations make is that dogs are often raised in large, squalid commercial breeding kennels for sale in pet stores. Just as animal rights groups call large animal farms "factory farms," they use the pejorative term "puppy mills" to refer to these kennels. And as with livestock and poultry farming, they say that commercial dog breeding is inhumane because it seeks to make a profit. The Humane Society of the United States accuses commercial breeders of engaging in "cruel commerce" that treats puppies "like so much merchandise."[24] Roger Caras, president emeritus of the American Society for the Prevention of Cruelty to Animals, says that "the mentality [of breeders] is that [the puppies] are not dogs, they are a cash crop."[25] According to HSUS, commercial kennel conditions are "squalid," "foul," "unsanitary," and "inhumane," and puppies are "Il-treated," "often ill," and "sick and traumatized."[26] The ASPCA likewise says that the kennels are "filthy" and "atrocious" and that cages are "small," "shoddily built," and "infrequently cleaned."[27]

While some commercial kennels are no doubt substandard and could be improved, neither the ASPCA nor HSUS offer evidence that conditions among the limited number of kennels they have investigated are typical of commercial kennels in general. The ASPCA says it recently "uncovered" 70 kennels in one Pennsylvania county, but gives no indication of what conditions were like at any of them. It contends that "many breeders . . . have been cited for numerous violations," but gives only one example and does not say how serious the other violations were. Based on another lone example, it says that "lack of veterinary care was illustrated" when a rabid kennel-raised golden retriever puppy resulted in six people having to receive rabies treatments. Despite lack of evidence of a widespread puppy-mill problem, it urges its members to write complaint letters to the USDA, which regulates commercial kennels.[28]

HSUS notes that "all fifty states have anticruelty laws [prohibiting] neglect and mistreatment of dogs in puppy mills." Moreover, it notes, "the Animal Welfare Act (AWA) . . . requires wholesale commercial dealers to be licensed, inspected, and regulated,"[29] including stipulations that "wastes must be removed from cages promptly, kennels must be disinfected twice-monthly, each puppy must have a veterinarian's certificate of health, and that no puppy can be shipped before reaching eight weeks of age."[30]

Apparently, however, neither group believes its primary mission is to help enforce such laws or to improve the treatment of kennel-raised dogs. At a 1992 press conference, HSUS chief investigator Robert Baker said, "I don't care if these people [commercial breeders] go to jail or not. I don't care what happens to them. I just don't want them in the business of deal-ing with dogs."[31] The ASPCA notes that shipping puppies between states, usually from kennels in the Midwest to pet shops in East and West coast states, "frequently [involves] numerous changes of plane and long waits in cold cargo terminals" that increase the likelihood of stress and injury.[32] However, in the early 1990s, it "sadly [announced]" the closing of its "Animalport" facility at John F. Kennedy International Airport "after years of dedication to the humane, safe transport of animals and their boarding during layovers. . . . Animalport personnel were called upon frequently to educate airlines and the public about safe travel for animals."[33] This occurred despite the ASPCA's near $20-million budget.

A public knowledgeable about the signs of good health in puppies would largely refrain from buying unhealthy animals, forcing less respon-sible breeders out of business and allowing better breeders to prosper. But instead of focusing on education, animal rights groups such as HSUS have announced boycotts of "puppy-mill puppies" and advised the public not to buy puppies from pet stores.[34] HSUS president emeritus John Hoyt told one audience, "Don't breed, don't buy, don't even accept giveaways. . . . The 'good' pet stores we shall encourage to become even better, which ulti-mately might mean selling no dogs and cats."[35] HSUS' Robert Baker like-wise advises potential buyers to "stop buying puppies in stores."[36]

However, only 500,000—8 percent—of the 6.2 million puppies born each year are sold in pet stores. The remaining 5.7 million are raised in households by show and amateur breeders or are mixed breeds born into typical American homes.[37] Most of these are sold directly to new owners or are given away to neighbors, family, and friends. It is actually "give-away" and low-cost dogs—not expensive dogs purchased in pet shops or from professional breeders—that are most likely to end up in shelters. According to a recent control-group study conducted by the Humane

Society of St. Joseph, Indiana, 41 percent of the dogs taken to its shelter were obtained for free and 51 percent were purchased for $100 or less. Only 9 percent cost more than $100. Moreover, only 2.5 percent were purchased in pet shops.[38] A more comprehensive study of 12 shelters found that the highest number of dogs taken to shelters—31 percent—were obtained from friends. Only 11 percent were from breeders and four percent from pet shops. Similar figures were found for cats.[39] It is likely that people who consider buying an expensive dog from a pet shop or breeder think carefully about their future responsibilities before making a purchase.

In summary, animal rights organizations have failed to produce evidence of a widespread puppy mill problem. Moreover, pet store puppies do not contribute significantly to shelter euthanasia. When animal rights groups use donors' contributions to criticize commercial dog breeding and to launch boycotts of pet shops, less money is available for such programs as low-cost spaying and neutering and dog-obedience training classes that could help to reduce euthansia.[40]

Mandatory Pet Licensing and Sterilization

Norma Bennett Woolf of the National Animal Interest Alliance notes that

> the chain of thought that blames the production of purebred puppies for the death of an unwanted mongrel in an animal shelter . . . assumes that dogs are 'one size fits all,' that a buyer will adopt an adult curly-coated 15-pound ball of fur of unknown origin and potential behavior problems when he really wants a Dalmation or Doberman puppy. . . . Yet repeated often enough and illustrated with pictures of forlorn dogs and cats in shelter cages or dead bodies in barrels, the accusations take hold and are turned into anti-breeding legislation in counties and cities throughout the country.[41]

In the last ten years, HSUS, the Fund for Animals, the Progressive Animal Welfare Society, and other animal rights groups have worked to enact costly dog licensing fees and mandatory pet sterilization laws in dozens of localities. In early 1993, HSUS called on local, county, and state legislators to enact voluntary or mandatory moratoriums on dog and cat breeding, mandatory pet sterilization laws, and other animal control measures. While HSUS president Paul Irwin said that "HSUS is not attempting to eliminate companion animals with these measures," the mandatory breeding ban contained these stipulations:

• "A two year moratorium would be imposed on all breeding" and would be lifted when a government-appointed task force "*so recommends.*"

• "During the moratorium, retail pet establishments would be prohibited from selling dogs and cats under the age of six months" (i.e., no puppies or kittens).

• "Penalties: For *each* puppy or kitten born in violation of the moratorium, the owner or person possessing the animal shall pay a penalty of $100. . . ."

• "All cat and dog owners [would be required] to purchase a license / mandatory ID tag. For those owners who want to keep their animals [fecund], a $100 *per year* surcharge would be required."

• "If an individual wanted to breed an animal, a breeder permit could be obtained" for an *additional* $100. "If a person breeds without a permit," the fine would be $250 *per litter* plus $10 for each animal.[42]

HSUS and the New Jersey Humane Society recently promoted a state bill (A2612) to require commercial breeders, defined as anyone "who owns or operates a breeding facility and sells or offers for sale more than five dogs or cats per year," to register with the state. Of course, a single litter often has more than five kittens or puppies. While the bill never left committee and was withdrawn before a vote, HSUS sought to impose the following stringent standards that would likely have driven many breeders out of business:

• Temperatures inside kennels to be maintained at 50 to 80 degrees for dogs over eight weeks of age and 65 to 80 degrees for puppies and kittens under eight weeks;

• Air to be circulated eight to 12 times per hour;

• Indoor dog runs of "appropriates sizes" to be provided for different breeds of dogs;

• Separate enclosures of "appropriate sizes" to be provided for cats;

• Dogs to receive twenty minutes of *unleashed* exercise per day.[43]

A first offense would result in a $5,000 fine and a five-year ban selling dogs and cats. Subsequent violations would earn a $10,000 fine and an additional five-year ban on sales.

In many other states and localities, animal rights groups have sought similar legislation. Recently in Los Angeles, the Board of Animal Commissioners, whose members include Gini Barrett, director of the western region of the American Humane Association, proposed a $500 tax on owners of unsterilized dogs. Those failing to pay the tax would be subject to an additional $500 fine if caught. The proposal, under consideration when this book went to print, has been endorsed by the animal rights group Animal Issues Movement (AIM). AIM has also endorsed a California Senate bill (621) to require a $250 annual permit for anyone who sells or gives away one or more dogs. Recently in Tucson, Arizona, the Ad Hoc Committee, whose members include nine animal rights groups, sought to impose a $100 annual license fee on owners of unaltered dogs. It also sought to charge breeders a $100 fee for each litter. Violators of the litter permit would be fined $200 to $2,500.

In promoting such laws, activists often point to San Mateo County, California as a model. In 1992, the county enacted an ordinance, applicable only to unincorporated areas, that required: payment of "differential license fees" for cats and dogs (i.e., $15 for an unaltered cat, $5 for an altered cat / $25 for an unaltered dog, $10 for an altered dog); breeding permits for owners wishing to breed a small number of dogs and cats; and fancier's permits for owners keeping between four and ten dogs and / or cats. Spearheaded by the Peninsula Humane Society (PHS), an anti-fur advocate that in 1988 helped pass a California ordinance allowing students to forego dissection, the law was passed despite the fact that dog and cat euthanasia in the county had dropped from 37,680 in 1970 to 8,378 in fiscal year 1990-1991.

A 1995 study by The Animal Council (TAC), a Millbrae, California-based organization, shows that during the first three years of the ordinance, euthanasia actually *increased* significantly in the affected parts of the county, reversing the prior downward trend. However, the downward trend continued in parts of the county unaffected by the ordinance. Licensing of cats and dogs also declined by 35 percent in the affected areas.[44] A 1993 study by the San Diego County Animal Control Advisory Board also found that the number of stray shelter cats claimed by owners decreased by 32 percent following enactment of a licensing law in that county.[45]

One possible reason for the euthanasia increase is that lower-income people with unlicensed pets may not wish to claim them for fear of being fined. TAC president Sharon A. Coleman concludes that "the risks of micromanaging individuals through criminal law and the ensuing unintended effects of avoidance behavior—less licensing and possibly less rabies vaccination—and loss of good will in a diverse population counterbalances any arguable benefits" of the ordinance.[46] Regarding cat licensing in general, the San Francisco Society for the Prevention of Cruelty to Animals concludes that "truly irresponsible cat owners won't be affected. If the law isn't enforced, they are free to ignore it. If it is enforced against them, they are likely to surrender or abandon their animals, which will only add to the number of animals killed."[47]

Costs

Traditional humane organizations have helped to significantly reduce shelter euthanasia over the last two to three decades by offering low-cost, voluntary spaying and neutering, dog-obedience classes, and information on responsible pet ownership. But the animal rights campaign against pet breeding and pet shops siphons resources away from these programs. Moreover, evidence suggests that breeding bans, high licensing fees, and similar laws may actually contribute to higher rates of euthanasia.

Insofar as animal rights groups succeed in persuading legislators to enact such laws, many responsible persons will find it difficult or impossible to obtain the pet of their choice. Even spaying and neutering, taken to an extreme, could have this effect. Gary Patronek of the Purdue University School of Veterinary Medicine, who has extensively studied the U.S. dog population, recently suggested that overly zealous pet sterilization may lead to a shortage of puppies from reputable sources: "We're almost a victim of our own success in getting the message out about spay and neuter. We may be facing a problem in the animal welfare community that no one anticipated. People want animals. If we don't want people to get animals from sources we think are inhumane, we should make sure they can get animals from sources we approve of."[48]

But groups such as the Humane Society of the United States insist that "only by spaying and neutering *all* pets, will we get a handle on this problem."[49] Of course, if "all" pets are sterilized, eventually there will no longer be any pets. In a recent TV interview, HSUS president emeritus John Hoyt held up a photo of a dog and said, "in the future, this is the kind of pet people should have." Reportedly, he was referring to the photo, not to the dog itself.[50]

The most obvious cost of pet abolition would be a loss of animal companionship. Outlawing pets would also affect people such as quadriplegics who need the assistance of animals. Friends of Animals has opposed the use of monkeys to help quadriplegics learn basic household and personal skills. People for the Ethical Treatment of Animals believes that working dogs live "lives of servitude" and that "optimally, human services for the disabled should be improved rather than relying on the breeding and exploitation of animals."[51]

Marthe Kiley-Worthington, a well-known animal behavioral scientist, suggests that a separation of humans and animals would not be beneficial to either. While addressing activists' efforts to end circuses, her remarks have direct implications for pets as well:

> Humans, although they may have access to innumerable beautiful television films, lectures and talks [featuring animals], although they may be taught . . . to respect them and so on, . . . never experience them, or have relationships with them. As a result, . . . humans grow up increasingly alienated from the natural biological world, from its joys and its traumas. They may have learnt to respect and admire animals as alien beings, . . . but the vast majority . . . will never [learn about or understand them through personal experience]. . . . The closer we live with [animals], the more we may find we have in common, but certainly the more chance we have of loving and respecting [them].
>
> It is widely assumed, given a chance, that [formerly domesticated] animals . . . would [go] off into the wilderness and live happily ever after, and that animals will always, or almost always, . . . prefer to associate and

live with members of their own species. . . . This is blatantly not the case. . . . Many dogs given the opportunity do not prefer association with dogs all the time, or indeed the majority of the time. . . . Cats . . . behave in much the same way, as do many other house pets. There has been little serious study of this question in the larger animals, but elephants, rhino, giraffe, eland, civet cats, duikers, horses, cattle and deer to name a few frequently choose human company, usually an individual human, in preference to other conspecifics.[52]

How successful animal rights groups will be in their campaign to "liberate" pets will largely depend on whether the public understands that the goal of the animal rights movement is not to improve the treatment of pets but to end their breeding and ownership altogether.

Notes

1. Susan Sperling, *Animal Liberators: Research and Morality* (Berkeley: University of California Press, 1988), pp. 66-67.

2. Pet Industry Joint Advisory Council, telephone conversation, March 19, 1993.

3. Michael W. Fox, *Inhumane Society: The American Way of Exploiting Animals* (New York: St. Martin's Press, 1990), pp. 170-171.

4. Friends of Animals, "Seal of Approval: How the American Kennel Club Sanctions Abuse," *ActionLine*, April / May 1991, p. 7; emphasis in original.

5. PETA, "Companion Animals: Pets or Prisoners?" undated.

6. John Bryant, quoted in PETA, "Statement on Companion Animals."

7. John Bryant, "Should Dogs Be Kept as Pets? NO!" *Good Dog*, February 1991, cited in Mark LaRochelle, former press secretary, Putting People First, "'Animal Rights' vs. Pets," undated sheet.

8. Statement of People for the Ethical Treatment of Animals, cited in LaRochelle.

9. Ingrid Newkirk, quoted in Katie McCabe, "Who Will Live, Who Will Die?" *Washingtonian*, August 1986, p. 115.

10. Ingrid Newkirk, quoted in "Just Like Us?" *Harper's*, August 1988, p. 50.

11. PETA, "Companion Animals: Pets or Prisoners," "Captured or Captive-Bred Birds," and "Fishes in Tanks: No Thanks!" factsheets, undated.

12. HSUS, "Close-Up Report," May 1992.

13. HSUS, "Pet Overpopulation Fact Sheet," undated.

14. IDA, "Companion Animal Overpopulation," website.

15. AHA figures, cited in "AHA Says 12 Million," *Animal People,* October 1993.

16. PETA, "Spaying and Neutering: A Solution for Suffering."

17. Gary Patronek and Andrew Rowan, "Flow Chart of the US Pet Dog Population," adopted from *Anthrozoos*, 1996 and 1994.

18. "AHA Says 12 Million," *Animal People*, October 1993.

19. *The Hartford Courant*, May 27, 1998.

20. Rod and Patti Strand, *The Hijacking of the Humane Movement* (Wilsonville, Oregon: Doral Publishing, Inc.: 1993), pp. 54, 62; *Animals' Agenda*, October 1991, cited in Strand, p. 62; and Tufts Center for Animals and Public Policy, cited in Putting People First, facsimile transmission dated April 24, 1993.

21. Tufts Center for Animals and Public Policy, cited in Andrew Rowan, "Pet Overpopulation: the Problem and the Remedy," *Our Animal Wards*, Fall 1991, p. 10.

22. Strand, p. 64.

23. Patronek and Rowan and Salman, M., New, J., Scarlett, J., Kass, P., Ruch-Gallie, R., and Hetts, S., "Human and Animal Factors Related to the Relinquishment of Dogs and Cats in 12 Selected Animal Shelters in the USA," on file with author.

24. HSUS "Puppy Mills Exposed," *Close-Up Report,* report dated 1991.

25. Roger Caras, quoted in "Not Fit for a Dog," *Life*, September 1992, pp. 38-39.

26. HSUS, "Puppy Mills Exposed."

27. American Society for the Prevention of Cruelty to Animals, "Puppy Mills: Why Federal Legislation Is Needed," sheet dated March 20, 1992.

28. ASPCA, "Prisoners of Profit," *ASPCA Animal Watch*, Winter 1996.

29. Humane Society of the United States, "Puppy Mills Exposed."

30. "The Puppy Mill Connection," *Animals*, November / December 1990.

31. "Not Fit for a Dog," p. 40.

32. ASPCA, "Puppy Mills: Why Federal Legislation Is Needed."

33. ASPCA, 1991, annual report, p. 17.

34. HSUS, "Puppy Mills Exposed."

35. John Hoyt, president emeritus, Humane Society of the United States, quoted LaRochelle.

36. "The Puppy Mill Connection."

37. Patronek and Rowan.

38. National Animal Interest Alliance, "Vet Visits, Obedience Schools Help Keep Dogs at Home," *NAIA News*, July / August 1996, website: www.naiaonline.org

39. Salman, M., *et. al.*

40. The Salman, M., et. al. study found that behavior problems were the second most common reason for dog abandonment ("human housing issues," e.g., moving into a rental building that does not allow dogs, was the main reason). The researchers found that 85 percent of dogs taken to shelters had not been trained before being obtained, 96 percent had not participated in obedience classes, and 99 percent had not been professionally trained.

41. Norma Bennett Woolf, "Are There Too Many Dogs and Cats?" *NAIA News*, July / August 1996.

42. HSUS, "Summary of the HSUS Recommendations: Pet Overpopulation," facsimile transmission dated March 24, 1993. Emphasis added.

43. National Animal Interest Alliance, "Dog Fanciers Outfox Anti-breeding

Advocates in New Jersey," *NAIA News*, March / April 1997.

44. "San Mateo County Pet Overpopulation Ordinance: A Legislative Failure," *NAIA News*, July / August 1995.

45. Cited in "SFSPCA: Mandatory Cat Licensing Is Ill-Conceived and Ill-Advised, *NAIA News*, May / June 1995.

46. Sharon A. Coleman, "The Animal Council Answers Peninsula Humane Society," *NAIA News*, July / August 1995.

47. "SFSPCA: Mandatory Cat Licensing Is Ill-Conceived and Ill-Advised."

48. Gary Patronek, quoted in National Animal Interest Alliance, "California Bill Charges $250 for Breeder Permit."

49. HSUS, "Pet Overpopulation Fact Sheet," undated, emphasis added.

50. Patti Strand, cited in Putting People First, facsimile transmission dated April 24, 1993.

51. PETA, "Companion Animals: Pets or Prisoners?"

52. Dr. Marthe Kiley-Worthington (visiting lecturer, School of Agriculture, University of Edinburgh), *Animals in Circuses and Zoos: Chiron's World* (Basildon, England: Little Eco-Farms Publishing, 1990), pp. 150-153.

Chapter VII

Shaping Public Opinion

Animal rights organizations understand the importance of conveying their ideas to the public. By organizing demonstrations, distributing leaflets, publishing newsletters, sending direct-mail appeals, filing high-profile lawsuits, securing celebrity endorsements and other means, they convey animal rights messages while seeking to build public opposition to animal use and ownership.

Using the Mass Media

Most Americans have learned about the animal rights movement through media coverage of demonstrations, radio and TV interviews with animal rights leaders, and the like. Activist Kevin Beedy, in discussing what he calls "the politics of media manipulation," advises activists that "what is certain is that the battles will be fought in the arena of mass media. Whether the object is to convince more people of a particular position or to convince politicians to act in the public's interest, no tool is proving as powerful as the television set."[1] Moreover,

> it is crucial for the animal liberation movement to take . . . control of how the issue is portrayed. . . . The most important thing to understand regarding the media's treatment of the news is that reporters seldom or never report facts. They report what they perceive to be the facts. . . . The object is to influence the way the reporter views and presents a particular issue. . . . Political victories . . . go to those better skilled in the tactics of political war.[2]

Likewise, animal rights author Tom Regan asks, "what will it take to win wide acceptance of the animal rights philosophy? Answer . . . the media. The media love a plane crash, a disaster, a conflagration, and that's how they cover the animal rights movement. A break in at a laboratory or an act of vandalism, that's a story. The media don't like talking about substantive ideas."[3] Another activist remarks, "a half minute on television is worth a lengthy to me when it comes to changing public consciousness. . . . In a world shrunken by mass media communications systems, political activists like ourselves can plant the seeds of revolution in millions of minds if we can just make it onto prime time."[4]

Many animal rights groups have arguably become skilled at "media manipulation." An activist guidebook published by People for the Ethical

89

Treatment of Animals offers suggestions on how to organize news conferences, issue press releases, prepare media kits, write letters to the editor, make public-service announcements, answer interview questions on radio and TV, stage demonstrations that use attention-getting signs and costumes, enlist the support of anti-nuclear and anti-war activists, and engage in civil disobedience.[5]

PETA has specialized in attracting celebrities and other well-known Americans to advance the animal rights cause. Past attendees of its annual Animals Ball and Humanitarian Awards gala, which is always covered by the entertainment media, include singer Michael Franks, the late astrologer Jeane Dixon, actress Rue McClanahan, former California Republican Representative Robert K. Dornan, former game show host Peter Marshall, Olympic gold medallist Matt Biondi, artist Peter Max, and rock singer Michael Jackson.[6] Among the celebrities PETA enlisted in 1997 alone were: Lisa Rinna of *Melrose Place,* who appeared on the cover of PETA's *Shopping Guide for Caring Consumers,* and *Baywatch* star David Chokachi, who did TV ads urging viewers to tell President Clinton not to block a proposed European ban on the import of U.S. furs derived from leghold traps. Bea Arthur of *The Golden Girls* also advised women to use alternatives to Premarin (see Chapter III), and vegetarian Jennie Garth of *Beverly Hills 90210* urged people to stop eating meat. As noted in Chapter II, however, some celebrities have broken with PETA over the issue of using animals in biomedical research.

March for the Animals

The June 1990 "March for the Animals," held in Washington, D.C., offers one example of how animal rights groups use the media. Promoted by a New York public relations firm "to alert the public to the plight of millions of animals who endure pain and exploitation each year because of the lack of legislation,"[7] activists carried signs reading "Animals Are Not Toys," "Animal Rights Not Human Wrongs," and "All Creatures Great and Small, Why Not Justice for Them All."[8]

March organizers closely monitored the media's coverage of the event, screening press badges and conducting a "media check-in," "credential distribution" and "one-on-one interviews . . . in specially marked areas . . . assessable only by properly credentialed press."[9] Close to 25,000 demonstrators marched around the White House and down Pennsylvania Avenue to a rally at the U.S. Capitol that featured a "star-studded line-up" of celebrities, including Kim Basinger, Melanie Griffith, River Phoenix, and Christopher Reeves. (Reeves was reportedly booed off stage after defending the use of some animals in research and calling for more moderate tactics.)[10] Said organizer Peter Linck, "it is important to have the endorsement of the Hollywood community because of the impact and visibility they represent."[11]

As part of the effort to "achieve justice for all animals,"[12] activists advocated passage of three of 60 animal-related bills then before Congress: the Refuge Wildlife Protection Act, to stop all hunting and trapping on public lands; the Consumer Products Safe Testing Act, to ban the use of animals in cosmetics and product safety tests to meet government safety, labeling, and transportation requirements; and the Veal Calf Protection Act, to ban the raising of veal calves in individual stalls.

Politicians sympathetic to animal rights, including Rep. Tom Lantos (D-CA), attended the march, as did representatives of at least four animal rights groups often mistaken for humane organizations: the American Humane Association, the American Society for the Prevention of Cruelty to Animals, the Animal Protection Institute of America, and the Humane Society of the United States. Other prominent groups at the march included: the American Anti-Vivisection Society, the Animal Legal Defense Fund, *Animals' Agenda* magazine, the Doris Day Animal League, FARM Sanctuary, Friends of Animals, the Fund for Animals, the Humane Farming Association, In Defense of Animals, the International Fund for Animal Welfare, Mobilization for Animals, the New England Anti-Vivisection Society, People for the Ethical Treatment of Animals, Psychologists for the Ethical Treatment of Animals, and *Vegetarian Times* magazine.[13]

A similar rally was held in Washington, D.C. in the summer of 1996. However, it attracted only a third the number of participants organizers had expected, suggesting that the animal rights movement may be waning.

The Save the Seals Campaign
In the late 1960s, activists began one of the first concerted efforts to build public opposition to hunting. Through the distribution of films, photographs, and articles about the Canadian harp seal hunt, which for centuries has been conducted each spring in the Gulf of St. Lawrence and off the coast of northeastern Newfoundland, groups such as the International Fund for Animal Welfare (IFAW), Greenpeace, and the Fund for Animals convinced new supporters that the hunt was cruel, unnecessary, and morally wrong. The late Cleveland Amory of the Fund for Animals enlisted the support of such celebrities as Henry Fonda, Burl Ives, Burgess Meredith, Mary Tyler Moore, and Loretta Swit, and Brian Davies of IFAW used $3 million in donations to buy ads in every major European newspaper. These alleged that killing baby harp seals for their skin, meat, and blubber caused pain as well as emotional suffering among adult females who "grieved" for their lost pups.

Throughout the 1970s, millions of donors in the United States, Canada, and Europe responded with contributions that provided "seed money" for the burgeoning animal rights movement. These were spent on further advertisements and publicity used to disseminate allegations about the nature of the hunt. As the campaign began to bring in millions of dollars, groups such as the Animal Protection Institute of America, the Humane Society of the United States, and the Seal Rescue Fund also joined the effort.

Due to mounting public opposition, the Council of the European Community voted in 1983 to ban the import of baby harp sealskin products to all EC countries, effectively eliminating 75 percent of the market for seal products. In 1987, Canada banned the commercial hunting of baby harp seals, although the hunting of adult seals has increased since a lull in the early 1990s.

The following excerpt from an IFAW newsletter is typical of the strategy used by organizations opposed to the hunt:

> For centuries, defenseless harp seals and hooded seals (mostly babies) have been subjected to the most *horrifying torture* every spring off the coast of Canada. . . . They are massacred for the luxury fur and leather industry— *or sometimes just to satisfy someone's dark lust to kill.* . . . Frightened baby seals of some ten days of age are separated from their mothers and (crying pitifully) are then brutally beaten over the head and sometimes the throat with clubs or murderous ice pick-like weapons. Bleeding from the nose and mouth, the baby seal is then rolled on its back and the skin is violently ripped from its still trembling body. . . . *Some baby seals suffer the dreadful pain of being skinned alive.* . . . Great tears [flow] from [the] grieving eyes [of the mothers].[14]

Although this was written in 1982, humane methods for killing baby harp seals had been developed and enforced as early as 1965. Each year, Canadian fisheries officers instructed prospective sealers in humane killing methods before issuing licenses. During the hunt, officers stationed on large sealing vessels supervised all operations. Helicopters were used to spot smaller ships from the air, and officers landed and observed hunters to ensure that regulations were followed.

The Seal Protection Regulations of 1965, developed in consultation with wildlife biologists and humane society personnel, included the following specifications: only a hakapik or club approved by regulators could be used to strike a seal; sealers must strike each animal three times on the forehead, causing immediate and irreversible unconsciousness and inability to feel pain; sealers must check that each animal is unconscious and unable to feel pain before skinning.

Janice Henke, an American delegate to the Convention on International Trade in Endangered Species (CITES) and author of a book on the seal hunt, notes that this method of killing is essentially the same as that used in slaughterhouses:

> Instant unconsciousness [results] from the first blow, and [is] made irreversible by the mandatory next two. Brain destruction is followed by

the next step: each pup is stuck with [a] knife in the chest, between the flippers, and the major arteries are severed [to release the blood]. Death within fifteen seconds is assured. . . . Dead bodies twitch, and most thrash from side to side in a swimming motion, as they bleed out. The compres sion of the spinal cord as the first blow is struck causes this reflex. It is identical to that seen in decapitated chickens, stunned hogs, or beef in a commercial slaughterhouse. For the sealer, the reflex action means he has done a good job. The pup is not conscious [and cannot feel pain].[15]

Female seals, or dams, nurse their newborn pups on the ice for a peri- od of ten days. After the tenth day, the dams completely abandon their young, having become preoccupied with finding new mates. In the days immediately following, the pups have not yet learned to find food on their own, and they cry almost constantly for their mothers. As Henke notes, "since she would have abandoned maternal care of [her] pup by the tenth day anyway, how strong can her feelings of loss be? There is no evidence that grief or loss as we know it exists for the harp seal, regardless of high- ly-colored claims to the contrary."[16]

Adult harp seals cry constantly in response to the surrounding cold, dry air. As Henke notes, this "is an entirely natural process, unaffected by events around them and no more indicative of their psychological state than is sweat on a horse in the sun. . . . Those who have claimed that the seal dams weep because they mourn the loss of their young have been either ignorant of seal physiology or guilty of deliberate and inexcusable untruth."[17]

Henke notes that before the EC voted to ban the import of baby harp sealskin products,

the humane aspects of seal clubbing were again explained, defended, and endlessly discussed. Distortions of this method which had been given to the public by IFAW and other groups were countered. The humane training programme which sealers have to undergo before being licensed was also outlined. National leaders and their representatives to the EEC agreed that the hunt was as humane as possible, and probably more so than the slaugh- tering of domestic stock in the leading [slaughterhouses] of Europe. . . . However, none of this mattered because the voting public was not aware of any of it. There was no way to reach the skeptical masses of people who would not have accepted another version of the cruelty issue anyway.[18]

In 1996, however, the Canadian government began raising the annual quota for adult harp seals, which had reached a low of 50,000 in the early 1990s. In 1998, the quota for Newfoundland's 6,000 licensed sealers was set at 275,000, its highest level in years. Through aggressive marketing, Newfoundland sealers are finding new markets for seal meat, oil, and pelts. Samples of seal sausage and seal pepperoni are now offered at food fairs across Canada, and Newfoundland's first seal tannery recently reopened. Seal penises and oil-pills are also being exported to Asia, where they are believed to have medicinal qualities.

Although the renewal of commercial sealing in no way threatens stocks, IFAW calls it "unsustainable," suggesting that seals will be pushed "to the brink of extinction."[19] Paul Watson, co-founder of Greenpeace, recently remarked, "the seal hunt will be shut down—make no mistake about it. If we have to drag the Canadian flag through the mud to do it, we'll do so."[20] But Newfoundland's fisheries minister Fred Efford counters, "we've been carrying on the seal hunt in Newfoundland for 200 years. There's no group in the world that's ever again going to stop it."

Since 1992, Newfoundland has lost 27,000 jobs due to a collapse of its codfish stocks. Some analysts believe increases in the number of (fish-eating) seals is partly responsible. Without the hunt, the seal population reached 4.8 million in 1994 and may be six million today. Efford asks, "Why are these so-called humanitarians not concerned about 400 communities in Newfoundland left without work?"[21] (See Chapter IV for a further discussion of how efforts to end the harp seal hunt have harmed both Canadian sealers and the seals themselves.)

The Save the Whales Campaign

In the late 1960s, activists launched a similar media campaign to "Save the Whales." In response to mounting public pressure, the International Whaling Commission (IWC), an international association formed to regulate whaling for the benefit of whales and whalers, began a temporary five-year moratorium on commercial whaling in 1986 so that scientific assessments of worldwide whale stocks could be made. The moratorium was extended in 1991 and again in 1992.

In 1993, the Scientific Committee of the IWC concluded that only five of 76 species of whales worldwide were threatened or endangered; the other 71 were abundant enough to sustain regulated hunting. Some scientists believe that the abundance of minke whales, one of the smallest species numbering some one million worldwide, limits the population of some endangered whale species, such as blue whales, because they are in competition for food.

Nonetheless, at the May 1993 meeting of the IWC in Kyoto, Japan, delegates voted 16 to 10 (with six abstentions) to continue the moratorium. Three months earlier, the U.S. House of Representatives, having received volumes of mail from animal rights activists, had voted unanimously for House Concurrent Resolution 34 to oppose any resumption of commercial whaling. The resolution, strongly promoted by the Humane Society of the United States and the Earth Island Institute, helped defeat a plan by Japan to hunt 50 minke whales in the North Pacific Ocean in 1993. As Janice Henke notes, the international scientific community recognizes that there is no biological basis for objection to either harvest of harp seals or minke whales, yet [an] animal rights minority [has] so skillfully communicated [its message] to the general public that international politics demands a continued ban on harvest in both instances. [People's thinking] has been carefully shaped by paid [animal rights] professionals. . . . Mass letter writing campaigns and petition campaigns [ensure that] each of these issues is managed by . . . political, not biological, realities.[22]

In 1993, Norway lodged a reservation to the ban and began hunting 136 minke whales along its coast. In 1998, the quota was set at 671, which in no way threatened the estimated 112,000 minkes living in the North Atlantic Ocean. Japan also planned to hunt about 600 minkes in 1998. In Norway, Japan, and many other coastal countries, whaling is vital to the economies of small communities. Whaling generally accounts for half the income of a Norwegian fishing vessel, and there are few alternative means of employment.

Interestingly, the Humane Society of the United States continues to publish materials suggesting that whales are threatened or endangered. Its website says, "twenty years ago the world finally realized that whale populations were perilously threatened by the whaling that had occurred in the oceans for more than a century. A long struggle to save the whales finally resulted in the 1986 [IWC] decision. . . ."[23] HSUS urges Americans to boycott Norwegian products, including fish, cheese, petroleum, and travel to Norway. It has also sought, unsuccessfully, to pressure the Clinton Administration to enact trade sanctions against Norway.

Ultimately, animal rights groups' opposition to whaling appears to be based on a belief that whales are somehow "sacred." But just as beef is part of the traditional American diet, whale meat has long been part of the Norwegian diet. This has prompted some critics to accuse anti-whaling organizations of cultural imperialism. Says Norwegian foreign minister Bjorn Tore Godal, "imagine India . . . threatening the U.S. with trade sanctions if it didn't accept the sanctity of the cow. The principle is the same."[24]

The Silver Spring Monkeys Case
The now-famous case of the Silver Spring Monkeys helped established a model for fundraising and media coverage still used by animal rights groups today. In 1981, less than a year after People for the Ethical Treatment of Animals was formed, PETA chairman Alex Pacheco began an undercover investigation at a biomedical research laboratory in Silver Spring, Maryland. He approached the laboratory's director, Dr. Edward Taub, as a college student seeking volunteer work.

Soon after agreeing to hire Pacheco, Taub left on a two-week vacation, leaving the facility in the care of Pacheco and other assistants. Upon returning, however, he discovered that police, armed with a search warrant, were confiscating research monkeys.

Sometime during Taub's absence, Pacheco took pictures showing unsanitary conditions and alleged cruelty to animals. These were turned over to the police. Money for a camera and walkie-talkies, which allowed Pacheco to take pictures while a guard posted outside watched for unexpected visitors, was provided by the late Cleveland Amory, president of the Fund for Animals.[25] Just before the search, PETA issued press releases to ensure broad media coverage of the raid.

One of Pacheco's photos showed a monkey tied crucifixion-style to a steel restraining device, its head jutting upward at a seemingly uncomfortable angle. While the origin of the photo is unclear (see endnote for a discussion of a related court case concerning the photo),[26] PETA immediately circulated it in the form of flyers and posters with the words, "This is Vivisection." Given wide distribution, they helped to draw new supporters into the animal rights movement. In what soon became a major membership and fundraising drive, PETA distributed direct-mail appeals saying, "money is urgently needed for civil legal costs, expert witnesses, other professionals, etc. for this ongoing project."[27]

The state prosecuting attorney, Roger Galvin (who would later help create the Animal Legal Defense Fund), brought 119 charges of animal cruelty against Taub. After five years in court, Taub was cleared of all counts but one: a failure to provide adequate veterinary care for six animals. While he was found guilty of this charge, the conviction was controversial: five veterinarians supported Taub's procedures while two others believed he had been negligent. In any case, the conviction was later overturned on a technicality, and four scientific societies exonerated Taub after independent investigations.[28]

Nonetheless, PETA's membership skyrocketed. What began as a loose-knit group of activists quickly became a million-dollar organization staffed by full-time employees. In fundraising mail, PETA still claims to have "successfully prosecuted" Taub in a "landmark victory" lawsuit.[29] It also sells a video narrating how "the first-ever police raid on a research laboratory" led to "the first and only U.S. criminal conviction of an experimenter on charges of cruelty to animals."[30] And until 1991, PETA solicited funds to gain custody of several monkeys that the National Institutes of Health had taken into custody after the raid. (See Chapter V, the Berosini Case, for a discussion of a similar PETA campaign that targeted the use of animals in education and entertainment.)

The Boys Town Kittens

Since the Silver Spring Monkeys Case, PETA has made similar allegations against other biomedical researchers. In August 1996, it submitted a 53-page report to the U.S. Department of Agriculture, which enforces the

Animal Welfare Act, a set of federal rules governing the care of research animals. It accused two researchers, Drs. Edward J. Walsh and his wife, JoAnn McGee, of conducting "hideous 'deafness' experiments" on cats and kittens at the Boys Town National Research Hospital in Omaha. Walsh and McGee, said PETA, "open kittens' skulls and sever a bundle of nerves at the base of their brains. . . ."[31] The "mutilated kittens [are] never given painkillers."[32]

These allegations followed a seven-month undercover investigation by an unidentified PETA informant who was hired as a security guard at the hospital. Immediately following PETA's complaint, the USDA made unannounced inspections of the Boys Town facilities. Before the investigations were complete, PETA held several protests outside the hospital and at the home of Walsh and McGee. It also circulated literature condemning the research as "cruel and wasteful."[33]

After 13 months of investigation, the USDA found no evidence of animal abuse at Boys Town. It concluded that animal-care staff and facilities complied with all major government regulations. A veterinarian from the National Institutes of Health also visited the hospital and approved a five-year renewal of an NIH grant. Neither agency filed formal charges against Boys Town and both closed their investigations.

Yet PETA continued to protest. Months later, eighteen protesters barged into an office of Rev. Val Peter, executive director of Boys Town, and handcuffed themselves to furniture. At another demonstration outside the hospital, a PETA intern masquerading as Satan (to represent the "cruelty" at Boys Town) told a reporter, "I've dressed as a carrot, a rat, a dissected frog, a cow, a fish . . . a variety of things like that."[34] PETA also continued to distribute leaflets outside the hospital and at local schools and churches, urging supporters to write complaint letters to Walsh and McGee's home address. One letter said, "We will kill you and every member of your family in the exact same way you killed the cats. No matter where you hide! We will splice open your heads and cut the nerves in your brains while you are alive."[35] According to Boys Town, some employees also received hate mail and bomb threats. Boys Town facilities around the country were also picketed, and a building and van at one facility near Orlando received $10,000 in damage.

Although researchers Walsh and McGee have moved on to experiments that use mice, Walsh was recently interviewed by the Foundation for Biomedical Research, a Washington, D.C.-based nonprofit that promotes the humane use of animals in research. He explained that the cat experiments examined congenital deafness, a condition that ranges from profound deafness to less extreme hearing loss in children. "The cat inner ear," he notes, undergoes "developmental change during the first weeks of life, changes that human fetuses undergo during the second and third trimesters of pregnancy. . . . [Therefore], it was necessary to perform the surgery on neonates, or newborns." The surgery that severed the nerves at the base of the kittens' brains was "conducted in an operating room using standard sterile procedures in deeply anesthetized subjects." In hearing experiments that followed, "the animals are deeply anesthetized throughout each and every recording session, ensuring that they experience no discomfort. . . ."[36]

Walsh believes his research has helped lay the groundwork for regenerating the sensory cells responsible for hearing in deaf individuals. He also notes that "our colleagues, generally speaking, are completely unwilling to talk about the issue publicly for fear that this small, aggressive, virulent group is going to target them next."[37]

Targeting Youth

Animal rights groups recognize that the nation's youth provide a promising source of new supporters, and their efforts at "youth outreach" may be having some effect. According to a 1991 Gallup poll, 41 percent of American teenagers support animal rights "very much" and another 26 percent support it "somewhat."[38] According to the *Wall Street Journal*, "teens have flocked to the movement after seeing endorsements by movie stars like Kim Basinger, Alec Baldwin, Candice Bergen, and River Phoenix and rock groups like the B-52s, R.E.M. and Indigo Girls."[39]

Part of this effort involves what could arguably be called a manipulation of some students' uneasiness about dissecting animals in biology classes. Joyce Tischler, executive director of the Animal Legal Defense Fund, says that "going after dissection enables us to reach out to the next generation with an animal-rights issue that they understand."[40] Sandra Bressler of the California Biomedical Research Association notes that "if you can persuade young people that there is something fundamentally wrong with using animals in research, then you are creating voting adults with views contrary to the research community."[41] In her book *Animal Liberators,* Susan Sperling suggests that "the long-range effects of animal rights on the practice of science in America . . . may occur in the gradual discouragement and fear surrounding the use of animal subjects rather than in the realm of laws and restrictions."[42]

Many animal rights groups believe that encouraging schools to let students opt out of dissection can serve as a first step toward implementing other animal rights policies. In an article entitled "Humane Educators: Compassionate, Not Crazy," published by the American Society for the Prevention of Cruelty to Animals, educator Shelia Schwartz says,

> it's so easy to integrate humane education into the curriculum, there's no reason you can't bring all the issues in, including wildlife, companion animals, hunting and trapping, even diet [i.e., hunting and trapping bans and vegetarianism]. . . . Students should at least know that they have a right to refuse to dissect, and don't have to watch either. We need to

provide them with information so they can make intelligent choices.[43]

Similarly, the Animal Rights Coalition Conference has called on activists to "get people into elementary and high schools to convince students about the evils of vivisection—gain entrance by developing 'how to take care of your pet' programs and then use entry to acquaint students with animal-rights issues."[44]

The Humane Society of the United States

A prominent group in this effort is the Humane Society of the United States. (See Chapter VIII for a discussion of the radicalization of HSUS.) HSUS operates a youth-education division called the National Association for Humane and Environmental Education (NAHEE). For $25, students ages 12 to 18 can join HSUS and receive its quarterly magazine, *HSUS News*. NAHEE also provides several publications, including:

• *KIND (Kids in Nature's Defense) News*, a newsletter featuring "celebrity interviews, puzzles, students' writing, and timely articles" for students grades two through six.

• *Alternatives to Dissection*, a booklet discussing "thirteen alternative biology projects."

• *Does the Idea of Dissecting or Experimenting on Animals in Biology Class Disturb You?*, a pamphlet offering "alternatives to dissection and harmful animal experiments in pre-college biology."

• *HSUS Student Action Guide*, a guidebook with instructions on forming "Earth / animal-protection" clubs at school.[45]

NAHEE's colorful website features several letters from teenage activists. One 15-year-old student tells others about "needless testing on animals," "the cruelty of fur coats," and "the torture that goes on behind the walls of the meat industry's factory farms." A 13-year-old complains that "a significant source of animal cruelty and destruction is the use of animals in laboratories." And a 16-year-old believes that whales will become extinct unless whaling is stopped.[46]

The website also features profiles of student activists, apparently to inspire others to take action. Eden Hommes, a high school student in Massachusetts, formed "the Animal Rights Club" after learning that she would have to dissect animals in anatomy class. When sophomore Tifanie Broderick discovered that high school students in a neighboring town were dissecting cats, she contacted animal rights organizations, which told her of "potential health risks involved in handling animals preserved in chemicals." Seventeen-year-old Paul Shapiro founded a 300-member animal rights group that conducts two demonstrations a month at circuses, rodeos, and fast-food restaurants. After reading literature from HSUS and PETA, 14-year-old Sarah Lantz began a "personal crusade" against dissection. "By the time [7th grade] started that fall, I had a definite set of beliefs. No meat. No fur."[47]

People for the Ethical Treatment of Animals

In a report widely distributed to biology teachers and parents, PETA opines that "while dissection may teach some understanding of anatomy, biology, and physiology, it also teaches a profound disrespect for the life it purports to study and fosters conflict and confusion in impressionable young people who are taught in other classes and perhaps at home and through religious instruction that life is precious."[48] One PETA newsletter shows a picture reprinted from a dissection supply company catalog in which several dead rats are said to have "lost their precious lives so that a child could say, 'Yuck!'" Another photo shows several dead animals in a plastic bag and is captioned, "Why mutilate one body, when you can buy a 'grab bag' of dead 'goodies?' For just $34.85 children can devalue eight life forms, including a once-beautiful starfish, a fetal pig and a frog."[49] The same article tells students, "You have a right to a violence-free education. We will help you in any way we can." Parents are advised to "[meet] with teachers and the school principal to discuss alternatives to cutting up animals in class." And activists should "lobby your school board to pass a resolution recognizing a student's right not to dissect or a ban on dissection."[50]

Since 1991, PETA has organized "National Cut Out Dissection Month," distributing green ribbons to schools to "symbolize the millions of frogs that have been dissected." Students are also asked to wear green armbands, post banners and stickers that say "Cut Out Dissection," and "petition and leaflet their classmates."[51] It advises, "write or call PETA for your free copy of our 'Cut Out Dissection' Kit. It contains everything you need to help stop the killing of the millions of frogs, rats, mice, cats, and other animals who are cut up in classrooms every school year."[52]

PETA also offers an all-day seminar, "Animal Rights 101," where teenage activists learn "how [to adopt] a cruelty-free lifestyle [and] a healthy and compassionate diet" as well as "how to put pressure on industries that exploit animals."[53] PETA staff members also speak regularly at elementary and secondary schools, colleges, and universities about animal research, "factory farming," dissection, and related issues.[54]

For children under ten, PETA offers a biannual magazine called *PETA Kids* that features cartoons, connect-the-dot puzzles, and "advice on how to become a vegetarian."[55] A recent issue tells school children to "give animals a break on your lunch break—don't eat em! . . . At almost every large supermarket, you'll find mock meats . . . that are tasty and good for you . . . . Write to PETA for our free 'Vegetarian Starter Kit.'" The same issue instructs, "look for backpacks and bookbags that are leather-free. Remember, a whole cow had to die for that little bit of leather trim."[56] For young children, PETA also provides tours of its zoo—the Aspen Hill Sanctuary and Memorial Park—where "schoolchildren of all ages" meet "the animal residents" and "[enjoy] a scrumptious vegan lunch." According to PETA, "in contrast to zoos, aquariums, and other animal exhibits where children experience animals as 'things' for humans to cage and control, Aspin Hill shows children that animals are individuals with lives worthy of respect."[57]

The American Society for the Prevention of Cruelty to Animals

The ASPCA publishes a quarterly newsletter entitled *"A" Is for Animal* that is sent to 10,000 teachers at schools throughout the country. While it features informative articles about wildlife conservation, the responsibilities of pet ownership, and related issues, it also seeks to "[get] students involved with legislative issues. . . ."[58] The ASPCA's corresponding Humane Education web page advises teachers to "have your class actively participate in the legislative process by writing letters, talking to politicians and researching the need for new animal protection laws in your community."

"A" Is for Animal provides at best a superficial overview of controversial issues. For example, the March 1998 issue asks teachers to have their students send petitions to the U.S. Department of Agriculture to protest its Animal Damage Control program. ADC spends $37 million a year trapping, hunting, and poisoning wolves, coyotes, and other wild animals that threaten cows, horses, sheep, and other livestock. According to the ASPCA, "this is cruel and unnecessary, since many effective, nonlethal means are available, such as guard animals, electronic devices and predator-exclusion fencing. . . . Your classes can gather other students' signatures on the petition, on which they have asked the USDA to stop killing wildlife and start educating ranchers in nonlethal ways to protect livestock." However, non-lethal methods of animal control are often more expensive than hunting, trapping, and poisoning. And contrary to the ASPCA's claims, they are not always as effective.

Another recent issue says that "up through the late 1980s, some tuna fishermen deliberately chased and captured dolphins in nets so they could catch the tuna underneath, and tens of thousands of dolphins were being killed. . . . Congress passed a law that all canned tuna sold in the United States had to indicate if it was 'dolphin safe" or not. Now . . . the President has signed a bill repealing that law, and soon 'dolphin deadly' tuna will be allowed into the U.S."[59] In fact, the International Dolphin Conservation Program Act of 1997 requires each tuna boat to have an independent observer on board to certify that any dolphins caught are released without harm. Tuna whose capture results in dolphin deaths cannot be labeled dolphin-safe. Under the previous law which prohibited net casting around dolphins, the U.S. lost half its tuna fleet and Mexico lost 6,000 jobs. Nonetheless, the ASPCA asks teachers to have their students write to the presidents of Van Camp and BumbleBee Seafoods with the message, "Keep Tuna Dolphin Safe: Please don't sell tuna caught by netting dolphins."

Direct Mail

Millions of Americans are on the mailing lists of animal rights organizations. The National Trappers Association notes that these groups

> provide marketing messages to satisfy our desire "to do something"—to support a "good cause". . . . Issues that "sell" can be identified by opinion polling and other market-research techniques. Texts, layouts, and even the color schemes and fundraising "newsletters" are fine-tuned accordingly. The "product" is promoted through protest rallies, boycotts and other media stunts. Computer-generated mailing lists are used to solicit funds from the part of the public selected as a potential "target" audience.[60]

The Alberta Society of Professional Biologists similarly notes that animal rights groups need

> overhead, trained staff, and an infrastructure. . . . These financial obligations . . . mean that organizations are economically and philosophically compelled to seek out new "products" or issues [such as allegations of animal cruelty] to offer to the public and their supporters. . . . Furthermore, all animal rights groups are in competition with each other for a larger share of the donor base and experience has shown that the public is more likely to respond to radical and extreme positions than conservative ones.[61]

Critics Rod and Patti Strand note that

> direct-mail solicitation has become so sophisticated that nonprofit animal rights organizations can select specific groups from the general public. . . . Mailing lists are organized [to] query respondents to find out whether they feel that illegal activities are justified. . . . Positive responses to this type of inquiry . . . produce contacts that could aid the covert side of the movement. . . . [If] properly screened and recruited, some [people] could be moved to translate their feelings into action.[62]

Interestingly, animal rights solicitations often include photographs of alleged animal abuse intended to evoke reactions of shock, disgust, and anger. Yet photographic film is made with a gelatin derived from cattle bones. Apparently, many animal rights groups believe it is acceptable to use a product of animal "exploitation" for their own fundraising purposes.

Fundraising Tactics

An examination of animal rights groups' direct fundraising mail shows several approaches used to raise funds:

• *Portraying isolated incidents of abuse as typical.* A solicitation of the Animal Protection Institute of America describes a "puppymill gone haywire" that was discovered in a "remote Nevada location" in the winter of 1991: "An investigator from API . . . discovered the scattered corpses of bassets, Boston terriers, cocker spaniels, poodles, Lhasa Apsos—cats, too!—as well as rabbits and chickens. . . . Here was a paw sticking out; over there, the tail of a kitten. Further on, still more of the frozen bodies. And everywhere—all over the property, death and more death—and with it the fear that, when the snows lifted in the Spring, still other bodies would be found."

The appeal concludes by asking for money to mount a "full-scale blockade" against "crackpot-style, crueler-than-cruel puppymills, . . . a common affliction throughout the U.S."[63]

• *Using vague, unidentified, or contrived photos.* A photo often seen in the anti-hunting / trapping solicitations of Friends of Animals, PETA, and other groups shows what many wildlife experts believe is a poorly staged scene of a road-killed raccoon placed in a steel-jaw leghold trap. Trapper Russ Carman notes the photo's discrepancies: while the foot held in the trap is badly mangled, there is no sign of blood; the trap is almost as large as the animal, a size prohibited in most eastern states where raccoons are commonly trapped; and the animal appears to be lying on asphalt, rather than in an area where traps are set.[64] Asked for details, a PETA spokesman could only say that the photo was provided by another animal rights group.[65]

A recent issue of PETA's *Animal Times* magazine shows a photo of what appears to be an abused mare on a Premarin farm. But according to a *Washington Post* reporter who spoke with the PETA employee who took the picture, it is actually a stallion with a leg wound and its genitalia photo-cropped. PETA president Ingrid Newkirk conceded that graphic artists placed text over the horse's genitalia, but said the animal's sexual identity was irrelevant. Nonetheless, the horse could not have been involved in Premarin production. (See Chapter III for a discussion of Premarin.)

Similarly, an Internet posting by In Defense of Animals describes "monstrous experiments" on cats at New York's Rockefeller University and shows several pictures of cats allegedly undergoing cruel experiments. But a barely noticeable disclaimer in fine print at the bottom of the article notes that "the images in this document are meant to reflect the plight of the laboratory cats now imprisoned and tortured in Rockefeller University laboratories and are not necessarily specific images of cats at Rockefeller University."[66]

• *Portraying animals in inaccurate or misleading ways.* In a fundraising letter of the White Plains, New York-based Committee to Abolish Sport Hunting, wild animals are portrayed as childhood cartoon characters rather than as predator and prey struggling for survival: "That's right, BAMBI will be safe from all those cruel hunters. . . . We need your help in our fight by sending us tax deductible donations. REMEMBER BAMBI, and YOGI THE BEAR are depending on you."[67]

• *Making false or unsubstantiated allegations of abuse.* This is probably the most common method of raising funds. An undated PETA solicitation describes a "ten-month undercover investigation" at Commonwealth
Enterprises, a farm in New York state that raises ducks for *foie gras* or
"fatty liver." According to PETA, the farm "force-feeds tens of thousands
of ducks via a pneumatic pump [until] their livers often swell to 6 times
their normal size. . . . We discovered ducklings being drowned in scalding
water, ducks being so full of food they couldn't walk [and] suffering ducks
with gaping wounds and broken bills. . . ."[68] Another PETA letter says that
because of its investigation, "for the first time in U.S. history, police raided
a factory farm."[69] However, following PETA's allegations Commonwealth
Enterprises was inspected by three veterinarians from the county Society
for the Prevention of Cruelty to Animals, by a committee formed by the
county district attorney, and by a task force formed by Governor Mario
Cuomo. None of the investigations substantiated PETA's charges.[70]

Based on a review of animal rights solicitations, Nancy Thorton of
Lansing, Michigan-based incurably ill For Animal Research (iiFAR) concludes that

> monkeys and chimps, with their resemblance to small, furry children, rank
> number one [in animal rights group's mailings]. Dogs and rabbits tie for
> second . . . cats are third. Mice are a very distant fourth, and rats don't
> seem to get much of a mention—even though rats and mice together make
> up 85 percent of the mammals used in labs. . . . Certainly no one has ever
> gone to the defense of such very common laboratory subjects as slugs,
> squid, mosquitoes, earthworms and fruit flies. . . . Any creature that doesn't
> look good on a poster will [be] ignored.[71]

Caution to Donors

Animal rights organizations make constant allegations of animal abuse
to attract media coverage, bring supporters into the movement, and raise
funds. They target an increasingly urban population that has little direct
experience with farm animals or wildlife and little understanding of the
importance of animals in biomedical research. But as detailed in this chapter and elsewhere, many of these allegations cannot be substantiated, and
others are simply false. Moreover, their aim is dishonest: animal rights
groups often say they want to improve animal treatment, but their actual
goal is to end animal use and ownership.

For potential donors, these considerations underscore the importance of
looking beyond an organization's stated rhetoric and closely examining its
views and agenda. Potential donors should ask direct questions about an
organization's views on animal research, livestock and poultry farming,
hunting and trapping, the use of animals in education and entertainment,
and breeding and owning pets—and they should receive direct answers, in

writing if requested. An organization should also be willing to provide an annual report, audited financial statement, and IRS 990 Form (which lists such basic information as revenue sources and executive salaries) if requested. Most importantly, potential donors should find out if an organization is working to improve the treatment of animals or to end the use of animals.

Notes

1. Kevin J. Beedy, "The Politics of Animal Rights," *Animals' Agenda*, March 1990, p. 18.

2. *Ibid.*, pp. 17, 18, 21.

3. Tom Regan, quoted in *Observer* (Charlotte, N.C.), October 2, 1988.

4. Trans-Species Unlimited (now called Animal Rights Mobilization), "Putting the Media to Work for Animals," *T S Update*, undated.

5. PETA, "Becoming an Activist: PETA's Guide to Animal Rights Organizing," undated guidebook.

6. Katie McCabe, "Beyond Cruelty," *Washingtonian,* February 1990, p. 186.

7. Solters, Roskin, Friedman, Inc., press release dated April 18, 1990.

8. "Thousands March on Capitol to Back Rights for Animals," *Washington Times*, June 11, 1992.

9. Solters, Roskin, Friedman, Inc., press release dated June 4, 1990.

10. "Animal Rights Activists Boo Moderation," *Washington Post*, June 11, 1990.

11. Peter Linck, quoted in press release of Solters, Roskin, Friedman, Inc., April 18, 1990.

12. *Ibid.*

13. National Alliance for Animal Legislation, "March for the Animals—Endorsing Organizations," press release dated June 6, 1990.

14. Brian Davies, International Fund for Animal Welfare, newsletter dated February 1982, quoted in Janice Henke, *Seal Wars* (St. John's, Newfoundland: Breakwater Books, Ldt., 1985), pp. 16-17; emphasis in original.

15. *Ibid.*, p. 26.

16. *Ibid.*, p. 60.

17. *Ibid.*, pp. 20, 60.

18. *Ibid.*, p. 75.

19. IFAW, "Commercial Exploitation & Trade of Wild Animals," website, www.ifaw.org.

20. Paul Watson, quoted in "Newfoundland Sealers Counter Protests with Marketing," AAP Newsfeed, March 12, 1998.

21. Fred Afford, quoted in *ibid.*

22. Janice Henke, letter dated June 2, 1993.

23. HSUS, "Anti-Whaling / Norway Campaign" website, www.hsus.org.

24. Bjorn Tore Godal, quoted in "Defying Global Ban, Norway Still Hunts Whales," *Chicago Tribune*, February 22, 1994.

CHAPTER VII

25. Peter Carlson, "The Great Silver Spring Monkey Debate" *Washington Post Magazine,* February 24, 1991, p. 17.

26. In a 1990 *Washingtonian* article, journalist Katie McCabe charged that Pacheco and a colleague "had staged the picture" of the monkey in the restraining device and that Pacheco admitted in court to having "allowed conditions in the laboratory to deteriorate, then shot the pictures depicting unsanitary conditions." McCabe also said that "the only incontrovertible act of cruelty was perpetrated by PETA" when it acquired the monkeys and "transported them 2,000 miles to Florida by truck." When a court ordered them returned to Silver Spring, they showed signs of severe stress. (Katie McCabe, "Beyond Cruelty," *Washingtonian,* February 1990, pp. 77, 185.)

Soon thereafter, Pacheco and PETA filed a $3 million lawsuit against McCabe for defamation, trade libel, and conspiracy. (*Alex Pacheco and People for the Ethical Treatment of Animals v. Katie McCabe,* case no. 90-CA01627 (D.C. Superior Court).) In 1991, *Washingtonian Magazine,* which provided McCabe's defense, agreed to publish corrections and clarifications to parts of the article and to "make an unspecified donation to the animal rights movement." ("Magazine Apologies in 3rd Suit," *Washington Post,* October 17, 1991.) Corrections included: "a lab assistant, not a PETA colleague . . . placed the monkey in the restraining chair. . . . While the lab assistant was out of the room, Mr. Pacheco took the photograph. . . . Mr. Pacheco did not testify that 'he himself had allowed conditions in the laboratory to deteriorate. . . .' It was not his duty to . . . clean the laboratory."

Bill Weaver, general counsel for Putting People First, "a nonprofit [group supporting] rights for humans and welfare for animals, noted that the out-of-court settlement was "a contract between the two parties, . . . not a court finding of the truth or falsehood of [McCabe's] statements. . . . Most significantly, . . . the case was settled before PETA provided full discovery to *Washingtonian*—so the real truth of the matter remains in the shadows." (Putting People First, undated news release; emphasis in original.)

27. Putting People First, *Amicus Curiae* brief in the case of *People for the Ethical Treatment of Animals et al. v. Bobby Berosini, Ltd. and Bohumil Berousek,* (Supreme Court of the State of Nevada), p. 16.

28. McCabe, p. 185.

29. People for the Ethical Treatment of Animals, "National Referendum," undated fundraising letter.

30. Putting People First, *Amicus Curiae* brief, p. 17.

31. PETA, "Boys Town Cat Experiments," website: www.peta-online.org.

32. PETA, "Cruel Kitten Experiments Protested at Boys Town," website.

33. Foundation for Biomedical Research, "PETA's Latest Trick: Turning Boys Town into a Villain," *FBR News,* March / April 1997, p. 5.

34. Ali Williams, quoted in "'Satan' Protests at Boys Town Office," *Provincetown Journal-Bulletin,* May 1, 1997.

35. "Tough Tactics in One Battle over Animals in the Lab," *New York Times,* March 24, 1998.

36. Edward J. Walsh, quoted in "PETA's Latest Trick: Turning Boys Town into

a Villian," pp. 5-6.

37. Edward J. Walsh, quoted in CNN transcript 9808-02, August 2, 1998.

38. "Animal Rights Battle Spills into Schools as Both Sides Target Next Generation," *Wall Street Journal*, August 2, 1992, p. B1.

39. *Ibid.*, pp. B1-6. PETA also sells a tape called *Tame Yourself* that includes the songs "Animal Rage," "Skin Thieves," "Bless the Beasts and the Children," and "Don't Kill the Animals."

40. Joyce Tischler, quoted in "If the Star Witness Croaks, Will the Case then Be Dismissed," *Wall Street Journal*, November 6, 1989.

41. Sandra Bressler of the California Biomedical Research Association, quoted in *ibid.*

42. Susan Sperling, *Animal Liberators: Research and Morality* (Berkeley: University of California Press, 1988), p. 203.

43. Shelia Schwartz, "Humane Educators: Compassionate, Not Crazy," *Manhattan Pet House Resident*, Summer 1992, p. 21.

44. Animal Rights Coalition Conference, "Action for Animals: A Rising Tide," cited in Putting People First, facsimile transmission dated February 10, 1993.

45. Humane Society of the United States, *HSUS Publications*, 1992, pp. 12-13, and *HSUS News*, Summer 1992, p. 20.

46. NAHEE, "Speak Up," website, www.nahee.org.

47. NAHEE, "A Course of Action," "Learn and Let Live," and "Shedding Light on Animal Issues," website.

48. PETA, "Dying for Biology: A Special Research and Investigations Case Report," undated report, p. 16.

49. PETA, *PETA News*, September / October 1990, p. 6.

50. *Ibid.*, p. 6.

51. PETA, annual review, 1991, p. 9.

52. PETA, "Back to School" issue, *PETA Kids*, 1998.

53. PETA, "Would You Like to Help Animals but Don't Know What to Do or Where to Start?" undated flyer.

54. People for the Ethical Treatment of Animals, annual review, 1990, p. 22.

55. "Animal Rights Battle Spills into Schools as Both Sides Target Next Generation," p. B6.

56. PETA, "Back to School" issue.

57. PETA, annual review, 1990, p. 22.

58. ASPCA, *"A" Is for Animal,* December 1997, website, www.aspca.org.

59. *Ibid.*

60. National Trappers Association, "Facts About Furs!" booklet dated 1988, pp. 33, 34.

61. Proceedings of the 1986 Symposium of the Alberta Society of Professional Biologists, quoted in *ibid.*, p. 34.

62. Rod and Patti Strand, *The Hijacking of the Humane Movement* (Wilsonville, Oregon: Doral Publishing, Inc.: 1993), pp. 64-66.

63. Animal Protection Institute of America, fundraising letter dated April 15, 1991.

64. Russ Carman, *The Illusions of Animal Rights* (Krause Publications: Iola, Wisconsin, 1990), p. 67.

65. Garett Smith of PETA, facsimile transmission dated January 19, 1993. According to Smith, the original photo says, "Credit: S.P.C.A. Monterey Calif. Courtesy: Assoc. for the Protection of Fur Bearing Animals."

66. IDA, posting on website: users.11broadway.com., June 24, 1998.

67. Luke Dommer, former president, Committee to Abolish Sport Hunting, quoted in Carman, p. 59; punctuation as in original.

68. PETA, undated fundraising letter; emphasis eliminated.

69. PETA, fundraising letter dated June 1998 and signed by president Ingrid Newkirk.

70. Putting People First, facsimile transmission dated April 10, 1993.

71. Nancy Thorton, incurably ill For Animal Research (iiFAR), "Whose Life Is It Anyway?" *iiFARsighted Report*, Spring 1989, p. 3.

CHAPTER VIII

How Animal Rights Undermines Animal Welfare

Over the last 15 years, increasing numbers of long-established humane organizations have adopted animal rights ideas and policies. Ingrid Newkirk, president of People for the Ethical Treatment of Animals, noted a decade ago that "humane societies all over the country are adopting the animal-rights philosophy, becoming vegetarian, and working harder to get inside labs."[1] This radicalization of humane organizations undermines animal welfare for a simple reason: it diverts funds from efforts to improve animal treatment to efforts to outlaw animal use and ownership.

While there is no thorough research documenting the extent to which this radicalization has occurred, anecdotal evidence suggests that the pattern is fairly widespread. For example, the American Humane Association, founded in 1877, now claims in fundraising letters that "animals in research . . . are subject to brutal experiments that frequently result in extreme pain" and that "the leghold trap [is] a gruesome device . . . that indiscriminately and mercilessly eats through the flesh of its ensnared victims."[2] The National Humane Education Society, founded 50 years ago, now urges its members to "express your opposition to hunting and trapping on public lands" and "eat a vegetarian diet."[3]

Perhaps some leaders of traditional humane organizations have actually been convinced by animal rights ideas. But perhaps others believe that promoting an extremist agenda helps them raise more money. John Hoyt, president emeritus of the Humane Society of the United States, says that "PETA successfully stole the spotlight. . . . Groups like ours that have plugged along with a larger staff, a larger constituency . . . have been ignored. . . . Since we haven't been successful in getting half a loaf, let's go for the whole thing."[4]

Critics Rod and Patti Strand note that "by using traditional humane societies as forums to promote extremist positions, animal rights groups have been able to operate under a mantle of mainstream acceptability and respectability."[5] One possible effect of this has been to make the most militant animal rights groups look less extreme—and therefore more credible. As environmental activist David Brower notes, "I founded Friends of the Earth to make the Sierra Club look reasonable. Then I founded the Earth Island Institute to make Friends of the Earth seem reasonable. Earth First! now makes us look reasonable. We're still waiting for someone to come along and make Earth First! look reasonable."[6]

Humane organizations have been radicalized by both gradual infiltration and outright takeovers by animal rights activists. Other organizations appear to have willingly adopted an animal rights agenda. This latter trend is particularly evident in the American Society for the Prevention of Cruelty to Animals and the Humane Society of the United States.

The American Society for the Prevention of Cruelty to Animals

The ASPCA was created in 1866 by humanitarian Henry Bergh as America's first humane society. Its original mission was to monitor slaughterhouse conditions and provide ambulatory service to carriage horses and other animals. Today it has a staff of 200, another 200 volunteers, and 425,000 members who pay a minimum $20 membership fee. Its income in 1996 was $19.6 million and it held $38.9 million in assets, $15.5 million in the form of cash and investments.[7]

Many ASPCA donors probably do not realize they are supporting an animal rights group. This is because ASPCA fundraising letters—the only information on the ASPCA some donors ever see—convey the impression of a traditional humane organization. For example, a frequently mailed letter about an abused dog begins, "His belly was empty. So empty it hurt. The back door would open and shut, and Astro would hope for food. But his owner never brought any. In fact, he didn't even look at Astro as he came and went. Astro drank out of a puddle near the stake he was chained to. The dirty water kept him alive, but then the puddle dried up. Astro had only a few days to live." Most readers would probably assume that the ASPCA's main purpose is to rescue dogs and cats from their abusers, since the letter continues, "Please send the largest gift you can to help the ASPCA save animals like Astro. . . . With your financial support, the ASPCA can reach out to animals like Astro and so many others."[8]

Similarly, the ASPCA's 1996 annual report, which features pictures of 17 cats and dogs, makes no mention of the organization's involvement in animal rights causes. It highlights only the ASPCA's traditional animal-welfare services, which are actually very few and minimally funded. It's the kind of report that would likely be sent to the ASPCA's 100 corporate and foundation supporters, again conveying the impression of a "be-kind-to-animals" charity.

The reality of the ASPCA is far different. President emeritus Roger A. Caras recently opined that "nothing is worse than reducing a living creature to a steak or chop wrapped in cellophane."[9] He declares the ASPCA "at one [with] vegetarians, vegans, antivivisectionists and other people generally thought of as 'activists.'" . . . Simply put, they have the same goals that we do. They want to see an end to pain, fear and suffering. We may not all set the same course to get where we want to go; we may have different agendas, priorities and tactics, different strategies, but we have the same purpose."[10]

When Caras became president in the early 1990s, he wrote two presidential addresses to members suggesting that the ASPCA's transition to animal rights has not been smooth. In one he said, "in the last two weeks alone I have received two letters declaring us outcasts because I had made anti-fur comments. Well, these individuals can take their donations and . . . contribute them elsewhere."[11] In another he remarked, "if you do not believe in our fundamental purpose, so be it. Step aside. We are going to win."[12]

Several years ago, the ASPCA opposed teaching children the song "Old MacDonald Had a Farm" because it portrays farm animals as happy and ignores the fact that they are raised for food.[13] In 1997, it complained about a British experiment designed to test the capacity of train windshields to withstand collisions with birds. Rather than firing dead chickens at the windshields, the ASPCA suggested that researchers "get a lifelike synthetic chicken" instead.[14] A recent article in the ASPCA's quarterly *Animal Watch* newsletter urged readers to "save" a turkey this Thanksgiving "instead of serving" one. Information on Farm Sanctuary, a nonprofit organization that "rescues" turkeys from farms, auctions, and slaughterhouses, was included. For $15, the article explained, donors could "adopt" two or three turkeys as pets or sponsor a turkey on Farm Sanctuary's ranch. According to the ASPCA, "this unique way of celebrating Thanksgiving carries a powerful message."[15] Another recent issue of *Animal Watch* urged readers to "eliminate animal products from your diet," to visit the website of a vegetarian organization (the Vegetarian Resource Group: www.vrg.org), and to read *Animal Liberation*, the so-called "Bible" of the animal rights movement.[16]

The ASPCA has also suggested that readers visit the website of the Rutgers University Animal Rights Law Center, which seeks to have animals legally recognized as persons rather than property, effectively prohibiting any animal use. It advises visiting the "wonderful Website" of the Animal Legal Defense Fund, which in the early 1990s created a legal defense fund for Fran Stephanie Trutt, an animal rights activist convicted for her involvement in planting a bomb outside the headquarters of the U.S. Surgical Corporation. In addition, it has linked its website (www.aspca.org) to 19 other national "humane organizations," eight of which are actually animal rights organizations where Internet browsers can learn more "about specific animal welfare issues:" the American Anti-Vivisection Society, the American Humane Association, the Animal Legal Defense Fund, the Doris Day Animal League, the Humane Society of the United States, the National Anti-Vivisection Society, Psychologists for the Ethical Treatment of Animals, and the World Society for the Protection of Animals.

By supporting numerous anti-"pet theft" federal and state bills, the ASPCA has sought to prevent biomedical research facilities from acquiring unwanted shelter animals. It contends that middleman Class B animal dealers "regularly steal family pets out of their own backyards and fraudulently acquire others by answering 'free to good home' ads. . . . If your pet became lost and then brought to a shelter, could you justify his or her possible fate on a laboratory table . . .?"[17] Yet there is no rigorous study showing that pet theft is a significant problem. Moreover, the USDA requires pounds to hold animals for five days and dealers to hold them an additional five to ten days, giving pet owners time to claim them. Bans on using unwanted shelter animals in research actually result in more animal deaths since a separate population of research animals must be specially bred (most shelter animals and research animals are eventually killed). This special breeding also raises the cost of biomedical research.

The ASPCA's Declining Humane Services

As the ASPCA has shifted to animal rights, it has dramatically reduced traditional humane services long offered to pets and stray animals in New York City. Although the ASPCA calls humane law enforcement "the backbone of our animal protection efforts," its 1996 annual report shows that it spent only eight percent of its budget on law enforcement that year.[18] It employs about 12 law enforcement agents in a city of 7.5 million. Moreover, while many cities and towns empower more than one humane society to enforce anti-cruelty laws, only the ASPCA enforces anti-cruelty laws in New York City.

For 100 years the ASPCA operated New York City's main shelter, but it ceased doing so at the end of 1994. That year, it received a $5-million city contract supplemented by $2 million in private contributions. Critics such as Levi French of the Henry Bergh Coalition say the ASPCA abandoned the shelter because "it was losing money"[19] But ASPCA public affairs director Peter Paris says it did so because city funding was inadequate and because euthanizing animals was "hard on the staff." He adds, however, that the main reason was because the ASPCA "wanted to focus more on national programs."[20]

According to its 1996 annual report, the ASPCA has "refocused its resources on the roots of the problem of companion animal overpopulation and abandonment."[21] However, it appears to spend only nominal amounts on this issue relative to its $20-million annual budget. It recently used $80,000 to purchase a "Care-A-Van," a 26-foot mobile van that travels to lower-income neighborhoods and provides spay and neuter services for a suggested fee of $25. Paris says van staff performed 900 surgeries in 1997. He adds that the ASPCA recently lobbied for a new New York state law that uses fees for vanity license plates to fund local shelters. In addition, the ASPCA operates a National Shelter Outreach program that trains local shelter and animal-control personnel in management, animal placement, and humane law enforcement. In 1996, ASPCA staff consulted with and provided training to personnel at more than 80 shelters. Of note is that training for local shelter and animal-control workers includes instruction on such topics as "Lobbying to Make a Difference: Working with Your Elected Officials," "Letter-Writing Campaigns and Other Effective Advocacy Tools," "Building Coalitions to Further Your Cause," "The Legislative Process: How a Bill Becomes a Law," and "Public Relations and Lobbying for Animal Welfare Agencies."[22]

The ASPCA has cut other New York City animal services. In the early 1990s, it "sadly announced" the closing of its Animalport facility at John F. Kennedy International Airport—a shelter for animals in transit—"after years of dedication to the humane, safe transport of animals and their boarding during layovers."[23] And in 1996 it closed a Brooklyn animal clinic that "offered quality medical care to anyone in the community concerned about her or his animal companions. It was a unique service that sorely will be missed."[24] Between 1989 and 1996, it also closed one of two animal adoption centers and two of three pet receiving centers. It also ceased operating 15 animal rescue ambulances and two mobile pet adoption vans. As a result, its own records show that it provided services to 176,373 animals in New York City in 1989 but to only 37,159 in 1996.[25]

The Humane Society of the United States

With a $46-million budget and 1.8 million members, the Washington, D.C.-based Humane Society of the United States (HSUS) is the largest animal rights organization in the country. Founded in 1954 and staffed by 200 employees, HSUS is sometimes confused with local humane societies that find homes for unwanted cats and dogs. But according to its own literature, "we are not . . . affiliated with any local animal shelters or humane organizations."[26] Indeed, HSUS' image as a traditional humane society no doubt helps account for its popularity with animal lovers, who pay annual membership dues of $10.00 (individual) and $18.00 (family).

HSUS' embrace of animal rights appears to have begun nearly 20 years ago. Its 1980 convention called for the "pursuit on all fronts . . . the clear articulation and establishment of the rights of animals."[27] At its 1984 convention, John McArdle, then-HSUS director of laboratory animal welfare, urged caution in openly promoting animal rights: "Avoid the words 'animal rights' and 'anti-vivisection' [anti-animal research]. They are too strange for the public. Never appear to be opposed to animal research."[28] In 1986, McArdle said that "HSUS is definitely shifting in the direction of animal rights faster than anyone would realize from our literature."[29] That same year, John Hoyt, HSUS president emeritus, remarked that "this new philosophy [animal rights] has served as a catalyst in the shaping of our own philosophies, policies and goals."[30] Longtime HSUS vice president of bioethics and farm animal protection Michael Fox has characterized "humane care" as "simply sentimental, sympathetic patronage,"[31] and believes that "Humans are different. We're not superior. There are no clear distinctions between us and animals. Animals communicate, animals have emotions, animals can think. Some thinkers believe that the human soul is different because we are immortal, and that just becomes completely absurd."[32]

Many HSUS personnel have come from PETA, according to Americans for Medical Progress (AMP), an Alexandria, Virginia-based nonprofit that promotes the humane use of animals in research. These include: Richard Swain, vice president of investigations; Jonathan Balcombe, Cristobel Block, and Virginia Bollinger, investigations section; Howard Edelstein, computer programmer; Leslie Gerstenfeld and Kimberly Roberts, international affairs; and Leslie Ison and Rachel Lamb, companion animals. HSUS has also recruited employees from other animal rights organizations. John Kullberg, HSUS' head of investigations, is the past president of the American Society for the Prevention of Cruelty to Animals (ASPCA). Wayne Pacelle, HSUS' vice president of government affairs and media, is the former executive director of the late Cleveland Amory's Fund for Animals, an anti-hunting group based in New York City. Pacelle once said, "We have no problem with the extinction of domestic animals [e.g., exotic breeds of livestock and poultry]. They are creations of selective human breeding."[33] Another key HSUS employee is emergency medicine doctor Peggy Carlson, formerly with the Physician's Committee for Responsible Medicine (PCRM), a medical and nutritional spokesman for PETA.[34]

HSUS was a major presence at the Animal Rights 1997 National Convention, held near Washington, D.C. HSUS speakers included Martin Stephens, vice president of animal research issues; Patricia Forkan, executive vice president; Howard Lyman, director of Eating with a Conscience Campaign, who discussed ways to use the media to promote animal rights; and Michael Fox, who has written, "the life of an ant and that of my child should be granted equal consideration."[35] HSUS also awards small grants to dozens of animal rights organizations each year. These have included Animal Rights Community, Animal Rights International, the Committee to Abolish Sport Hunting, the International Society for Animal Rights, the New England Anti-Vivisection Society, and the World Society for the Protection of Animals.

It is worth noting that while HSUS operates programs to train shelter workers, it runs no animal shelters and makes no significant contributions to them. When the Washington (D.C.) Humane Society, a separate organization, almost closed its shelter in 1995 due to a lack of funds, HSUS did nothing despite its multi-million-dollar budget. Ironically, that same year HSUS withdrew an offer to build and operate at its own expense a model animal shelter in the District of Columbia. In exchange, HSUS wanted three to five acres of city land and tax-exempt status for all its real estate holdings in the city. Negotiations ended when HSUS sent a letter to former Mayor Marion Barry saying it would not proceed unless it could "own absolutely" the land, a condition the city was unable to meet.

Takeovers

While some traditional humane organizations willingly adopt animal rights ideas, others are taken over by activists. One of the first cases occurred in Great Britain in 1985 when supporters of the terrorist Animal Liberation Front captured the 90-year-old British Union for the Abolition of Vivisection. According to observer David Henshaw, BUAV by the 1970s had "settled into a state of [complacency] and, thanks to a generous flow of legacies, wealthy decrepitude." With assets of over half a million pounds and a steadily declining membership, BUAV was "ripe for takeover."[36]

Activists took over BUAV in a series of stages, described by Henshaw as "a revolution generating its own momentum."[37] In the late 1970s, animal rights author Richard Ryder, an "eminently respectable middle-class representative of the decent, moderate wing of the animal rights movement," became BUAV president, and militant activists were soon hired into prominent positions.[38] These included Ronnie Lee, founder of the Animal Liberation Front; Kim Stallwood, a friend of Lee who would later become the first executive director of People for the Ethical Treatment of Animals; and John Beggs, who reportedly cursed stray dogs taken in at BUAV's offices and who often said publicly that he "personally couldn't stand animals."[39]

At BUAV's 1985 annual meeting, activists took full control of the organization by busing in two hundred black-clad "young people . . . of anarchistic aspect" to vote out conservative members of the executive committee. One journalist "was threatened with physical violence if he refused to leave; microphones were switched off, four-letter words flew in batteries of targeted abuse; and older antivivisectionists of a delicate disposition were reduced to floods of tears."[40]

The BUAV takeover has served as a model for U.S. and Canadian activists. In the mid-1980s, three animal rights groups—People for the Ethical Treatment of Animals, the Fund for Animals, and the Toronto Humane Society (an organization worth CAN $20 million in assets that was itself taken over in 1986)—launched a campaign to acquire the Boston-based New England Anti-Vivisection Society, then one of the oldest and wealthiest humane groups in the U.S. The takeover coalition recruited Vicki Miller, co-founder of the Canadian animal rights group Ark II and newly-elected president of the radicalized Toronto Humane Society, to persuade NEAVS president Robert Ford to resign following allegations that he was earning a "hefty" salary for part-time work.

In the meantime, hundreds of applications for voting memberships arrived at NEAVS headquarters, and the wife of then-PETA legal counsel Gary Francione purchased another 300 memberships. An "Action Campaign Fund" was also established to pay for activists' airfare to NEAVS' 1987 annual meeting.[41] The coalition successfully elected their own nominees to NEAVS' 13-member board.

A year later, a fiscally-conservative slate of candidates organized a "Save NEAVS Committee" to challenge what critics called PETA's undue control of the organization, saying that PETA planned "to give $3 million in NEAVS funds to several groups, including the Physicians' Committee for Responsible Medicine."[42] The committee also charged that PETA had "created false stories, altered facts, staged photographs and outright lied to reporters, the public, employees and other activists to manufacture certain images about the organization and its 'leaders,'" and that it was "not encouraging local action in the Boston area but [was] seeking to control it from Washington."[43]

At NEAVS' 1989 meeting, incumbents beat the Save NEAVS candidates by a seven-to-one margin. Officers and board members elected included PETA chairman Alex Pacheco and PETA president Ingrid Newkirk; John McArdle, a former officer of the Humane Society of the United States; the late Cleveland Amory, president of the Fund for Animals; Gary Francione, former PETA legal counsel; and Neal Barnard, president of the Physicians Committee for Responsible Medicine.

In 1998, the Massachusetts Superior Court issued a ruling in settlement of a two-year-long battle over control of NEAVS. Judge Margaret Hinkle found that Newkirk, Pacheco, Barnard, and three other NEAVS trustees all "breached their fiduciary responsibilities" in 1996. This included removing trustee Cleveland Amory "without cause," "delegating to the executive committee . . . excessive power and authority," and "failing to allow Theo Capaldo to stand for election as the duly nominated sole candidate for president" at NEAVS' 1996 annual meeting. Judge Hinkle noted that PETA had received significant funding from NEAVS and that Capaldo was unlikely to support further funding. Following the takeover, NEAVS' assets declined from $8.6 million in 1989 to $5.8 million in 1995.

Two other takeovers are noteworthy:

• In 1987, supporters of the Animal Liberation Front prompted nine directors and eighteen employees of the London-based National Anti-Vivisection Society to resign or face firing. Their positions were taken by ALF supporters.[44]

• In 1985, activists prompted four conservative directors of the well-financed Peninsula Humane Society in San Mateo County, California to resign. PHS soon launched an anti-fur campaign, lobbied for state legislation to allow high school students to refuse to dissect animals, and helped enact the nation's first mandatory pet sterilization law. The takeover had the approval of then-HSUS officer John McArdle, who at the time was helping local humane groups become more "activist."[45]

Caution to Donors

Donors should realize that when humane organizations adopt an animal rights agenda, contributions will not support efforts to improve the treatment of animals but will instead be used in campaigns to end animal use and ownership. There is obviously a need for animal welfare groups to monitor compliance with anti-cruelty laws, conduct animal cruelty investigations and bring perpetrators to justice, and otherwise promote better treatment for animals. But the radicalization of humane organizations siphons money away from these efforts. Moreover, animal rights groups attack individuals, businesses, and concerns that use animals rather than cooperate with them to improve animal well-being. This means that these parties must spend money to defend themselves, again leaving fewer resources to improve animal treatment.

Fortunately, as more humane organizations have adopted animal rights views, new organizations have formed to promote humane treatment and educate the public about responsible animal use. Animal-use trade associations, including organizations representing biomedical researchers, farmers and others, have placed new emphasis on improving animal care. Animal lovers may wish to support some of these organizations, which are listed in Appendix I.

Given the pattern of radicalization among humane organizations, the best and simplest advice for potential donors is to be well informed about an organization's views and agenda before making any contribution.

Notes

1. Ingrid Newkirk, quoted in Katie McCabe, "Who Will Live, Who Will Die?" *Washingtonian*, August 1986, p. 117.

2. AHA, undated fundraising letter signed by executive director Robert F.X. Hart.

3. NHES, "Responsible Caring Takes Many Forms," undated brochure.

4. John Hoyt, quoted in Carol Matlack, "Animal-Rights Furor," *National Journal*, September 7, 1991, p. 2145.

5. Rod and Patti Strand, *The Hijacking of the Humane Movement* (Wilsonville, Oregon: Doral Publishing, Inc.: 1993), p. 57.

6. David Brower, quoted in Robert James Bidinotto, "Environmentalism: Freedom's Foe for the '90s," *Freeman*, November 1990, p. 415.

7. ASPCA, 1996 annual report, financial statement.

8. ASPCA, fundraising letter dated February 1998 and signed by Roger A. Caras, president.

9. Roger A. Caras, "The Way It Seems to Me," *ASPCA Animal Watch*, Spring 1998.

10. Caras, "The Way It Seems to Me," *ASPCA Report*, Fall 1991.

11. Caras, "The Way It Seems to Me," *ASPCA Report*, Summer 1992, ellipses in original.

12. Caras, "The Way It Seems to Me," *ASPCA Report*, Fall 1991.

13. "Going to the Dogs?" *Washington Times*, October 12, 1990, p. E-8.

14. "Enlightened and Inhumane," *ASPCA Animal Watch*, Summer 1997.

15. "Let's Talk Turkey!" *ASPCA Animal Watch*, Fall 1997.

16. ASPCA, "Saying Grace," *Animal Watch*, Fall 1998, pp. 30-31.

17. "A Superlative Relationship," *ASPCA Animal Watch*, Summer 1997.

18. ASPCA, 1996 annual report, p. 11 and financial statement.

19. Levi French, telephone conversation, July 13, 1998.

20. Peter Paris, telephone conversation, July 17, 1998.

21. ASPCA, 1996 annual report, p. 7.

22. ASPCA, "National Shelter Outreach," website, www.aspca.org.

23. ASPCA, 1991 annual report, p. 17.

24. ASPCA, 1996 annual report, p. 13.

25. ASPCA, "Facts 1989," 1996 annual report, and website.

26. HSUS, "About the HSUS," website, www.hsus.org.

27. HSUS, *Animal Rights and Human Obligations*, 1981 publication.

28. John McArdle, quoted in McCabe, p. 115.

29. McArdle, quoted in *ibid.*, p.116.

30. John Hoyt, quoted in McCabe, "Katie McCabe Replies," *Washingtonian*, October 1986, pp. 109-110.

31. Michael Fox, quoted in 1988 *Newsweek* interview, cited in McCabe, "Beyond Cruelty," p. 190.

32. Fox, quoted in *ibid.*, p. 192.

33. Wayne Pacelle, quoted in Putting People First, facsimile transmission dated March 24, 1992.

34. AMP, "What's Happening with Our Humane Groups? Inside the Humane Society of the United States," October 1996, and "A Wolf in Sheep's Clothing: The HSUS—PETA Connection," n.d.

35. Michael W. Fox, Inhumane Society (St. Martin's Press: New York, 1990).

36. David Henshaw, *Animal Warfare: The Story of the Animal Liberation Front* (London: Fontana Paperbacks, 1989, p. 158.

37. *Ibid.*, p. 159.

38. *Ibid.*, p. 159.

39. *Ibid.*, p. 161.

40. *Ibid.*, pp. 161-162.

41. Putting People First, *Amicus Curiae* brief in the case of *People for the Ethical Treatment of Animals et al. v. Bobby Berosini, Ltd. and Bohumil Berousek*, Supreme Court of the State of Nevada, p. 11.

42. *Animal Rights Reporter*, April 1989, cited in Putting People First, "Animal Extremist Relations—Infiltration & Vendetta," 1990 information sheet.

43. New England Anti-Vivisection Society, "Fact Sheet on PETA," sheet dated 1987.

44. Henshaw, pp. 164-165.

45. *San Mateo Times*, December 18, 1985.

CHAPTER IX

Criminal Actions and Terrorism

In the last 15 years, an extremist fringe of the animal rights movement has committed hundreds of illegal and terrorist acts in the U.S., including vandalism, raids, and arson directed at biomedical research facilities, livestock and poultry farms, and other animal-use concerns. The U.S. Justice Department studied animal rights violence from 1977 to June 1993 and reported 313 incidents, 20 percent of which were directed against university medical and research facilities. Another 16 percent were targeted at fur retailers and 14 percent at individuals and private residences, mostly biomedical researchers, their families, and homes. Food production facilities, markets, delis, butcher shops, private and federal research facilities, and department stores were also significant targets.[1] While half the incidents were minor types of vandalism, the theft and release of animals accounted for 25 percent of all incidents. Threats against individuals comprised another nine percent. Major vandalism, arson, bomb threats, firebombings, and bomb hoaxes were also significant crimes.

The FBI also reports 80 incidents of animal-rights-inspired arson in the last ten years alone. In fact, the number of incidents appears to be increasing. Animal Liberation Frontline, a on-line clearinghouse for information on "animal liberation activities and activists," reports nearly 200 "actions" in 1997 alone.[2] As of 1998, animal rights terrorists were claiming almost one violent act per day.

Nor are these incidents limited to the United States. In the 1980s alone, animal rights groups worldwide carried out some 6,000 illegal and terrorist acts at an estimated loss of $40 million annually. Groups are active in Australia, Austria, Belgium, Brazil, Canada, Denmark, England, Finland, France, Germany, Greece, Holland, Ireland, Italy, Japan, the Netherlands, Norway, Poland, Scotland, Slovakia, Spain, South Africa, Sweden, and Switzerland. One group responsible for these incidents is the Animal Rights Militia (ARM), an underground organization that has generated poisoning hoaxes in England and Canada. In 1984, it claimed to have poisoned Mars candy bars on store shelves in England because Mars Candy had conducted tooth decay experiments on animals. The company withdrew the candy and suffered huge financial losses. In 1992, Canadian Cold Buster food bars were pulled from store shelves in Canada after ARM claimed to have poisoned them because the manufacturer was involved in animal research.

The zeal with which animal rights violence is often carried out is sobering. Earth First!, an environmental and animal rights group, has called on terminally ill and suicidal people to die for the environmental and animal rights movements by blowing up dams, power plants, fur warehouses, and paper mills. It has also requested anonymous donations so that "Eco-Kamikazes" can obtain explosives, airplanes, boats, and rocket launchers and has even called for research into "a species specific virus" to destroy mankind.[3]

According to former U.S. Justice Department official Joseph Morris, animal rights terrorist manuals prepared in Great Britain and intercepted by U.S. law enforcement agents are "extraordinarily sophisticated," explaining how to form cells (underground local groups), build and plant bombs, cover trails, and use the media following raids. They also contain advice for "disguising members of terrorist organizations as members of non-terrorist informational organizations."[4] One unidentified 18-page manual offers instructions on sending bomb threats, destroying vehicles, forcing cars off the road, purchasing untraceable equipment, gathering intelligence, bypassing security systems, dealing with the police, damaging furs, tapping phone lines, bugging rooms, stealing animals, and causing maximum damage in laboratory raids.[5] A manual currently available on the Internet discusses how to elude the police, bypass bugging devices, sabotage vehicles, glue and drill out locks, and build incendiary devices. Among its advice: wear "oversized shoes from a thrift shop to avoid leaving tell tale footprints;" cover shoe soles with duct tape; buy clothes from a thrift shop and throw them away afterwards so that clothing fibers left at the crime scene cannot be traced; dispose of gloves since fingerprints may be left on the inside; sharpen crowbars or bolt cutters after a break-in "since slight markings on the tool can leave traceable markings on what [has been] opened."[6]

In the United States, most animal rights violence and terrorism has been carried out by the Animal Liberation Front, an underground organization classified by the FBI as a terrorist group. (See Appendix IV for examples of some of ALF's activities.)

Formation of the Animal Liberation Front

ALF originated in Great Britain, where as early as 1962 a group called the Hunt Saboteurs Association was harassing fox and bird hunters.[7] Some activists, unhappy with merely disrupting hunts, formed a splinter group, the Band of Mercy, which in 1972 began engaging in more violent acts such as vandalizing hunters' vehicles and raiding biomedical research laboratories.

In 1973, the Band of Mercy set fire to and partially destroyed an animal research center. Leader Ronnie Lee explained that "the building was set fire to to prevent the torture and murder of our animal brothers and sisters by evil experiments."[8] The attacks escalated until 1975 when Lee and fellow activist Cliff Goodman were arrested and sentenced to three years in jail. Released on parole one year later, the two men parted when Goodman wanted to pursue animal liberation legally and Lee did not.

In 1976, Lee and 30 others formed the Animal Liberation Front. Within weeks, the raids and arsons resumed, but under a more sophisticated strategy. Lee's year in jail had allowed him to learn the methods of the Irish Republican Army.[9] ALF assumed the IRA's organizational structure of decentralized, loosely connected local groups or "cells." These often carry out operations autonomously and communicate little with one other, making investigations and arrests more difficult. Lee assumed a commanding role within ALF, engaging in little direct action so as to avoid serving time again. He did, however, serve as an above-ground spokesman, supplying explanations for raids to the media.

Within ten years, ALF had grown to an estimated 1,500 activists and 2,000 supporters causing some £6 million in damage annually to British businesses and biomedical research facilities.[10] ALF's own records of its activities from the period February to May 1986 make sobering reading:

• Bedfordshire, 3 April: "the windows of several [Muslim] butchers' shops were smashed, and the tyres of a lorry belonging to one of them slashed."

• Cheshire, 27 March: "about £15,000 damage was caused in an attack on an abattoir [slaughterhouse] in Macclesfield. Two [trucks] were set on fire, and the tyres slashed [on] a Mercedes car."

• Cumbria, 16 April: "nearly two thousand fish . . . were released into Lake Windermere from the premises of the Freshwater Biological Association, where they were being kept in tanks and subjected to cruel experiments for the benefits of factory fish farming. Thirty-five ALF activists took part."

• Dorset: "one of the most active areas of the country with about forty attacks on animal abuse targets in the period February to May; the first of these was on 6 February, when two posh cars belonging to the Adams family, who run a battery [chicken] farm, were damaged with paintstripper and etching fluid (acid) at Canford Magna. Over the period butchers' shops were damaged in Poole, Bournemouth, Winton, Burnley-Willis, Moordown, Southbourne and West Parley. . . ."[11]

Lee went to jail a second time after mice taken from a breeding center were found in his home. Released after eight months, he was again arrested in connection with a series of department store firebombings and sentenced to 10 years in prison. Yet even without his leadership, the raids and bombings continued, including a 1989 bombing that destroyed the Senate House at Bristol University.[12] Lee had left ALF strong enough to survive without him.

Scotland Yard has classified ALF as a terrorist organization, in the same category as the Irish Republican Army, the Palestine Liberation Organization, and the Black September Movement.[13]

Ties Between ALF and PETA

According to the FBI, ALF's first raid in the U.S. occurred in 1982, two years after People for the Ethical Treatment of Animals was formed.[14] ALF's history in this country can be traced to PETA chairman Alex Pacheco's involvement in the British antivivisection movement in the late 1970s. According to his own account, Pacheco spent the years 1978 and 1979 in "animal-related experiences," including time aboard the Sea Shepherd, a ship owned by the Fund for Animals and used to ram fishing and sealing ships.[15] Following one ramming incident that nearly sank a whaling ship, Pacheco was briefly imprisoned. Upon release, he joined the Hunt Saboteurs Association—the still-intact predecessor of the Animal Liberation Front—to disrupt fox hunts and vandalize hunters' cars. A self-described pacifist, Pacheco nonetheless says, "I had a lot of fun. . . . There was a lot of excitement."[16] While in Great Britain, Pacheco met Kim Stallwood, a friend of then-ALF leader Ronnie Lee.

Pacheco came to the United States in 1980 and met future PETA president Ingrid Newkirk, then an animal disease control officer with the District of Columbia. With 18 others, he and Newkirk founded PETA later that year. Soon thereafter, Stallwood arrived from England and became PETA's first executive director. According to a sworn deposition by Gary Thorud, a former PETA fundraising official, Stallwood "had been a member of ALF and came over to train [Pacheco] and [Newkirk] in America [and] was very proud of that relationship. . . . [Pacheco] also told me that he brought [Stallwood] over in the initial stages to train and then finally just to work for them."[17] In other testimony, Thorud said, "Pacheco once told me anything is acceptable in the names [sic] of animals . . . including killing for the animals."[18]

According to Pacheco, PETA serves as a "PR firm for ALF." It has run full-page pro-ALF ads in its publications and distributed press statements for ALF. One statement says, "[ALF's] activities comprise an important part of today's animal protection movement. . . . Without ALF break-ins, . . . many more animals would have suffered." Supporters are advised to "offer a permanent home to rescued [i.e., stolen] animals," to "support PETA's Activist Defense Fund, which helps pay legal fees of individuals accused of liberation-related activities," and to consider "[taking] a job to keep a particular laboratory or animal supplier under surveillance. All contacts are kept in strict confidence."[19]

In 1985, following criticism of ALF in *Animals' Agenda,* a popular animal rights magazine, Newkirk defended the group, suggesting that "device and chicanery" might help stop animal research: "If there were a chance in hell that a bomb threat would make the difference, wouldn't we dial the phone? If we think how serious the situation is for non-humans, we should be rioting in the streets. Because we choose not to riot, should we feel secure in our living rooms advising others not to riot either?"[20]

Two years later, Newkirk said that ALF consists of normally law-abiding citizens driven to break "archaic laws designed to hurt and imprison and slaughter others with whom these people empathize." Since "liberationists" pose no "realistic risk" to human life, she opined, "they cannot be properly labeled 'terrorists.'"[21] When asked in an interview if PETA "collaborated with [ALF] at all in planning some of the raids in which they destroyed property," Newkirk replied, "if we had we wouldn't say so. We don't discuss anything to do with that. We would never place [ALF] in jeopardy."[22] Similarly, Pacheco has said that "I won't get up and denounce the people who risk their freedom to save animals."[23]

PETA: Defending Criminal Actions and Terrorism

Several incidents in which PETA has defended ALF attest to the candor of Newkirk's and Pacheco's remarks:

• When ALF activist Roger Troen was arrested in connection with theft, burglary, and conspiracy following a 1986 raid at the University of Oregon, PETA paid $27,000 in legal fees and, after Troen's conviction, another $34,900 in fines.[24] Later, PETA launched a fundraising effort to defend another activist who had broken a shop window and thrown paint on furs. Said former PETA fundraising official Gary Thorud,

> they discovered they made money off that, so they did it again and again and again. . . . I discovered that we were illegally funding [Troen] with money solicited for other causes. . . . Then I said, you can't raise money to support a convicted felon, or an admitted felon. Then they were using money without mentioning it, the money they had got to defend [the man who] broke the window and threw paint on furs.[25]

• In 1989, ALF raided and set fire to a research facility and administration building at the University of Arizona. More than 1,200 animals were stolen and $500,000 in damage caused. Among the animals taken were 30 mice infected with crypto sporidium, known to be deadly to malnourished children, AIDS patients, and other immuno-suppressed persons.[26] The next day, PETA issued press statements and distributed videotapes taken during the raid,[27] one of which was "transmitted via satellite from [PETA headquarters] to channel 9 [in Tucson, Arizona, and] shown on three major television stations. . . ."[28]

• Three months later, ALF raided the Texas Tech University Health Science Center, causing $55,000 in damage and stealing five cats used to study Sudden Infant Death Syndrome, a condition that kills some 8,000 infants annually. The next day, PETA issued press releases for ALF. Ten weeks later, it filed a formal complaint with the National Institutes of Health, charging that the center had committed 15 violations of federal animal protection laws. Several officials, four scientists, and two staff members of the National Heart, Lung and Blood Institute investigated the center and pronounced the allegations unfounded.

• In 1991, following a raid and three-alarm fire at a food co-op, PETA issued a statement saying, "we cannot condemn the Animal Liberation Front. . . . They act courageously, risking their freedom and their careers to stop the terror inflicted every day on animals in the labs."[29]

PETA also urges its members to defend ALF. In one activist guide-book, readers are told how to answer questions that reporters or critics of the animal rights movement might ask, such as, "How can you justify the millions of dollars worth of property damage done by the Animal Liberation Front?" Response: "The ALF breaks inanimate objects such as stereotaxic devices and decapitators in order to save lives. The ALF raids have given us proof of the abuse of tax dollars and have resulted in shut-ting down labs."[30]

In a pamphlet entitled "Activism and the Law," PETA offers advice to those contemplating criminal actions to "liberate" animals. Remarking that "no struggle against exploitation has been won without [illegal actions]," PETA says, "judges dismiss cases for cryptic, technical reasons" and "today's legal system is a nightmare for the police officer: a poker game in which all the best cards seem to be in the defendant's hand." Readers are asked to consider a hypothetical case in which a couple is stopped by the police "in the vicinity of the burglary of a primate research center:"

> As he reaches into a coat pocket to pull out a wallet, one of the officers spins him around, pats down his clothing, and pulls out the sole contents of the other pocket: a map of the research center with the surveillance camera and burglar alarm locations clearly marked. The officers order Brown to open his pack. He refuses to do so, stating that the pack contains only camping gear. The officers arrest Brown, search his pack and discover burglary tools and stolen research files.[31]

Readers are then asked to think about the suspects' legal situation when brought to trial. One critic notes that "this pamphlet is surely one of the few cases where a tax-exempt organization provides written legal counsel prior to the commission of a crime."[32]

Ironically, many ALF raids have led to the deaths of animals. *Animal People* magazine reports that in the first half of 1996 alone, 3,000 animals died as a result of ALF actions. When ALF released minks from the L.W. Bennett & Sons fur farm near East Bloomfield, New York, 2,000 starved in the late winter snows or were hit by cars. In England, 1,000 pheasants released from a farm at Wherwall Estate, Andover starved, froze to death, or suffocated while huddling together for warmth after activists smashed the heating system. In 1991, 5,000 turkeys suffocated after an ALF activist allegedly sabotaged the electrical system at Nicholas Turkey Breeding Farms in Lincoln, California.[33] And in 1997, five ALF activists released

1,500 minks from the Ebert Fur Farm in Blenheim, Ontario, 300 of which were killed by pneumonia, in-fighting, or cars.[34]

Costs and Remedies

The 1993 U.S. Department of Justice report cited above concludes that

> animal rights extremism in the United States has significantly affected the enterprises and industries it has victimized. The effects include the direct costs of physical destruction or stolen property, the collateral costs of enhanced security, higher insurance rates, and lost clientele, and the indirect costs of disrupted, delayed, or cancelled research. These compounded effects on targeted animal enterprises have not been reliably quantified.[35]

Some attempts have been made to calculate the costs of animal rights violence and terrorism. A 1993 report by the American Association of Medical Colleges found that of 126 medical schools responding to a survey, 76 reported losses totaling more than $4.5 million and 33,000 hours of labor due to demonstrations, break-ins, vandalism, lost grants, and other disruptive incidents during the preceding five years. Activist-precipitated construction delays and the installation of new security cost the schools another $6.8 million during the period. The schools also estimated current and on-going expenses approaching $17.3 million and 170,000 hours of labor for security personnel, insurance, record-keeping, and compliance with recent regulations.[36] The Department of Justice study found that security costs for most targeted industries had risen 10 to 20 percent because of animal rights violence.

Moreover, the AAMC study concluded that medical students have been deterred from careers in biomedical research and some biomedical researchers have left the animal research field: "harassments of faculty and staff . . . has been experienced in an estimated 3,800 incidents during the 5-year period. They range from bomb and death threats to picketing of family homes, graffiti, and threatening letters and phone calls."[37] Steven Wise, a scientist at the National Institutes of Mental Health, warns that a significant loss of biomedical researchers could exact a price in human lives: "If the chain of scientific talent is broken, society won't be able to reverse that trend easily. In five or 10 years, when we desperately need good scientists to solve another health emergency like AIDS, the scientific talent just will not be there."[38]

Recently, inroads have been made in gathering information on animal rights terrorist groups and in apprehending suspects. In 1998, activist Douglas Joshua Ellerman was sentenced to seven years in prison as part of a plea bargain agreement to avoid a 35-year sentence for his role a 1997 bombing of the Utah-based Fur Breeders Agricultural Cooperative, which caused $1 million in damage. This is the most severe sentence imposed to date on any animal rights activist. Five other activists were also indicted as suspects in a rash of crimes against animal enterprises in the Salt Lake City area: Ellerman's brother, Clinton Colby Ellerman, who has received a two-year sentence; Andrew N. Bishop of Ithaca, New York; Alexander David Slack of Sandy, Utah; Adam Troy Peace of Huntington Beach, California; and Sean Albert Gautschy of Salt Lake City. Two other activists, Peter D. Young and Justin Samuel, were also indicted recently under charges of releasing thousands of minks on farms in Iowa, South Dakota, and Wisconsin. They could each receive sentences of 82 years.

As of mid-1998, at least eight animal rights terrorists had been imprisoned or released on probation. These included Rodney Coronado, who was sentenced to 57 months for aiding an abetting arson and handling stolen property. In the early 1990s, a federal grand jury also subpoenaed Ingrid Newkirk and Alex Pacheco of PETA to provide fingerprints and handwriting samples to the FBI as part of a five-state federal task force investigation into ALF raids at Michigan State University and elsewhere.[39]

In addition to longstanding state statues that prohibit breaking and entering, theft, receiving stolen goods, arson, harassment, and conspiracy, laws specifically designed to protect biomedical research laboratories, their employees, and animal subjects have been enacted in at least 34 states. Other state laws prohibit any person from intentionally, willfully, and without permission releasing any animal that is lawfully used in science, research, commerce, agriculture, or education. In Colorado, such actions are a Class 6 felony and guilty parties must pay restitution for damages. In Nebraska, perpetrators are also liable for damages. In South Dakota, damaging, destroying, or stealing property or animals from research or agricultural facilities is also a felony, and victims may bring civil suits against perpetrators. Legislation in Missouri, South Carolina, and Texas forbids similar acts, which are classified as either misdemeanors or felonies. The Missouri law requires guilty parties to pay restitution while in Tennessee a victim may apply for an injunction or temporary restraining order.[40]

In 1992 President Bush also signed the Animal Enterprise Protection Act, amending Title 18 of the U.S. Criminal Code to outlaw theft of or damage to equipment, records, or other property (including animals) at research laboratories, farms, zoos, aquariums, circuses, rodeos, and similar concerns. Introduced by Representative Charles Stenholm (D-TX) and Senator Howell Heflin (D-AL), the bill passed unanimously in both the U.S. House and Senate and carries penalties ranging from one year to life imprisonment as well as restitution for damages.[41]

Enactment of the Animal Enterprise Protection Act is seen by many as significant. Legal expert David T. Hardy says that

> police at the city or county level, let alone [university] security squads, are no better placed to deal with [ALF's] cellular organization and international connections than they would be with the Islamic Jihad or the Italian Red

Brigade. . . . What is necessary is . . . a vigorous commitment of law enforcement resources at the national level, compilation of national data on illicit activities, projections, and undercover leads, and a task force specifically dedicated to penetrating and arresting the threat to biomedical research.[42]

Notes

1. U.S. Department of Justice, *Report to Congress on the Extent and Effects of Domestic and International Terrorism on Animal Enterprises,* August 1993.

2. Animal Liberation Frontline, "USA Diary of Actions, 1997," website: www.animal-liberation.net.

3. "Eco-Kamikazes Wanted," *Earth First! Journal,* September 22, 1989, p. 21.

4. Joseph Morris, former official, U.S. Justice Department, quoted in Katie McCabe, "Beyond Cruelty," *Washingtonian,* February 1990, pp. 188-189.

5. "Action for Animals," unidentified manual suggesting terrorist activities, dated 1986.

6. Animal Liberation Frontline, "The A.L.F. Primer," website, www.animal-liberation.net.

7. David Henshaw, *Animal Warfare: The Story of the Animal Liberation Front* (London: Fontana Paperbacks, 1989), p. 12.

8. *Ibid.,* pp. 14-15.

9. *Ibid.,* p. 50.

10. *Ibid.* p. 52.

11. Animal Liberation Front, "Action Report," quoted in Henshaw, p. 53.

12. Henshaw, p. 202.

13. Peggy Peck, "Animal Rights: Terrorists Strike Medicine," *Physician's Management,* June 1989.

14. David T. Hardy, *America's New Extremists: What You Need to Know about the Animal Rights Movement* (Washington, D.C.: Washington Legal Foundation, 1990), p. 25. However, some unofficial sources date ALF's U.S. activities to 1977, when two dolphins were reportedly stolen from the Hawaii Marine Lab in Honolulu. See *Liberator,* U.S. edition, 1988.

15. Alex Pacheco and Gary Francione, "The Silver Spring Monkeys," *In Defense of Animals* 135, Peter Singer, ed. (New York: Harper & Row, 1985), cited in Hardy, p. 26 and footnote.

16. Peter Carlson, "The Great Silver Spring Monkey Debate," *Washington Post Magazine,* February 24, 1991, p. 16.

17. Gary Thorud, quoted in Putting People First, *Amicus Curiae* brief in the case of *People for the Ethical Treatment of Animals et al. v. Bobby Berosini, Ltd. and Bohumil Berousek* (Supreme Court of the State of Nevada), p. 7.

18. Gary Thorud, quoted in *Animal Rights Reporter,* September 1990, p. 3.

19. PETA, statement cited in Putting People First, pp. 7-8.

20. Ingrid Newkirk, "Support, Not Criticize, ALF Actions," *Animals' Agenda,* June 1985.

21. Ingrid Newkirk, "PETA Will Continue Aid to Animal Liberationists," *Montgomery Journal,* Sept. 15, 1987.

22. Ingrid Newkirk, quoted in Putting People First, p. 4.

23. Alex Pacheco, quoted in Carlson, p. 29.

24. McCabe, p. 189.

25. Deposition of Gary Dennis Thorud, *Bobby Berosini Ltd. v. People for the Ethical Treatment of Animals,* case no. A276505 (District Court, Clark County, Nevada), pp. 49-50.

26. *Washington Post,* May 30, 1989.

27. University of Arizona, *Animal Liberation Front Break-In,* 1989.

28. Putting People First, p. 8.

29. PETA, press statement dated June 19, 1991.

30. PETA, "Becoming an Activist: PETA's Guide to Animal Rights Organizing," undated guidebook.

31. PETA, "Activism and the Law," quoted in Putting People First, p. 9.

32. *Ibid.,* p. 9.

33. "ALF Raids Kill Animals," *Animal People,* August / September 1996.

34. "Mink Free, But Not Metro Detroiters," *Detroit News,* April 2, 1997.

35. U.S. Department of Justice, *ibid.*

36. American Association of Medical Colleges, "Cost of Animal 'Rights' Activities and Use of Animals in Medical Curricula," facsimile transmission dated May 18, 1993.

37. *Ibid.*

38. Steven Wise, quoted in Katie McCabe, "Who Will Live, Who Will Die?" *Washingtonian,* August 1986, p. 153.

39. *Campus Life,* March 8, 1992, and Americans for Medical Progress, news release dated July 21, 1992. The raid at Michigan State caused at least $125,000 in damage and destroyed 32 years of research on the effects of toxins in minks as well as on fertility problems in humans and endangered species.

40. "Summary of 1992 State Legislation Affecting Animal Research," *Foundation for Biomedical Research Newsletter,* September / October 1992, pp. 4-5.

41. Putting People First, facsimile transmissions dated August 5, August 20, August 26, August 28, and September 1, 1992.

42. Hardy, pp. 37, 44.

Conclusion

The 1993 edition of this book warned that the animal rights movement would continue to grow as long as significant numbers of Americans failed to understand its ultimate goal—to abolish all uses and ownership of animals. Since then, more Americans have undoubtedly come to realize that the animal rights movement does not seek to improve the treatment of animals, and more will come to realize this in time.

Although many, if not most, Americans have by now heard the animal rights message, their attitudes and behavior do not appear to be changing. A recent survey by the Harrisonburg, Virginia-based Responsive Management polling firm concluded that only three percent of Americans "live by the animal rights doctrine." Ninety-seven percent of those surveyed had eaten chicken or consumed dairy products during the past two years. Ninety-two percent had eaten beef, 81 percent had worn leather, 76 percent owned a pet, 57 percent visited a zoo, 39 percent fished, 24 percent had gone to a circus, and 17 percent had hunted. Moreover, 79 percent agreed that "animals can be used by humans as long as the animal does not experience undue pain." Eighty-six percent agreed that "people should have the freedom to choose to wear fur." And 92 percent disapproved of "protesting fur clothing in a harassing manner."[1] Another survey of Illinois residents found that 71 percent approved of trapping for animal damage control and 70 percent for population control.[2]

What the Movement Has Accomplished

A brief summary of the animal rights movement's accomplishments gives some indication of its overall strength and the effects it might have on American society in the near future:

• *Research Animals.* No major legislation affecting the use of animals in biomedical research has been enacted since 1985 when Congress passed costly amendments to the Animal Welfare Act. While animal rights groups appear to be focusing more on other areas of animal use, such as livestock and poultry farming, biomedical research facilities and individual researchers continue to be targeted in campaigns to halt specific research projects. Michael DeBakey, the renowned heart surgeon and an outspoken critic of the movement, believes that "the devastation, delay and outright intimidation that animal rights groups are imposing on the scientific community are greater than at any time in the history of biomedical research."[3]

• *Farm Animals.* Unlike in Europe, animal rights groups in the U.S. have failed to enact any legislation outlawing specific animal husbandry practices such as single-stall housing for veal calves. Moreover, the number of animals raised for food is increasing, primarily because Americans are eating more chicken. However, the terrorist fringe of the movement appears to be stepping up attacks on farms and related concerns such as butcher shops and furriers.

• *Wildlife.* Animal rights groups have succeeded in using statewide ballot initiatives to impose restrictions and bans on particular types of hunting and trapping. But pro-hunting and trapping groups have helped to defeat an equal number of these measures. Moreover, all 50 states now have laws that protect hunters from harassment by animal rights activists. In the international realm, both Norway and Japan have resumed limited whaling even though the International Whaling Commission continues to decree a worldwide moratorium on commercial whaling. Despite activists' earlier success in banning the hunting of baby harp seals in Canada, adult harp seals are increasingly hunted. The United Nations Convention on International Trade in Endangered Species (CITES) recently eased a 1989 ban on international trade in ivory. Under an "experimental" agreement, Zimbabwe, Namibia, and Botswana will sell 59 tons of stockpiled ivory to Japan in 1999. Congress also recently passed an amendment to the Marine Mammal Protection Act that lifts a seven-year U.S. embargo on tuna caught by Mexican fishing vessels and changes the definition of "dolphin-safe" tuna favored by activists.

• *Animals in Education and Entertainment.* At the behest of animal rights groups, a handful towns and cities have passed ordinances that prohibit certain types of animal exhibits and performances, such as rodeo calf roping. Activists also continue to target zoos, aquariums, rodeos, carriage horse operators, and other individuals and concerns that use animals to teach and entertain, often at significant cost to these parties. Nonetheless, circus, zoo, and rodeo attendance is stable or increasing slightly.

• *Pets.* Activists have persuaded some localities to impose costly fees on owners who wish to keep their dogs and cats fecund or breed them. But associations representing breeders and pet owners have thwarted many of these efforts. Moreover, the number of pets in American households has remained relatively constant in recent years.

Is the Movement Waning?

Rod Strand of the Portland, Oregon-based National Animal Interest Alliance, a coalition of farmers, sportsmen, veterinarians and others, believes that animal rights groups are floundering on the public-relations front: "The public is more aware of the animal rights agenda. They're not as naive as ten years ago."[4] Norma Bennett Woolf, also of NAIA, concurs, noting that recent demonstrations by PETA-affiliated groups to dissuade Americans from eating at McDonald's and other fast-food restaurants that serve meat have been met with scorn.[5]

However, animal rights organizations may be gaining effectiveness in the legislative arena, where they now have 15 years experience. Moreover, membership levels and funding bases of animal rights groups have remained constant or grown somewhat in the last few years. But the heavy growth in membership and funding seen in the 1980s has definitely waned. Perhaps most significantly, individuals, organizations, and industries targeted by the animal rights movement have become well organized in recent years, sharing intelligence on animals rights groups and thwarting their efforts to pass legislation. Animal rights author Peter Singer notes that "we took our opponents, to some extent, by surprise. At first they laughed at us. They didn't take us seriously. That allowed us a sympathetic hearing with the media and made it relatively easy to get a lot of attention. It's now become harder."[6] Wayne Pacelle of the Humane Society of the United States agrees: "The medical lobby, the farm lobby, the hunting lobby, just to name a few, are far more conscious of our activities and are increasingly proactive. It used to be that they reacted to our advances, [but] now they're taking the initiative to thwart our efforts."[7]

Kim Stallwood, formerly with PETA, believes the media may even be growing tired of the movement: "The animal rights movement has fed the media's craving for novelty and conflict by staging attention-grabbing publicity stunts, often involving celebrities, and by engaging in debate, sometime acrimoniously, with establishment figures such a medical doctors and leaders of business and industry. These strategies have reinforced a perception held by many members of the print and electronic media, namely, that animal rights is a fringe issue."[8] A Lexis-Nexis search done by this author found that the number of major stories on animal rights published by leading U.S. newspapers appears to have peaked around 1995.

In their 1994 book *The Animal Rights Movement in America*, Lawrence and Susan Finsen compare the movement to the social crusades led by Mohandas Gandhi and Martin Luther King, Jr. They conclude that the movement must adhere to three basic principles espoused by Gandhi and King if it is to succeed: nonviolence, "an absolute commitment to truth," and "an appeal to the highest moral principles."[9] But by any reasonable standard, the animal right movement violates all three. A wing of the movement is engaged in criminal actions and terrorism, and these incidents appear to be increasing. As detailed throughout this book, allegations of animal cruelty made by animal rights groups are almost invariably untrue or unsupported. Finally, the movement would achieve outcomes that are highly immoral by traditional standards. Charles Griswold, a philosophy professor at Howard University, remarks that "the animal rights movement illustrates the incoherent nature of a moral passion become immoral by virtue of its extremism. In the name of the laudable quality of humaneness, the use of animals for food, clothing and medical experimentation is prohibited. Research that could save your child's life, or save you from an excruciating disease, is declared unethical. The result is inhumanity toward man."[10]

Perhaps the biggest sign of the failure of the animal rights movement in America is that more animals are being used each year. This is largely because more chickens are being raised for food.[11] Animal rights leader Gary Francione laments that "until a larger segment of society accepts, for example, that our enjoyment of the taste of meat does not—cannot, as a moral matter—justify killing animals for food, legal change for animals will necessarily be limited. . . . Any demand for justice for non-humans will fall on deaf ears unless and until those concerned about the issue understand that much more work needs to be done to educate in order to gain the necessary social support to make legal change meaningful."[12]

Yet common sense suggests that the overwhelming majority of Americans—and indeed of the world's population—will never accept the premise that it is wrong to humanely use animals. While the observation may seem trite, animals have been used in many ways throughout the world from time immemorial, and the vast majority of people have had no serious moral qualms about this. It seems virtually impossible that even a small percentage of people will ever be convinced that humans and animals are morally equal and that animal use is inherently wrong. On the contrary, the more animal rights groups succeed in conveying their message of animal equality and animal non-use to the public, the more likely their agenda will founder.

This does not mean that the animal rights movement is unimportant. As detailed throughout this book, it has already imposed significant costs on many individuals, businesses, and concerns that depend on animals, and it will continue to do so. Moreover, animal rights activism has harmed all of society: who can say what life-saving medical research has been destroyed by animal rights raids or how many promising young medical students have avoided the animal research field for fear of attack by animal rights groups. Nonetheless, the more the public comes to understand the movement's actual agenda, the more animal rights groups will be forced to struggle to achieve even minor victories.

Notes

1. Responsive Management, "Americans' Attitudes toward Animal Welfare, Animal Rights and Use of Animals," final report, October 1996.

2. *Ibid.*

3. Michael DeBakey, "Hype and Hypocrisy on Animal Rights," *Wall Street Journal,* December 12, 1996.

4. Rod Strand, telephone conversation, June 16, 1997.

5. Norma Bennett Woolf, telephone conversation, June 16, 1997.

6. Peter Singer, quoted in "A Conversation with Peter Singer, Part I," *Animals' Agenda,* March / April 1994.

7. Wayne Pacelle, quoted in "Wayne Pacelle, Unplugged, Part II," *Animals' Agenda,* website: arrs.envirolink.org/aa/index.html.

8. Kim Stallwood, "The Four Challenges Facing the Animal Rights Movement," *Animals' Agenda*, May / June 1994.

9. Lawrence and Susan Finsen, *The Animal Rights Movement in America* (Twayne Publishers: New York, 1994), cited in "Wither Animal Rights," *Animals' Agenda*, July / August 1994.

10. Charles Griswold, Jr., quoted in Sharon M. Russell and Charles S. Nicholl, eds., "Reply to Singer's 'Blind Hostility,'" *Proceedings of the Society for Experimental Biology and Medicine,* February 1996, vol. 211, no. 2, pp. 149-150.

11. Still, in other areas such as biomedical research, the number of animals used has been declining for years. The American Association for Laboratory Animal Science notes that animal use in biomedical research has declined 20 to 50 percent in the last 20 to 25 years. "Frequently Asked Questions about Animal Research," website, www.aalas.org.

12. Gary Francione, "Animals as Property," 1996 article on website of Rutgers Animal Rights Law Center, www.animal-law.org.

APPENDIX I

Organizations Promoting Humane Animal Treatment and Responsible Animal Use

GENERAL

Animal Welfare Council
PO Box 2007
Weatherford, TX 76086
www.animalwelfarecouncil.org

Individuals, businesses, and concerns involved in the responsible use of animals in entertainment, sports, and industry. Promotes improved animal welfare practices and counters allegations of animal abuse made by animal rights organizations.

National Animal Interest Alliance
PO Box 66579
Portland, OR 97290
(503) 761-1139
www.naiaonline.org

Business, agricultural, scientific, and recreational concerns that promote humane animal treatment. Hosts conferences, monitors animal rights campaigns, and offers the media factual information about animal use.

RESEARCH ANIMALS

Americans for Medical Progress
421 King Street, Suite 401
Alexandria, VA 22314
(703) 836-9596
www.amprogress.org

Conducts several programs to educate the public about the importance of animals in biomedical research. Its Hollywood Information project seeks to dissuade celebrities from supporting the animal rights movement.

**Association for Assessment and Accreditation of
Laboratory Animal Care
International**
11300 Rockville Pike, Suite 1211
Rockville, MD 20852
(301) 231-5353
www.aaalac.org

Employs experts to conduct on-site inspections of research facilities,
evaluating them for humane animal treatment.

California Biomedical Research Association
1008 Tenth Street, Suite 328
Sacramento, CA 95814
(916) 558-1515
www.ca-biomed.org

Educates the public about the contributions of animal research to human
health. Programs target students in particular.

Foundation for Biomedical Research
818 Connecticut Avenue, NW, Suite 303
Washington, DC 20006
(202) 457-0654
www.fbresearch.org

Conducts educational programs to help the public understand the need
for animal testing in biomedical research. A 501(c)(4) affiliate lobbies
and litigates to prevent undue regulation of animal research.

incurably ill For Animal Research (iiFAR)
PO Box 27454
Lansing, MI 48909
(517) 887-1141
website in development

A grassroots patient-based organization that supports the humane use of
animals in biomedical research. Members include survivors of diseases
who have benefited from animal research.

Health, Safety and Research Alliance of New York
PO Box 874
Goshen, NY 10924
(914) 291-1944
website in development

Educates the public about product safety testing involving animals.

Massachusetts Society for Medical Research
73 Princeton Street, Suite 311
North Chelmsford, MA 01863
(978) 251-1556
www.msmr.org

Publishes curriculum materials to educate children about animal research.

FARM ANIMALS

Animal Industry Foundation
1501 Wilson Boulevard, Suite 1100
Arlington, VA 22209
(703) 524-0810
www.aif.org

Educates the public about animal agriculture and its contribution to human life. Its website includes links to several livestock and poultry trade associations.

WILDLIFE

National Trappers Association
PO Box 3667
Bloomington, IL 61702
(309) 829-2422
www.nationaltrappers.com

Educates the public about the need for trapping to manage and conserve wildlife.

Wildlife Conservation Fund of America
801 Kingsmill Parkway
Columbus, OH 43229
(614) 888-4868
www.wcfa.org

Conducts national programs to educate the public about the necessity of hunting and trapping.

ANIMALS IN EDUCATION AND ENTERTAINMENT

American Zoo and Aquarium Association
8403 Colesville Road, Suite 710
Silver Spring, MD 20910
(301) 562-0777
www.aza.org

Promotes zoos, aquariums, and wildlife parks as educational institutions and encourages the breeding of endangered and threatened species in captivity.

Circus Fans Association of America
1445 Monroe Drive, Suite 33
Atlanta, GA 30324
(404) 872-8680
www.circusweb.com/CFA

Seeks to create enthusiasm for the circus and preserve it for future generations. Its affiliated National Circus Preservation Society promotes "reasonable and practical legislation" to protect circus animals.

International Professional Rodeo Association
2304 Exchange Avenue
PO Box 83377
Oklahoma City, OK 73148
(405) 235-6540
www.intprorodeo.com

Works to improve the treatment of rodeo animals by writing rules and policies governing professional rodeo.

Professional Rodeo Cowboys Association
101 Prorodeo Drive
Colorado Springs, CO 80919
(719) 593-8840
www.prorodeo.com

Enforces animal welfare guidelines to protect rodeo animals from abuse.

PETS

Many local humane societies do excellent work in finding homes for dogs, cats, and other pets. Many are also hard pressed for funds. However, as Chapter VIII discusses, some of these organizations have adopted an animal rights agenda. Investigate your local humane organization carefully before contributing.

APPENDIX II

American Society for the Prevention of Cruelty to Animals

424 East 92nd Street
New York, NY 10128
(212) 876-7700
www.aspca.org

SUMMARY

Founded in 1866 as America's first humane society, the ASPCA has increasingly adopted an animal rights agenda in the last 15 years. It opposes hunting and trapping, the wearing of fur, greyhound racing, the use of unwanted shelter animals in biomedical research, and modern livestock and poultry farming. A recent ASPCA article advises readers to "eliminate animal products from your diet." In a recent address, president emeritus Roger Caras said that the ASPCA is "at one" with "ethical vegetarians, vegans, antivivisectionists and other people generally thought of as 'activists.'"

The ASPCA's shift to animal rights has coincided with a drastic reduction in services long offered to pets and stray animals in New York City, where the organization is headquartered. In 1989, it helped 176,000 animals through adoptions, spaying and neutering, and care in hospitals and shelters. In 1996, however, it helped only 37,000 animals through these services. (See Chapter VIII for a fuller discussion of the radicalization of the ASPCA.)

FOUNDED
1866

IRS STATUS
501(c)(3)

STATED PURPOSE
To "provide effective means for the prevention of cruelty to animals throughout the United States."

MEMBERSHIP
425,000

OPERATING OFFICER
Larry Hawk, President

POLITICAL ACTION COMMITTEE
None

PUBLICATIONS
A is for Animal (quarterly teacher newsletter)
Animal Factories (book by James Mason and Peter Singer claiming that modern livestock and poultry farming is cruel)
Animal Rights Handbook: Everyday Ways to Save Animals' Lives (book urging readers to help "put an end to the torture of veal calves and chickens on factory farms . . . to stop the use of rabbits and monkeys in painful (and unnecessary) laboratory tests . . . to protect wild animals from being killed in fiendish leghold traps")
ASPCA Animal Watch (quarterly magazine)
ASPCA Complete Pet Care Manuals (guides for pet owners)
In Defense of Animals (compilation of essays by animal rights advocates, edited by animal rights author Peter Singer)
For Kids Who Love Animals: A Guide to Sharing the Planet (children's companion volume to *Animal Rights Handbook*)
JAAWS (quarterly journal with articles on animal husbandry and the use of animals in biomedical research, co-published with the animal rights group Psychologists for the Ethical Treatment of Animals)
Throwaways (video documentary on stray animals)
Tee shirts, caps, mugs, pet emergency first aid videos, educational games

INCOME (1996)
$19.6 million

Contributions and grants (59%)
Bequests (16%)
Animal hospital and fees (13%)
Other (12%)

FUNDING SOURCES (partial list)

American Express Company
ARCO Foundation
Chase Manhattan Bank
Chemical Bank
Citibank
Walt Disney Company Foundation
Geraldine R. Dodge Foundation

Robert Wood Johnson Foundation
Morgan Guaranty Trust Company
Pfizer, Inc.
Reader's Digest Foundation
US West Foundation

DONORS
$20 annual membership

PROGRAMS
• Humane Education (magazines, books, publication kits, pet care manuals, videos, workshops, and classes for students, teachers, parents, and pet owners)
• National Animal Poison Control Center (24-hour caller-paid hotline offering advice about animal poisonings)
• Animal Placement (placed nearly 2,000 animals in adoptive homes in 1996, down from nearly 17,000 adoptions and returns in 1989)
• Bergh Memorial Animal Hospital (veterinary hospital in Manhattan offering vaccinations, spaying and neutering, surgery, and other services)
• Humane Law Enforcement (enforces anti-cruelty statutes in New York City and New York state)
• Care-a-Van (mobile van offering low-cost pet spaying and neutering)
• Legal (drafts and lobbies for national, state, and local laws to ban hunting and trapping, greyhound racing, the use of single-stall housing for veal calves, etc.)

ACTIVITIES
• In 1985, opened a lobbying office in Washington, D.C., "to monitor, initiate and lobby for animal protection legislation."
• Helped organize New York City's 1990 Earth Day to "[highlight] the common ground the organization shares with the environmental movement."
• In 1991, "drafted legislation to further the rights of tenants to keep companion animals and to 'tax' puppy mills in order to strengthen the Animal Welfare Act. Other efforts included the continuing fight to improve conditions for veal calves and other farm animals, participation in a coalition to address the cruelty of canned hunts . . . and ongoing moves to better protect exhibition animals and endangered species such as the African elephant."
• Also in 1991, "successfully lobbied for passage of a New Jersey bill to ban the sale of wild-caught birds [and] drafted and lobbied for state bills that would: prohibit harmful animal experimentation by elementary and secondary school students, provide low-cost spaying and neutering of dogs and cats, prohibit the Draize eye and skin irritancy test for cosmetics

testing, strengthen animal fighting statues and provide standards for animal care at pet shops."

- Won a joint federal lawsuit in 1992 to expand the Animal Welfare Act to include birds, mice, and rats. However, the case was later successfully appealed for lack of standing.
- Also in 1992, lobbied for the "Animal Population Control Fund" to establish low-cost spaying and neutering for dogs and cats in New York state.
- Ceased operating New York City's largest animal shelter in 1994, which it had done for 100 years. Also recently closed its only other shelter.
- Filed a joint lawsuit in 1996 to stop a Canada goose hunt in Clarkstown, New York.
- In 1996, helped organize four successful state ballot initiatives in Colorado, Massachusetts, Oregon, and Washington to ban leghold traps and the hunting of bears, cougars, and bobcats.
- Also in 1996, closed a Brooklyn animal clinic, reducing the number of its clinics from two to one.
- In 1996, contributed $58,000 to anti-hunting ballot initiatives in Colorado, Idaho, and Massachusetts.
- In 1998, joined ProPAW, a coalition of animal rights groups, to ban leghold traps in California through a ballot initiative.
- Recently ceased operating 15 animal rescue ambulances and two mobile pet adoption vans in New York City.

APPENDIX III

Animal Legal Defense Fund

127 Fourth Street
Petaluma, CA 94952
(707) 769-7771
www.aldf.org

SUMMARY

The Animal Legal Defense Fund seeks legal recognition of animal rights. Executive director Joyce Tischler says that "only the Animal Legal Defense Fund has the expertise to deliver the legal services that can be crucial to saving an animal's life. . . . At ALDF, we've learned that in order to protect animals, we must speak to animal abusers in a language they understand. We haul them into court and make them answer to the law for their criminal actions."

In the 1981 case of the "Silver Spring Monkeys," ALDF vice president Roger Galvin, a former Maryland state attorney then with a predecessor organization called Attorneys for Animal Defense, successfully prosecuted animal researcher Edward Taub on one of 17 counts of animal cruelty. The conviction, however, was later overturned. (See Chapter VII for a discussion of the case.)

After the Animal Liberation Front raided the University of Pennsylvania Medical School Head Injury Clinic in 1985, ALDF represented members of People for the Ethical Treatment of Animals who had used stolen videotapes to stop federal funding of the clinic. ALDF also arranged a plea bargain for another PETA member, Jeanne Roush, who was accused of stealing 180 beavers from an abandoned beaver farm.

Following a well-publicized 1987 incident in which ALDF successfully defended a California high school student who refused to dissect a frog, ALDF opened a toll-free hotline to provide legal referrals to high school and college students wishing to avoid dissection. Through on-going debate and litigation, ALDF hopes to eliminate dissection in schools. More recently, ALDF has opposed animal cloning on the grounds that it will be used to engineer cattle for "maximum yield" and create "a menagerie of cloned animals available for human organ transplant."

FOUNDED
1981. Resulted from a merger of Attorneys for Animal Defense and the Lawyers' Committee for the Enforcement of Animal Protection Law.

IRS STATUS
501(c)(3)

STATED PURPOSE
To "[save] animals wherever they are in peril: in laboratories, on farms, and in the wild."

MEMBERSHIP
50,000, including 700 attorneys

OPERATING OFFICERS
Joyce S. A. Tischler, executive director
Steve Ann Chambers, president

POLITICAL ACTION COMMITTEE
None

PUBLICATIONS
Animal Law (law journal published annually by students of the Northwestern School of Law of Lewis & Clark College)
Animals' Advocate (quarterly newsletter)
Attorney Update (quarterly bulletin of U.S. animal law cases)

INCOME (1997)
$2,057,990

Contributions (89%)
Investments (3%)
Interest and dividends (1%)
Rents (1%)
Membership dues (1%)
Other (5%)

DONORS
$15 annual membership

PROGRAMS
• Lawsuits
• Lobbying
• Model state and local legislation and ordinances (to ban leghold traps, the use of unwanted shelter animals in research, the sale of fur, etc.)

- Affiliate student law groups at approximately ten law schools
- Animal Cruelty ActionLine (identifies alleged animal abuse cases and offers legal assistance to prosecutors)

ACTIVITIES
- Sued the U.S. Patent and Trademark Office in 1988 to stop the patenting of genetically engineered animals and to overturn a patent granted to Harvard University for developing a genetically altered mouse.
- Sued the National Institutes of Health in 1989 for allegedly delaying the issue of final regulations to the 1985 Animal Welfare Act. Also sued the U.S. Department of Agriculture to force issuance of final regulations for enforcing amendments to the 1985 Animal Welfare Act (*ALDF v. Lyng,* U.S. District Court for the District of Columbia).
- Successfully sued the California Fish & Game Commission in 1989 to stop black bear hunting on the grounds that an environmental impact report had not been prepared. Following the release of the report in 1990, the hunt was resumed (*Fund for Animals v. California Fish & Game Commission,* California Court of Appeals).
- Created a legal defense fund for Fran Stephanie Trutt, an activist convicted in connection with planting a bomb outside the headquarters of the U.S. Surgical Corporation.
- Continued a lawsuit in 1990 to challenge the Navy's use of dolphins as guards for nuclear submarines in Washington state (*PAWS v. U.S. Navy*).
- Filed a lawsuit in 1990 to defend activists sued for defamation in connection anti-fur demonstrations (*Zeller Furs v. Concerned Citizens for Animals,* State Court, Massachusetts).
- Filed a 1990 lawsuit to challenge the composition of the Massachusetts state wildlife protection board so that animal rights activists could become members (*ALDF v. Massachusetts Fisheries & Wildlife Board,* State Court, Massachusetts).
- Successfully sued the University of Vermont in 1991 to gain access to animal care committee meetings (*ALDF v. University of Vermont,* Vermont Supreme Court).
- Filed a lawsuit in 1991 against the New England Aquarium to challenge the transfer of a dolphin from the aquarium to the Navy (*Kama v. New England Aquarium*, U.S. District Court, Massachusetts).
- Filed a 1991 lawsuit to stop a deer hunt in Massachusetts, alleging that bald eagles would be harmed (*American Bald Eagle v. Metropolitan District Commission,* U.S. District Court, Massachusetts).
- Won a joint federal lawsuit in 1992 to force the U.S. Department of Agriculture to include mice, rats, and birds under provisions of the Animal Welfare Act. However, the case was successfully appealed for lack of legal standing.
- Lost a 1993 lawsuit to change the composition of the Massachusetts Fisheries and Wildlife Board to include animal rights activists.

- Lost a lawsuit to halt otter trapping in Missouri in 1997.
- Representing itself, Psychologists for the Ethical Treatment of Animals, and the Association of Veterinarians for Animal Rights, won a 1997 law suit to force the National Academy of Sciences to include animal rights activists on committees that prepare NAS' *Guide for the Care and Use of Laboratory Animals,* a set of rules for National Institutes of Health grant recipients. However, Congress several months later amended a law, the Federal Advisory Committee Act, that excluded NAS from the "open committees" sought by ALDF.
- Secured a temporary restraining order in 1998 to prevent the killing of 21 wild horses and six wild foals from Utah likely infected with equine infectious anemia, an incurable disease transmitted by biting insects.
- Has operated a toll-free "Dissection Hotline" to give legal referrals to high school and college students seeking to avoid dissection.
- For years has requested members and supporters to sign the "first-ever" "Animal Bill of Rights" petition for use in lobbying Congress:

> I, the undersigned American Citizen, believe that animals, like all sentient beings, are entitled to basic legal rights in our society. Deprived of legal protection, animals are defenseless against exploitation and abuse by humans. As no such rights now exist, I urge you to pass legislation in support of the following basic rights for animals:
> - The right of animals to be free from exploitation, cruelty, neglect and abuse.
> - The right of laboratory animals not to be used in cruel or unnecessary experiments.
> - The right of farm animals to an environment that satisfies their basic physical and psychological needs.
> - The right of companion animals to a healthy diet, protective shelter, and adequate medical care.
> - The right of wildlife to a natural habitat, ecologically sufficient to a normal existence and a self-sustaining species population.
> - The right of animals to have their interests represented in court and safe-guarded by the law of the land.

APPENDIX IV

Animal Liberation Front

underground organization:
no known address or
contact information

SUMMARY

Classified by the FBI as a terrorist organization, the Animal Liberation Front has claimed responsibility for, or has been suspected of, hundreds of acts of vandalism, arson, and theft of animals in the United States in the last 15 years. ALF's origins can be traced to 1972, when British animal rights activists Ronnie Lee and Cliff Goodman formed an anti-hunting group called the Band of Mercy to harass hunters in Great Britain.

The Band of Mercy also sought to end animal research, and in 1973 claimed responsibility for a double arson at an animal research laboratory. In a note left behind, Lee said, "the building was set fire to to prevent the torture and murder of our animal brothers and sisters by evil experiments. . . . We are a non-violent guerilla organization dedicated to the liberation of animals from all forms of cruelty and persecution at the hands of mankind. Our actions will continue until our aims are achieved." Lee also once said, "if it's impossible to protect animals without using violence, then violence is justifiable. Indeed there are times when to refrain from violence would be immoral."

Impressed by Band of Mercy's activities, 30 British activists formed the Animal Liberation Front in 1976. Lee became ALF's chief organizer and was jailed twice in connection with illegal activities. The attacks continued and broadened to include farms, retail shops, and department stores.

In the early 1980s, ALF became active in the United States. Its effectiveness here can be attributed to at least two factors. First, it relies on relatively autonomous "cells"—regional groups that have little contact with one another and that are patterned after the Irish Republican Army—to carry out attacks. This makes the arrest of perpetrators more difficult. As a spokesman for the British Union for the Abolition of Vivisection once said, "if [someone] . . . is interested in participating in an animal liberation action, [he] gets together with some close friends of like mind, or by [himself], undertakes the operation. That's it. That's the ALF." Second, ALF uses above-ground animal rights groups, such as People for the Ethical Treatment of Animals, to publicize its cause. (For a discussion of the ties between ALF and PETA, see Appendix XIV and Chapter IX.)

ALF has claimed responsibility for acts of vandalism and terrorism in

149

at least 25 countries. Says one British ALF activist, "I can support petrol bombing, bombs under cars, and probably shootings at a later stage. It's a war."

FOUNDED
1976 in Great Britain and believed to have begun activities in the United States in the early 1980s.

IRS STATUS
None

STATED PURPOSE
To end the "cruel" treatment of animals through vandalism, arson, and animal "rescue" operations directed at animal research laboratories, farms, fur stores, and similar concerns.

MEMBERSHIP
Unknown. As many as several hundred activists may be involved in the U.S.

OPERATING OFFICER
Unknown

ORGANIZATION
Unknown

Spokesmen / Supporters
Animal Liberation Frontline (www.animal-liberation.net)

North American – A.L.F. Supporters Group
Box 69597
5845 Yonge Street
Willowdale, ONT M2M 4K3
CANADA

North American A.L.F. Press Office
Box 103
Osseo, MN 55369
(612) 601-0978

People for the Ethical Treatment of Animals
(see Appendix XIV)

POLITICAL ACTION COMMITTEE
None

BOARD MEMBERS
Unknown

PUBLICATIONS
The A.L.F. Primer (discusses how to conduct criminal actions and terrorism)
The Final Nail (advice on how to destroy fur farms, stores, and related concerns)
Notes from the Underground (describes how one activist became involved in "animal liberation")
Underground Magazine (published by the North American A.L.F. Supporters Group)

INCOME
Unknown

DONORS
Unknown

PROGRAMS
- Criminal actions and terrorism (e.g., vandalism, raids, and arson directed at animal research laboratories, fur farms, fur stores, meat processing plants, and similar concerns)
- Theft and release of laboratory and farm animals

ACTIVITIES
- Sent letter bombs to British political party leaders in 1982.
- Raided the University of Pennsylvania Head Injury Clinic in 1984, stealing 60 hours of research videotape and causing $60,000 in damage.
- Fire-bombed the homes of four scientists in Great Britain in 1985.
- Released 1,000 animals, damaged computers, poured blood on files, and spray-painted slogans on laboratory walls at the University of California at Riverside in 1985, causing $700,000 in damage.
- Raided a University of Oregon psychology lab in 1986, releasing 125 monkeys, rabbits, hamsters, and rats.
- Broke into a Rockville, Maryland, animal research lab in 1986 and stole four chimpanzees being used to develop hepatitis B and AIDS vaccines.
- Raided and set fire to an animal diagnostic facility under construction at the University of California at Davis in 1987, stopping research on how toxic substances affect endangered bird species. Damage totaled $4.5 million—the highest amount caused by an act of animal rights

151

terrorism in the U.S.

- Burnt down a chicken warehouse and meat processing plant in San Jose, California, in 1987.
- Claimed responsibility for raiding the Loma Linda University Medical Center laboratory in California in 1988; at least seven dogs were stolen and red paint was splattered on walls and office equipment. In a subsequent statement, ALF criticized Dr. Leonard L. Bailey, a Loma Linda surgeon, for performing a baboon-to-baby heart transplant on the infant "Baby Fae" in 1984.
- Fire-bombed several British department stores and businesses in 1988 which sold furs or were associated with animal research.
- Claimed responsibility for throwing acid on the windows of an Atlanta furrier in 1988. Said owner Toni Lucci, "They [the vandals] hurt me monetarily, and I think that's what they wanted to do. But then they were getting more aggressive with the little notes that said, 'murderer.' I was scared because I was a woman alone there. I didn't need that. To walk away from the business, it cost me $50,000, which was devastating."
- Sent bomb threats to Stanford University researchers in 1989 after they had announced the infection of laboratory mice with the AIDS virus.
- Broke into a University of Arizona animal research lab in 1989, stealing 1,200 frogs, mice, rabbits, and pigs; subsequently set fire to the lab and an administration building, causing $500,000 in damage. Among the animals taken were 30 mice infected with crypto sporidium, known to be deadly to malnourished children, AIDS patients, and other immuno-suppressed people.
- Raided the Texas Tech University Health Sciences Center in 1989, stealing electronic equipment and five cats; estimated damages were $55,000.
- Blew up the Senate House at Bristol University in Great Britain in 1989.
- Claimed responsibility for stealing several rabbits, guinea pigs, and rats from the Cook County Hospital in Chicago in 1991. A statement found at the scene read, "These so-called scientists are lucky they only lost their animal captives and are not behind bars. Theirs are not deeds of science or medicine, but of shocking, sadistic insanity."
- Claimed responsibility for a 1991 three-alarm fire at a mink-food processing plant. A press release said the fire was set "with the hopes of causing maximum economic damage to an industry that profits from the misery and exploitation of fur animals."
- Claimed responsibility for vandalizing an office and setting fire to a barn at an Oregon State University mink research farm in 1991.
- Fire-bombed a Canadian fish company in 1991.

- Claimed responsibility for setting fire to a Michigan State University animal research laboratory in 1992, causing at least $75,000 in damage. Ingrid Newkirk and Alex Pacheco, president and chairman, respectively, of People for the Ethical Treatment of Animals, were subsequently subpoenaed by a grand jury to provide fingerprints and handwriting samples as part of a federal task force investigation into the incident.
- Between 1995 and 1997, suspected of a rash of 40 incidents in Utah including broken windows, vandalism, and arson.
- In 1996, set fire to the Alaskan Fur Company in Minnesota, causing $2 million in damage.
- Set fire to the Cavel West Horse Rendering plant in Redmond, Oregon in 1997, causing $1 million in damage. Because the plant provided horse bone tissue used in correcting birth defects in children, future surgeries in the area had to be postponed indefinitely.
- In 1997, suspected of releasing 5,000 minks and 100 foxes from a farm in Sioux City, Iowa. While half the animals were captured, many died of stress, starvation, or were run over by cars.
- In 1997, released 10,000 mink—the largest number of animals released from any facility in the U.S.—from the Arritola Mink Farm in Mt.Angel, Oregon. At least 3,000 died, including 2,000 babies trampled by activists and savaged by adult mink. Losses totaled $750,000.
- Claimed responsibility for a 1997 fire at a veal-processing plant in Lauderdale, Florida.
- In 1998, suspected of setting a two-alarm fire that destroyed a veal-processing plant near Tampa, Florida, causing $500,000 in damage. "A.L.F" had been spray-painted on the side of the plant.

APPENDIX V

Animal Protection Institute of America

PO Box 22505
Sacramento, CA 95822
(916) 731-5521
www.g-net.com/api.htm

SUMMARY
The Animal Protection Institute, founded in 1968 as a humane organization, has in recent years embraced an animal rights agenda. In the 1970s and 1980s, it worked with other burgeoning animal rights organizations to successfully end the hunting of baby harp seals in Canada (see Chapter VII for a discussion of the hunt). It has also been a leader in efforts to end the use of leghold traps and has recently led a campaign to ban xenotransplantation, the replacement of human organs with animal organs. API contends that xenotransplants are morally wrong, impractical, and could lead to "a disastrous worldwide epidemic from a deadly virus that leaps from animals to humans."

FOUNDED
1968

IRS STATUS
501(c)(3)

STATED PURPOSE
"To advocate for the protection of animals from cruelty and exploitation."

MEMBERSHIP
75,000

OPERATING OFFICER
Alan H. Berger, executive director

POLITICAL ACTION COMMITTEE
None

PUBLICATIONS
"Animal Alternatives in Education" (brochure offering alternatives to dissection)
Animal Issues (quarterly magazine formerly called *Mainstream*)
A.P.E. News (free biannual publication for teachers and educators)
Bulletin (bimonthly animal activism update)
"The Fallacy of Sport Hunting" (anti-hunting brochure)
"Premarin: Just Say NO!" (brochure discouraging the use of the estrogen replacement therapy Premarin)
"What's Really in Pet Food" (investigative report on pet food)
Greeting cards, sports bottles, t-shirts, and other merchandise

INCOME (1996)
$1,732,438

Contributions (91%)
Investments (8%)
Rents (1%)

DONORS
$25 annual membership
$35 international membership

PROGRAMS
- Lawsuits, lobbying, and advocacy against xenotransplants and hunting and trapping, including sealing and whaling

ACTIVITIES
- With other animals rights groups, helped to end the hunting of baby harp seals in Canada in 1987.
- In 1996, released a study of the pet food industry entitled "What's Really in Pet Food," contending that "preservatives, flavoring, food coloring, and deceptive labeling all help disguise ingredients unfit for anyone's consumption."
- Successfully sued the National Park Service in 1997 to stop a deer hunt in Ohio's Cuyahoga Valley National Recreation Area.
- In 1998, joined several other animal rights groups in a successful ballot initiative campaign to end trapping in California.
- Has sought unsuccessfully to have General Mills redesign its tapered Yoplait yogurt containers, contending that wild animals such as skunks get their heads caught in discarded containers and die.
- Has advocated passage of a national Presumed Consent Law which would presuppose that everyone wants to be an organ donor unless otherwise indicated.

- Has recently campaigned against the use of Premarin, an estrogen replacement therapy made from the urine of pregnant mares (see Chapter III).
- Has organized protests against the Scripps Institute's use of high-intensity, low-frequency sound devices in the ocean, contending that marine animals are harmed.
- Has opposed efforts by Washington state's Makah Indian tribe to hunt grey whales, a traditional source of food.
- Protested the construction of a dolphin show stadium at Marine World / Africa USA.

APPENDIX VI

Animal Rights International

PO Box 214, Planetarium Station
New York, NY 10024
(212) 873-3674
no website

SUMMARY

Animal Rights International has successfully pressured several cosmetics and household products companies to end the use of animals in research that tests the safety of consumer products. In 1979, ARI organized the Coalition to Abolish the LD50 and Draize Tests to urge cosmetics companies, including industry leader Revlon, to develop alternatives to animal testing. Revlon agreed to award Rockefeller University $750,000 to study non-animal research methods following demonstrations, letter-writing campaigns, an international boycott, and full-page ads in major newspapers, underwritten by the New York City-based grant-maker Millennium Guild. Other cosmetic companies have since implemented similar programs.

More recently, ARI has printed full-page ads in the *New York Times* and elsewhere alleging that chickens raised by Perdue Farms, the nation's fourth largest chicken producer, live in overcrowded conditions that encourage cannibalism, disease, and mass hysteria. Calling the charges "vague and totally groundless," Perdue has countered with advertisements of its own. ARI believes that "the Perdue campaign will become a catalyst for industry-wide change and will catapult factory farming onto the national agenda in the 1990s." (See Chapter III.)

Under the leadership of recently deceased Henry Spira, a leader of the civil rights and trade union reform movements of the 1960s and 1970s, ARI'S approach became arguably more moderate than most animal rights groups'. Said Spira, "I don't see the usefulness of pushing yourself into a corner where you are going to generate the most resistance. What's interesting is what can be done. People and institutions can only move so much at one time." Nonetheless, his ultimate goals were radical: "My dream is that people will come to view eating an animal as cannibalism. . . . Clearly, animal rights and eating animals don't mesh."

FOUNDED
1985

IRS STATUS
501(c)(3)

STATED PURPOSE
To support alternatives to product testing on animals and to reform the treatment of farm animals.

MEMBERSHIP
None

OPERATING OFFICER
Peter Singer

POLITICAL ACTION COMMITTEE
None

PUBLICATIONS
   Strategies for Activists (handbook by Henry Spira discussing his activities in the civil rights, labor, and animal rights movements)
   Brochures, pamphlets

INCOME (1991)
$96,993

Contributions, gifts, grants (99%)
Savings, investments (1%)

DONORS
Not available

PROGRAMS
   • Alternatives to the Lethal Dose 50 and Draize Eye Irritancy Tests
   • Ending "factory farming"

ACTIVITIES
   • Published articles in the *Food Drug Cosmetic Law Journal, Fellowship,* newsletter of the Johns Hopkins Center for Alternatives to Animal Testing, *Animals' Agenda, and Animals' Voice.*
   • Publicized campaigns in the *Washington Post, New York Post, Associated Press, Newsweek, Fortune, Congressional Quarterly, Boston Magazine, Vegetarian Times, Washington Times,* and Baltimore *City Paper.*

- Used ten full-page ads in December 1991 editions of the Washington Times to protest the appointment of "chicken king" Frank Perdue to the University of Maryland's board of regents. Perdue was accused of "lying to the government," "ripping off the consumer," "evading a manslaughter charge," "ruining the environment," "abusing animals," "business with the Mafia," and "endangering the lives of . . . workers."
- Successfully lobbied for the repeal of New York City's Metcalfe-Hatch Act, which allowed researchers to use unwanted shelter animals in biomedical research.
- Has run ads in major newspapers that promote vegetarianism by showing a dog in a sandwich bun with the caption, "Why Would Anybody Eat Their Best Friend?"

APPENDIX VII

Animal Welfare Institute

PO Box 3650, Georgetown Station
Washington, DC 20007
(202) 337-2332
www.animalwelfare.com

SUMMARY

Founded in 1951 as a humane organization, the Animal Welfare Institute has increasingly adopted an animal rights agenda. Its lobbying arm, the Society for Animal Protective Legislation, has helped pass nearly all of the 15 major federal laws affecting animals. These include the Humane Slaughter Act of 1958, the Laboratory Animal Welfare Act of 1966, the Endangered Species Act of 1969, the Marine Mammal Protection Act of 1972, and the Improved Standards for Laboratory Animals Act of 1985. President and director Christine Stevens' many political connections, including her husband, a former Democratic National Committee treasurer, have greatly aided AWI in the legislative realm.

Since 1954, AWI has awarded the Albert Schweitzer Medal for "outstanding achievement in the advancement of animal welfare." Recipients include Rachel Carson (1962), author of *Silent Spring*; Sen. Robert Dole (1986) for leading efforts to amend the Animal Welfare Act in 1985; Astrid Lindgren (1988), a Swedish children's book author for helping to ban "factory farming" practices in Sweden; Michael Tillman (1994) for helping to maintain a worldwide moratorium on commercial whaling; and the late Henry Spira (1996), director of Animal Rights International (see Appendix VI).

FOUNDED
1951

IRS STATUS
501(c)(3)
Society for Animal Protective Legislation (est.1955), 501(c)(4) lobbying arm

STATED PURPOSE
"To [reduce] the sum total of pain and fear inflicted on animals by man."

APPENDIX VII

MEMBERSHIP
9,500

OPERATING OFFICER
Christine Stevens, President and Director

POLITICAL ACTION COMMITTEE
None

PUBLICATIONS
Animal Welfare Institute Quarterly (newsletter that reports on the treatment of "captive animals" in laboratories and on farms; also summarizes international meetings, laws, and treaties affecting animals; distributed annually to 20,000 teachers, scientists, animal-interest organizations, public libraries, and medical and veterinary schools)

Animals and their Legal Rights (441-page book discussing U.S. and foreign laws affecting animals)

Animals, Nature, and Albert Schweitzer (by Ann Cottrell Free)

The Bird Business: A Study of the Commercial Cage Bird Trade (by Greta Nilsson)

Down on the Factory Farm (video "documenting cruel confinement and showing alternative housing systems")

Endangered Species Handbook (book containing "projects for classrooms and science fairs")

Factory Farming: The Experiment that Failed (86-page compilation of *AWI Quarterly* articles)

Facts about Furs (257-page book on "the way furs are obtained throughout the world")

Other books, pamphlets, and videos on domestic and wild animals

INCOME (1990)
$750,574

Contributions (93%)
Memberships (3%)
Sales, dividends, other (3%)

DONORS
$25 annual membership

PROGRAMS
- Laboratory Animals (to monitor the treatment of animals used in biomedical research, including site visits and analysis of U.S. Department of Agriculture inspection reports)

164

- Wildlife Trade (to investigate wild bird, mammal, and ivory trades)
- Save the Whales (to monitor international whaling activities, boycott whaling products, and "bring a permanent end to commercial whaling")
- Trapping (to campaign against steel-jaw leghold traps in the U.S. and abroad)
- Farm Animals (to "halt . . . intensive farming practices and replace them with methods which are both humane and economical")

ACTIVITIES
- Lobbied to enact the Humane Slaughter Act of 1958, requiring large farm animals to be rendered unconscious prior to slaughter.
- Lobbied for the Laboratory Animal Welfare Act of 1966, requiring animal dealers and research laboratories to meet federal standards of care.
- Lobbied for the Endangered Species Act of 1969, requiring the Secretary of the Interior to list threatened and endangered species and prohibiting the import of such species for commercial use.
- Lobbied for the Marine Mammal Protection Act of 1972, prohibiting the killing of any marine mammal without a permit.
- Lobbied for 1985 amendments to the Animal Welfare Act that in 1990 cost animal research laboratories, zoos, animal dealers, and auction operators an estimated $1 billion in compliance costs.
- Has used "Betsy Beaver," a 24-foot high inflatable beaver, in campaigns to ban leghold traps.
- Has presented lectures and held workshops at biology teachers' conventions and university student meetings on alternatives to dissection.
- Launched a "Pastureland Farms" campaign featuring a video showing "humanely" raised pigs for "farmers and others [wanting] pigs . . . to live their brief lives free of cruelty imposed by pork factory practices."
- Has led efforts for a worldwide ban on whaling and the sale of ivory.
- Has organized exhibition booths and distributed anti-dissection materials at conventions of the National Science Teachers Association and National Association of Biology Teachers.

APPENDIX VIII

Farm Animal Reform Movement

PO Box 30654
Bethesda, MD 20824
(301) 530-1737
www.farmusa.org

SUMMARY

As a "national, nonprofit, public-interest organization formed in 1981 by animal, consumer, and environmental protection advocates," the Farm Animal Reform Movement seeks to end the raising of farm animals for food. FARM uses three main methods in seeking this goal:

• Portraying meat consumption as disgusting. For example, FARM once flew an airplane over Florida beaches with a banner reading, "Eating Dead Animal Bodies Is Gross."

• Claiming that meat, poultry, and dairy products are unsafe. FARM newsletters often carry reports of isolated outbreaks of food poisoning and charge that the U.S. Department of Agriculture inadequately inspects meat.

• Alleging that farm animals are abused because of modern livestock and poultry farming methods: "The vested interests of American agribusiness [have] discovered that there is a great deal of money to be made on the backs of the least empowered groups in our social structure: farm workers, future generations, and of course, farm animals."

FARM helps coordinate a nationwide network of 1,000 grassroots activists in all 50 states who organize demonstrations around the country, including a protest against the opening of the 10,000th MacDonald's restaurant in Dale City, Virginia, and rallies outside recent Democratic National conventions. FARM believes it "must continue our quest for the ultimate solution [i.e., vegetarianism] by working to change the consumer's violent diet and industry's exploitative mindset. . . ."

FOUNDED
1981

IRS STATUS
501(c)(3)

STATED PURPOSE
To "eliminate all raising of animals for food."

MEMBERSHIP
13,000

OPERATING OFFICER
Alex Hershaft, President

POLITICAL ACTION COMMITTEE
None

PUBLICATIONS
Activism 101 (introduction to political activism)
Animal Factories (book by Peter Singer and James Mason on modern animal farming)
Chicken for Dinner? (video on chicken farming)
Cookbook for People Who Love Animals (vegetarian cookbook)
FARM Report (quarterly newsletter for members)
Health Costs of Meat Consumption (1996 report alleging high health costs of eating meat)
Healthy, Wealthy, and Wise (video on vegetarianism)
Recipes for Life ("tasty plant-based recipes")
Sentenced for Life (video on egg production)
Tee shirts, tote bags, bumper stickers, envelop stickers, buttons, slides, photographs

INCOME (1991)
$102,580

Contributions (64%)
Conference (18%)
Grants (9%)
Merchandise (5%)
Interest (4%)

DONORS
$20 annual membership

PROGRAMS
- CHOICE (Consumers for Healthy Options in Children's Education (encourages "school lunch action groups to fight for plant-based menu options" in schools)
- Compassion Campaign (to inject the notion of animal rights into

Presidential election debates)
- Great American Meatout (to highlight the "destructive" impact of meat production and consumption and to persuade Americans to "kick the meat habit" through local events such as booths with vegetarian foods)
- Letters from FARM (places activists' letters-to-the-editor in publications throughout North America)
- National Veal Ban Action (to end the production of "milk-fed" veal)
- World Farm Animals Day ("vigils and other somber events" to memorialize "the 9 billion [farm] animals" killed annually in the U.S.)

ACTIVITIES
- In 1981, held the first "Action for Life" conference "to turn hundreds of concerned folks into dedicated activists."
- Beginning in 1986, helped introduce several bills in California, Massachusetts, Maryland, and New York to end the production of "milk-fed" veal and the slaughter of injured animals at stockyards.
- In 1983, 1985, 1988, 1989, and 1990, participated in civil disobedience at stockyards, government offices, and farm industry conventions.

APPENDIX IX

Friends of Animals

777 Post Road, Suite 205
Darien, CT 06820
(203) 866-5223
www.friendsofanimals.org

SUMMARY

Founded in 1957 to provide nationwide, low-cost spaying and neutering for cats and dogs, Friends of Animals has since become a leading animal rights organization. As early as 1980, FoA was distributing "Tips for Hunt Saboteurs" that outlined ways "to ambush the hunter." In 1988, it declared hunting sabotage "a [FoA] national policy" and suggested such activities as rubbing rotten eggs into duck hunting blinds, spraying deer beds with repellent, and playing wolf howl tapes. Through television ads, radio announcements, demonstrations, letter-writing campaigns and other means, FoA also coordinates campaigns against whaling, sealing, and the use of fur and ivory.

FoA president Priscilla Feral, a former president of the Connecticut chapter of the National Organization for Women, believes that "we owe a great deal to the Animal Liberation Front. Without this group, our movement would not have come this far." (See Appendix IV and Chapter IX for a discussion of this terrorist organization.) FoA has also criticized the Veterans Administration for funding Helping Hands, a charity that uses organ grinder monkeys to help quadriplegics learn basic household and personal skills.

While FoA spent $2,249,125—nearly half its budget—on spaying and neutering of cats and dogs in 1996, 90 percent of this funding ($2,029,614) came from pet owners who paid for this service.

FOUNDED
1957

IRS STATUS
501(c)(3)
Committee for Humane Legislation, 501(c)(4) lobbying arm

STATED PURPOSE
"To prevent cruelty to and exploitation of domestic and wild animals."

APPENDIX IX

MEMBERSHIP
200,000

OPERATING OFFICER
Priscilla Feral, President and Executive Director

REGIONAL OFFICES
New York City
1841 Broadway, Suite 812
New York, NY 10023

Washington, D.C.
2000 P Street NW
Suite 415
Washington, DC 20036

Others
Los Angeles
Jerusalem

POLITICAL ACTION COMMITTEE
None

PUBLICATIONS
Tips for Hunt Saboteurs
ActionLine (quarterly newsletter)
FOA Quarterly
Skin Trade Primer (book)
Shopper's Guide to Cruelty Free Products
Brochures, pamphlets, and videos

INCOME (1996)
$4,904,995

Contributions (50%)
Spaying and neutering service fees (41%)
Investments and sales (9%)

DONORS
$25 annual membership

PROGRAMS
• Protests, boycotts, letter-writing campaigns, and lawsuits against hunt-

ing and trapping, leghold traps, stores that sell furs, and pet stores that sell pure-bred dogs
- Low-cost spaying and neutering of 65,000 pet cats and dogs annually in the United States
- Wildlife Sanctuary (in New York state)
- Puppy Mills (campaign to shut down commercial dog breeding kennels)
- FoA Chimp Sanctuary (in Ghana)

ACTIVITIES
- Joined the New Brunswick [Canada] Society for the Prevention of Cruelty to Animals in 1969 to protest the killing of baby harp seals in the gulf of the St. Lawrence River. Launched a campaign the following year to stop the killing of seals on the Pribilof Islands in Alaska. A televised documentary of the hunt, featuring former FoA president Alice Herrington, generated numerous protest letters to Congress and helped lead to passage of the Marine Mammal Protection Act of 1972.
- Helped enact a New Jersey law in 1984 banning the manufacture, sale, possession, use, and transport of leghold traps.
- Initiated a $500,000 fundraising drive in 1989 to provide anti-poaching assistance to Kenya and Tanzania.
- Picketed the Game & Fresh Water Fish Commission in West Palm-Beach, Florida, in 1988 because of its sponsorship of the Florida Youth Deer Hunt. Following the demonstration, activists went to the hunting site to spread human hair and deer repellent and later sent protest letters to 1,500 legislators, community leaders, and the media.
- Protested at the Hopkinton, Rhode Island, town hall in 1988 against a 15-cent bounty on woodchucks. FoA members dressed as groundhogs and staged a mock shooting.
- Sponsored a half-page ad in an April 1989 edition of the *New York Times* to protest the proposed "obscene" auction of two pairs of African elephant tusks by the Sotheby's auction house. Entitled "Why Auction Elephant Tusks in the Midst of an Elephant Holocaust?" the ad claimed that

greed and insensitivity are driving the elephant . . . to extinction. . . . In fact, unless effective action is taken soon, the African elephant will be gone within four to five years. . . . [We] are asking the American people to do three things: (1) to immediately stop buying ivory; (2) to ask jewelry and gift shops to discontinue all trade in this product, and to boycott famous action houses like Sotheby's that deal in ivory; (3) to petition the U.S. Government to support the inclusion of the elephant in Appendix I [endangered species listing] of CITES.

Sotheby's withdrew the tusks from sale by buying them from an unidentified owner, then donated them to a museum.
- Protested drug addiction research using animals at the University of California at Los Angeles in 1990. Keynote speaker and actress Sally Struthers called on the United Nations to issue a declaration of animal rights.
- Has advised its members on "What You Can Do" to address "the single argest factor contributing to the loss of animal life, environmental degradation and global climate change (human population growth):"

  - Limit your family size to two or fewer children and encourage others to do likewise.
  - Make conservation and respect for all life a part of your way of life.
  - Contact your Congressional representative. Urge him or her to back H. Con. Res. 180, adopting the United Nations Amsterdam Declaration on population as official U.S. policy, increase U.S. international family planning assistance to $650 million per year, and restore funding to the U.N.F.P.A.
  - Learn more about efforts to halt population growth. . . .

- Has lobbied for the Veal Calf Protection Act (to prohibit the raising of veal calves in single stall housing) and the Steel-Jaw Leghold Trap Prohibition Act (to ban use of leghold traps)
- Blockaded the Fendi and Revillon Fur Salon in New York City in 1996.
- In 1996, contributed $6,500 to an anti-hunting ballot initiative in Alaska.
- Sponsored two dozen demonstrations at pet stores in Connecticut in 1998 to protest the selling of pure-bred dogs raised at commercial kennels.
- Supported a 1998 New York City proposal (Intro No. 321) that would require pet owners, breeders, and pet stores with unaltered dogs and cats to buy special permits. The ordinance would also limit the number of litters a female dog could produce annually.
- Has urged a boycott of Federated Department Stores (Bloomingdale's, Macy's, Sterns, Aeropastale, the Bon Marche, Goldsmith's, Lazarus, Rich's, and Charter Club) for selling furs.
- Through lawsuits and media campaigns has opposed the killing of gray wolves in Alaska.

APPENDIX X

Fund For Animals

200 West 57th Street
New York, NY 10019
(212) 246-2096
www.fund.org

SUMMARY

Founded in 1967, the Fund for Animals is a leading opponent of hunting and trapping. In the early 1970s, recently deceased president Cleveland Amory appeared on NBC's *Today Show* and called for the hunting of hunters. A Hunt the Hunters Hunt Club, he said, would conduct "a carefully regulated open season on hunters" with trappers caught in traps and bow hunters shot with bows and arrows. When a reporter once asked Amory about two hunters who awaited rescue after becoming caught on a mountain ledge, he replied, "I'm rooting for the ledge."

The Fund for Animals was the first animal rights organization to enlist the support of celebrities to promote animal rights. It has filed numerous lawsuits at the federal and state levels to stop hunting and has challenged laws that protect hunters from harassment by animal rights activists. It is also a leader in efforts to introduce animal rights ideas to children.

FOUNDED
1967

IRS STATUS
501(c)(3)

STATED PURPOSE
"Dedicated to the protection of wildlife, saving endangered species, and promoting humane treatment of animals through public education and legislation."

MEMBERSHIP
200,000

OPERATING OFFICER
Marian Probst

POLITICAL ACTION COMMITTEE
None

PUBLICATIONS
The ABC's of Animal Rights (book for children by Janet Tubbs)
Animal Crusaders (quarterly newsletter for elementary school teachers)
Armchair Activist (semi-annual newsletter for members)
The Best Cat Ever (book by Cleveland Amory and one in a series of animal rights children's stories)
The Cat and the Curmudgeon (book by Cleveland Amory)
The Cat Who Came for Christmas (book by Cleveland Amory)
Ethical Eating: Common Questions on Vegetarianism
The Guns of Autumn (CBS documentary on hunting and trapping)
Man Kind? Our Incredible War on Wildlife (book by Cleveland Amory that criticizes hunting and trapping)
Ranch of Dreams: The Heartwarming Story of America's Most Unusual Animal Sanctuary (book by Cleveland Amory about the Fund for Animal's Black Beauty Ranch in Texas)
What's Wrong with Hunting (video for students)
Tee shirts, buttons, bumper stickers

INCOME (1997)
$5,251,264

Contributions and bequests (81%)
Investments (19%)

DONORS
$20 annual membership

PROGRAMS
- Campaigns against hunting and trapping, including protests, ballot initiatives, and lawsuits
- Black Beauty Ranch (facility in Texas for 600 "rescued" animals)
- Low-cost spay / neuter clinics in New York City, Houston, and San Antonio
- Wildlife rehabilitation center in Ramona, California
- Rabbit sanctuary in South Carolina
- Campaigns against the use of unwanted shelter animals in biomedical research

ACTIVITIES
- Worked for passage of the Marine Mammal Protection Act of 1972.
- Helped pass the Endangered Species Act of 1973.

- Opened the Black Beauty Ranch in Texas for "rescued" animals.
- Filed a lawsuit against Los Angeles County in 1983 that resulted in a 1986 ruling requiring county shelters to certify that shelter animals released for research are "humanely" treated.
- In 1988, claimed a "landmark legal victory" by winning a cease and desist order that ended a pigeon shoot in Reno, Nevada.
- Joined the National Audubon Society in a 1989 lawsuit against the National Park Service to end trapping in Jean Lafitte National Historical Park, Louisiana.
- In 1987, filed an unsuccessful lawsuit against the National Park Service to stop buffalo hunting in Yellowstone National Park.
- In 1988, protested quail shooting by President-elect George Bush at the Lazy F Ranch near Beeville, Texas.
- Filed a successful lawsuit with the Animal Legal Defense Fund in 1989 to end the hunting of black bears in California for one season.
- In 1991, "stalked and berated" hunters during the opening of bow hunting season in New York state.
- Secured a temporary restraining order in 1991 to stop the killing of 25 bison in Yellowstone National Park. Park officials had hoped to study the animals' organs and tissues for signs of disease.
- In 1994, supported a successful statewide ballot initiative in Oregon to ban the use of baits and hounds to hunt bears and cougars. Also supported a successful Arizona ballot initiative to end commercial trapping on public lands in Arizona.
- In 1996, contributed $5,000 to an anti-hunting ballot initiative in Colorado.
- With a coalition of animal rights groups, filed a successful lawsuit in 1997 to stop a deer hunt in Ohio's Cuyahoga Valley National Recreation Area.
- In 1998, filed a lawsuit against the Kentucky Fish and Wildlife Commission for denying "non-sportsmen" (i.e., animal rights activists) the right to vote for officers of the wildlife commission.
- Ran an ad in a Wyoming newspaper in 1998 offering young hunters free mountain bikes if they turned down their elk hunting permits. There were no takers.
- Has participated in annual International Whaling Commission meetings, urging a worldwide ban on the hunting of whales.
- Has offered a "Thanksgiving Amnesty" program for Future Farmers of America and 4-H students who raise turkeys for stock shows and eventual slaughter. In cooperation with other animal rights groups, has operated "turkey drop-off points" in several Texas cities for students who want their animals to live at the group's Black Beauty Ranch near Athens, Texas.

APPENDIX XI

Humane Society of the United States

2100 L Street, NW
Washington, DC 20037
(202) 452-1100
www.hsus.org

SUMMARY

In resources and membership, the Humane Society of the United States is the largest animal rights group in the country. Despite HSUS' on-going campaigns against modern animal agriculture, rodeos, hunting, trapping, pet breeding, and other animal uses, its public image as a "be-kind-to-pets organization" arguably allows it to "[collect] mainstream contributions from an unsuspecting public," according to critics Rod and Patti Strand.

HSUS' 1980 convention called for the "the clear articulation and establishment of the rights of all animals." At a recent gathering of HSUS members, president emeritus John A. Hoyt said that "in promoting the rights of animals we are doing so in a world where animals do not have equal status; indeed cannot and will not have equal status. The human species . . . will never concede equality to animals and will, I predict, resist with increasing vehemence all attempts to endow them with such." In a 1990 interview, HSUS vice president Michael Fox said that "Humans are different. We're not superior. There are no clear distinctions between us and animals."

HSUS has led the anti-fur campaign in the United States. Under the direction of Hoyt, HSUS in 1988 introduced the strategy of targeting anti-fur messages at consumers, an approach first used in Europe and based on the arguably successful campaigns of the Holland Anti-Fur Committee, Swiss Animal Protection Society, and Royal Society for the Prevention of Cruelty to Animals in Great Britain. Hoyt unveiled the plan at an annual meeting of the World Society for the Protection of Animals in Toronto, saying it was intended to make "those who wear fur feel uncomfortable in public." (See Chapter VIII for a fuller discussion of the Humane Society of the United States.)

FOUNDED
1954

APPENDIX XI

IRS STATUS
501(c)(3)

STATED PURPOSE
"To improve the lives of animals, both domestic and wild."

MEMBERSHIP
1,750,000

OPERATING OFFICER
Paul G. Irwin, President and Treasurer

REGIONAL OFFICES
Great Lakes
Gulf States
New England
South Central
Southeast
West Coast
North Central
Mid-Atlantic
Mid-West

Affiliates
Center for Respect of Life and Environment
EarthVoice
Humane Society International
HSUS Wildlife Land Trust
International Center for Earth Concerns
National Association for Humane and Environmental Education

POLITICAL ACTION COMMITTEE
None

PUBLICATIONS
   Animal Activist Alert (quarterly newsletter informing members of current animal-related legislation)
   Animal Rights (pamphlet discussing "animal rights")
   Animal Rights and Human Morality (book exploring the issue of whether animals should have legal and moral rights)
   Animal Welfare and Nature: Hindu Scriptural Perspectives (monograph reviewing Hindu perspectives on animals and humans)
   Animals and People (quarterly newsletter for teachers)

Close-Up Report (monthly report relating results of HSUS cruelty investigations)

HSUS News (quarterly newsletter for members)

KIND (Kids in Nature's Defense) News (newspaper for school children)

New Assault on Rodeo (guide for grassroots activists on "ending this cruel American sport")

Shame of Fur Campaign Packet (activist kit with suggestions on organizing anti-fur campaigns)

Shelter Sense (newsletter for shelter employees)

Brochures, pamphlets, videos, tee shirts, posters, buttons, bumper stickers

INCOME (1996)
$46,000,000

Dues and contributions (36%)
Bequests (30%)
Gifts and grants (24%)
Investments (7%)
Sales, other (3%)

DONORS
$10 annual membership for individual, $18 for family

PROGRAMS
- Shame of Fur (to persuade consumers that wearing fur is "cruel" and "unfashionable;" involves posting anti-fur messages on billboards and busses, organizing protests against fur stores, and airing anti-fur radio announcements)
- Breakfast of Cruelty (campaign against pork and egg manufacturers intended to prompt reforms in the way hogs and chickens are raised; HSUS says that "Behind virtually every slice of bacon and every innocuous looking egg lurks a long, hidden history of unbearable suffering")
- Primate Project (to end "the cruel trade in wild primates for research purposes;" HSUS has successfully lobbied for a ban on government funds to animal research centers using formerly wild chimpanzees)
- Government Alternatives Project (to force federal funding agencies to reform animal testing methods)
- Humane Charter Project (to encourage private funding agencies to adopt HSUS' animal research guidelines)
- Military Project (to make information on Department of Defense animal research publicly available)
- National Association for Humane and Environmental Education (youth program providing sample curricula and newsletters to promote

alternatives to dissection and encourage the formation of youth animal protection clubs at schools)
- Annual Russell and Burch Award (to recognize contributions in reforming lab animal treatment)
- Beautiful Choice (to urge personal-care products companies to take the following pledge):

From this day forward, we pledge:
- that cosmetics and other personal-care products marketed by this company as part of the "Beautiful Choice" campaign have not been tested on animals either by this company or by any outside organization;
- that this company has neither tested the ingredients of such products on animals nor requested such tests of an outside organization;
- that this company will support efforts by The Humane Society of the United States to end the use of animal testing for cosmetics and other personal-care products.

ACTIVITIES
- "Has been a leader in eliminating the use of shelter animals in research;" has also sought to end animal use in cosmetics and product safety tests.
- "Has supported state and local efforts to pass mandatory spay / neuter laws."
- Has "fought against efforts to legalize dog and horse racing."
- Has "[worked] through both legal and legislative channels to eliminate hunting and trapping on national wildlife refuges."
- Launched an investigation into dog kennels near Tallahassee, Florida, that led to the prosecution of four persons in connection with training greyhounds for races by chasing live rabbits.
- Announced support for a moratorium on patenting genetically altered animals.
- Protested the U.S. Air Force's planned killing of jackrabbits causing a hazard on the runways of McClellan Air Force Base in California.
- Petitioned the U.S. Department of the Interior in 1989 to list the African elephant as an "endangered" rather than "threatened" species in an effort to outlaw ivory sales in the United States.
- Protested at the Japanese Embassy in 1989 against Japanese whaling activities.
- Filed a lawsuit in 1989 to stop a deer hunt at the Mason Neck National Wildlife Refuge in Virginia.
- Participated in the 1990 Earth Day in Washington, D.C., "to raise public awareness of the environmental threats to our planet and the animals with whom we share the earth (habitat depletion, rainforest destruction, pollution of our waters, etc.) and to build a strong base of

public support to force environmental changes in the workplace and our daily habits."

- "[Called] for a partnership among the churches and conservation, environmental, and animal-protection communities [to encourage] religious leaders and environmentalists to work together to establish a global environmental ethic throughout the world."
- Sent letters in 1991 to 8,000 District of Columbia area residents asking them to urge Giant and Safeway supermarkets to sell eggs laid by non-caged hens. Giant began selling "organic nest-fresh eggs" at 70 cents to $1 more per dozen, but Giant vice president for consumer affairs Odonna Matthews said sales were "very, very slow." Safeway decided not to sell the eggs because an adequate supply could not be guaranteed.
- Threatened to sue *Encyclopedia Britannica* in 1992 after HSUS vice president Michael Fox wrote a 1991 entry that said the following: "Another common use of dogs, especially purpose-bred beagles, is in biomedical research. Such use, which often entails much suffering, has been questioned for its scientific validity and medical relevance to human health problems. . . ." *Encyclopedia Britannica* received hundreds of protest letters from scientists, and Robert McHenry, general editor of *Britannica*, admitted the entry was "unbalanced and unnecessarily inflammatory."
- Won a joint federal lawsuit in 1992 to force the U.S. Department of Agriculture to include mice, rats, and birds under provisions of the Animal Welfare Act. However, the case was later successfully appealed for lack of legal standing.
- Called on the 1992 U.S. delegation to the Convention on International Trade in Endangered Species to support Appendix I (most endangered species) listing for all African elephants after six southern African countries—Botswana, Malawi, Namibia, South Africa, Zambia, and Zimbabwe—proposed Appendix II (threatened) status. HSUS said that "Ivory fever . . . a sickness [affecting] man [with symptoms of] greed and an arrogant disregard for life and for the right of a majestic species" is leading to a "renewal of the 'vory trade' that 'means, without a doubt—without question—the decimation and eventual extinction of [elephants]." When the Zimbabwean government in 1991 announced a plan to kill 15,000 elephants living in overpopulated herds, HSUS said "Zimbabwe's proposed cull seems to be nothing more than a thinly veiled ploy to convince the world that elephants are not endangered. . . ."
- In 1996, contributed $259,905 to anti-hunting ballot initiatives in Idaho and Massachusetts. Wayne Pacelle, an HSUS vice-president, contributed $5,000 to a Colorado initiative.
- Sided with the Sierra Club and Earth Island Institute in denouncing the International Dolphin Conservation Program Act of 1997, which allows tuna net casting around dolphins.

APPENDIX XII

In Defense of Animals

131 Camino Alto, Suite E
Mill Valley, CA 94941
(415) 388-9641
www.idausa.org

SUMMARY

Originally called Californians for Responsible Research, In Defense of Animals has organized several campaigns in its 15-year history to halt animal research at universities and in the military. After secretly obtaining photos of dogs used at a University of California at Davis research laboratory, IDA threatened civil disobedience until the animals were released to people willing to adopt them. It filed a lawsuit against the U.S. Army that prompted the release of greyhounds used in studies of how broken bones heal. It also supported IDA investigator Ben White, who cut nets holding 40 dolphins in Japan.

Like other animal rights groups, IDA seeks to "lay siege to the concept of animal ownership." It believes that "the concept of seeing animals as 'things' or 'property' is an outdated belief. . . . They are not our property. We are not their owners."

FOUNDED
1983

IRS STATUS
501(c)(3)

STATED PURPOSE
"Ending the exploitation and abuse of animals by protecting their rights, welfare and habitat."

MEMBERSHIP
70,000

OPERATING OFFICER
Elliot Katz, President

POLITICAL ACTION COMMITTEE
None

PUBLICATIONS
"50,000 Reasons to Boycott Proctor and Gamble" (brochure)
"Fur: A Dying Fashion, a Dead Investment" (brochure)
IDA Magazine (quarterly newsletter)
In Defense of Animals (compact disc featuring songs by Pearl Jam, Michael Stipe, Lush, Primus, Helmet, and others)
In Defense of Animals Vol. 2 (compact disc featuring White Zombie, Bjork, Beastie Boys, Morphine, and others)
"Twelve Things You Can Do" (brochure)
Other brochures and pamphlets

INCOME (1996)
$1,620,485

Contributions (88%)
Investments (11%)
Sales (1%)

DONORS
$20 annual membership

PROGRAMS
- They Are Not Our Property (to persuade the public that the use of animals is morally wrong)
- Procter & Gamble Boycott (to protest P&G's use of animals in product safety testing)
- Pet Theft (to prevent biomedical research facilities from acquiring unwanted shelter animals for use in research)
- Lawsuits (targeted at biomedical research facilities in efforts to halt animal research in progress)
- Grassroots Campaign (offers advice to activists on how to use the mass media, investigate animal research facilities, and organize other campaigns against animal use)

ACTIVITIES
- Supported IDA investigator Ben White, who "liberated" 40 dolphins held in nets off the coast of Japan.
- Ended experiments on 180 beagles at the University of California at Davis after secretly obtaining photos of the animals and threatening civil disobedience.
- Filed a successful lawsuit to end a U.S. Army experiment that used greyhounds to study how bones heal.

- In 1997, joined 38 other animal rights organizations that called on President Clinton to declare a moratorium on federally funded research using non-human primates.
- In 1998, criticized the Alamogordo, New Mexico-based Coulston Foundation for holding over 100 "retired" U.S. Air Force chimpanzees that IDA wanted placed in sanctuaries.
- On-going boycott against Proctor & Gamble for using animals in product safety tests.

APPENDIX XIII

International Fund for Animal Welfare

411 Main Street
Yarmouth Port, MA 02675
(508) 362-6268
www.ifaw.org

SUMMARY
The International Fund for Animal Welfare was founded in 1969 to end the commercial hunting of harp and hooded seals in Canada. While the hunting of baby harp seals has been outlawed, IFAW continues to oppose the hunting of adult seals. It also seeks to abolish whaling, leghold traps, hound hunting in Great Britain, and what it calls the "unsustainable hunting" of African elephants.

FOUNDED
1969

IRS STATUS
501(c)(3)

STATED PURPOSE
"To stop commercial [animal] exploitation, to help animals in crisis and distress, to protect habitat for animals."

MEMBERSHIP
2,000,000 worldwide

OPERATING OFFICER
Frederick O'Regan

OTHER OFFICES

Australia
Belgium
Canada
China
Great Britain

France
Germany
Holland
Russia
South Africa

POLITICAL ACTION COMMITTEE
Yes

PUBLICATIONS
Peace on Ice (video)
Seal Song and Savage Luxury (book)
Seasons of the Seal (book)

INCOME (1996)
$11,700,000

DONORS
$15 suggested minimum annual membership

PROGRAMS
- Emergency Relief (rescues animals involved in disasters)
- Pet Rescue (provides grants to animal shelters worldwide)
- Scientific Research and Conservation (studies the social behavior of animals, seeks to preserve wildlife habitat)

ACTIVITIES
- Began a campaign in 1969 that resulted in a 1987 ban on hunting baby harp seals in Canada.
- Helped pressure the International Whaling Commission to enact a five-year worldwide moratorium on commercial whaling in 1986. The moratorium has since been extended.
- Assisted in animal rescue operations following the Exxon Valdez oil tanker spill in 1989.
- In 1992, helped 300 hippos during a drought in South Africa.
- Has unsuccessfully sought to end the tradition of using hounds to hunt foxes in Great Britain.
- Helped organize a 2,500-person demonstration against Canada's commercial seal hunt outside the 1998 federal Liberal convention in Ottawa.
- Filed a lawsuit in 1998 to force the Canadian government to end international trade in seal penises.
- In 1998, used billboard messages, newspaper and audio ads, and videotapes in efforts to unseat eight Tory MPPs in Canada who support hunting.

APPENDIX XIV

People for the Ethical Treatment of Animals

501 Front Street
Norfolk, VA 23510
(757) 622-7382
www.peta-online.org

SUMMARY

People for the Ethical Treatment of Animals is arguably the best known animal rights group in the U.S. Through demonstrations, lobbying, lawsuits, workshops, publications, celebrity fundraising events, and investigations of alleged cruelty, PETA seeks to advance its official motto that "Animals are not ours to eat, wear or experiment on."

PETA president Ingrid Newkirk, a former animal control worker with the District of Columbia, has often been criticized for her belief in human-animal equality: "I don't believe human beings have a 'right to life.' That's a supremacist perversion. A rat is a pig is a dog is a boy." In one interview, she said, "Six million Jews died in concentration camps, but 6 billion broiler chickens will die this year in slaughterhouses."

PETA chairman Alex Pacheco, a one-time candidate for the Roman Catholic priesthood, co-founded PETA with Newkirk in 1980 and helped propelled the organization into headline news the following year by alleging that an animal researcher in Silver Spring, Maryland, was abusing chimpanzees. (See Chapter VII for a discussion of the so-called "Silver Spring Monkeys Case.")

PETA is an outspoken supporter of the terrorist group the Animal Liberation Front. Following a 1986 ALF raid on a University of Oregon animal research lab, PETA said that

> ALF action goes beyond acts of protest. Animals will always be rescued where possible, but the main purpose of the action is often economic sabotage. Property and 'things' hold no sacred value—the opposite, in fact, if they are used to cause pain and death. To stop the very real violence of torture and killing, inanimate objects must be rendered unusable. When equipment is broken, work cannot go on as usual with a new batch of victims, insurance rates go up and so do security costs, making the enterprise less profitable.

Following a 1992 raid on a Michigan State University animal research lab for which ALF claimed responsibility, Newkirk and Pacheco were subpoenaed by a federal grand jury to provide fingerprints and handwriting samples to the FBI and U.S. Bureau of Alcohol, Tobacco and Firearms as part of a five-state federal task force investigation into ALF activities. (See Chapter IX and Appendix IV for a fuller discussion of PETA and its connections to the Animal Liberation Front.)

FOUNDED
1980

IRS STATUS
501(c)(3)

STATED PURPOSE
"To [establish] the rights and [improve] the lives of all animals—by educating, changing lifestyles and exposing abuse wherever it occurs."

MEMBERSHIP
600,000

OFFICERS
Chairman and Founder
Alexander F. Pacheco

Co-Founder and President
Ingrid Newkirk

POLITICAL ACTION COMMITTEE
None

PUBLICATIONS
Animal Rights (musical album)
Catalog for Cruelty-Free Living (32-page catalog of non-animal-tested consumer products)
The Compassionate Cook (vegetarian cookbook)
Compassionate Living (guide to buying "cruelty-free" products)
Cooking with PETA (vegetarian cookbook)
GRRR! The Zine that Bites Back (quarterly magazine for school children)
Monkey Business (describes the Silver Spring Monkeys Case)
PETA News (quarterly magazine for members)
PETA Kids (biannual magazine for children, including advice on becoming a vegetarian)
PETA's Animal Times (quarterly magazine)
Save the Animals! 101 Easy Things You Can Do (guide offering sug-

gestions for living a "cruelty-free" lifestyle)

Shopping Guide for Caring Consumers (guide to companies that do not test on animals)

Tame Yourself (musical sequel to Animal Rights)

Tofu Cookery (vegetarian cookbook)

250 Ways to Make Your Cat Adore You (animal rights pet care book)

Fliers, posters, brochures, action alerts, leaflets, videos, tee-shirts, postcards, household products

INCOME (1997)
$13,876,586

Contributions (94%)
Sales (3%)
Investment income (3%)

DONORS
$20 annual membership

PROGRAMS
- Fur Is Dead (includes anti-fur newspaper ads and radio announcements by actresses Rue McClanahan, Bea Arthur, and Betty White of television's "Golden Girls")
- Animals in Entertainment (to protest rodeos and "abuse" of animals in movies and circuses)
- Meat Stinks (includes vegetarian food booths at fairs and festivals, anti-meat television commercials and radio announcements featuring former Beatles member Paul McCartney, Chrissie Hynde, country singer k. d. Lang, and other campaigns against milk, hot dogs, chicken, and turkey to change "the way America eats")
- Caring Consumers (includes boycotts of companies that test consumer products on animals, certification of products as "cruelty-free," and the introduction of anti-animal testing shareholder resolutions at annual meetings of cosmetic companies)
- Compassion Corps (grassroots network of activists that organize boy cotts, demonstrates, and otherwise "[strike] back at powerful organizations with vested interests in animal abuse")
- Animal Rights Christmas Carols (annual Christmas Day concert out side the National Zoo in Washington, D.C., featuring such lyrics as: "On the 12th day of Christmas, the ALF set free 12 grateful turkeys, 11 lions roaring, 10 birds a-soaring, 9 pet shop puppies, 8 trapped coyotes, 7 crippled kittens, 6 blinded rabbits, 5 chimpanzees, 4 micro-pigs, 3 veal calves, 2 guinea pigs and a rat from a laboratory")
- National Fish Amnesty Day (to protest fishing)

ACTIVITIES

- Stopped a U.S. Department of Defense project in 1983 that was studying bullet wounds in dogs, cats, and goats.
- Used videotape stolen by the Animal Liberation Front from the University of Pennsylvania Head Injury Clinic in 1985 to persuade the National Institutes of Health to suspend government funding of the clinic on the grounds that researchers had allegedly made callous remarks and smoked while conducting non-sterile research on baboons.
- Boycotted clothing manufacturer Benetton in 1988 for conducting animal research. Benetton later ended the tests.
- Led a protest in 1989 against forest officials in San Bernardino, California, who were planning to move or destroy a colony of beavers that had nearly destroyed one of only two remaining Aspen tree stands in Southern California.
- Supported a Virginia pet store employee who hid a ferret that had bitten a five-year-old boy, forcing him to undergo several painful rabies injections. Said PETA spokesman Carol Burnett, "The discomfort of a human does not outweigh the right of the animal to live. . ."
- "Following on the British pattern . . . undertook plans to swallow up undermanned and overendowed old-line rivals, flying dozens of PETA members to the New England Anti-Vivisection Society meeting, at which they elected PETA's directors to NEAVS' board and gained control of NEAVS' eight million dollar fund balance."
- Distributed over one million door hangers nationwide in a 1989 "Avon Killing" campaign to protest Avon's use of animals in product tests. Avon (as well as Revlon) later stopped the tests.
- Filed a lawsuit in 1988 alleging that federally funded research at 17 San Francisco area labs was adversely affecting "air quality, traffic congestion, land use, noise, waste disposal, water availability, human health and socio-economics including public services, public finance, housing and education [in] individual communities and cumulatively to the San Francisco Bay area . . ." The charges were dismissed due to lack of legal standing.
- Prompted the "Wheel of Fortune" television game show in 1990 to stop giving fur coats as prizes.
- Sought a temporary restraining order in 1991 to stop the National Institutes of Health from euthanizing two of four remaining "Silver Spring" monkeys. Said PETA president Ingrid Newkirk, "NIH hopes to destroy the evidence of its failure to monitor federally funded animal research, its many documented lies to Congress in this case and its grossly inhumane treatment of the Silver Spring monkeys.
- Euthanized 18 rabbits and 14 roosters at its Aspen Hill Sanctuary and Memorial Park in Maryland because of "overcrowding." Said PETA president Ingrid Newkirk, "We really didn't have anything else to do. And so euthanasia was carried out with a great deal of concern."

Responded Peter J. Gerone of the Tulane Regional Primate Center, "With the $10 million that [PETA] brought in last year in revenue, they couldn't build some hutches for some rabbits to keep them alive?"

- Ran a newspaper ad in 1991 comparing the slaughtering of farm animals to the crimes of mass-killer Jeffrey Dahmer: "Milwaukee . . . July 1991. They were drugged and dragged across the room. . . . Their legs and feet were bound together. . . . Their struggles and cries went unanswered. . . . Then they were slaughtered and their heads sawn off. . . . Their body parts were refrigerated to be eaten later. . . . It's still going on. If this leaves a bad taste in your mouth, become a vegetarian."

- Prompted cosmetic manufacturer Neutrogena to stop animal testing in 1992.

- Launched boycotts of L'Oréal, Procter & Gamble, and Bristol-Myers Squibb in 1992 to protest animal product testing.

- Launched a 1992 fundraising drive attacking General Motors Laboratories for using animals to study the effects of automobile crashes. According to GM, impact studies comprise less than 10 percent of its research, ninety percent of the animals tested are rats and mice, and such research has led to the development of seat belts, air bags, child-safety seats, impact-absorbent construction, and crash helmets. An earlier PETA-sponsored shareholder resolution to stop the testing was defeated by a wide margin.

- Charged that animal researchers at Wright State University in Ohio had abused laboratory animals in 1992. PETA member Virginia Bollinger, who had earlier infiltrated the lab, was arrested and charged with tampering with research records and disorderly conduct.

- In 1997, praised PETA activist Alison Green for throwing a tofu cream pie in the face of fashion designer Oscar de La Renta in an Oregon department store. La Renta works with fur.

- In 1997, helped pass legislation in Rhode Island allowing students to opt-out of animal dissections.

- In 1997, joined several other animal rights groups to urge President Clinton to declare a moratorium on the use of non-human primates in biomedical research.

- In 1998, set up an anti-circus Internet website under the domain name "ringlingbrothers.com." PETA agreed to transfer the name to Ringling Bros. and Barnum & Bailey Circuses in exchange for withdrawal of a lawsuit alleging trademark infringement.

- In 1998, praised PETA activist Melynda Duval for throwing a pie in the face of Procter & Gamble chairman John Pepper at a governor's banquet. PETA said the reason for the attack was P&G's use of animals in product testing. A PETA spokesman remarked, "sometimes a polite word doesn't do it. That's why we sometimes do unusual things, such as slinging tofu cream pies."

- In 1998, unsuccessfully sought to halt NASA's Neurolab research project, which placed 2,000 animals on board the space shuttle Columbia to study the effects of microgravity on the nervous system. The research sought to better understand and dizziness, vertigo, jet lag, insomnia, and depression—conditions that affect millions of people.

- In 1998, asked members to write protest letters to ABC's *America's Funniest Videos*, which has shown such "abuse" as a monkey carrying a crying kitten up a tree.

APPENDIX XV

Physicians Committee for Responsible Medicine

5100 Wisconsin Avenue, NW, Suite 404
Washington, DC 20016
(202) 686-2210
www.perm.org

SUMMARY

Although the Physicians Committee for Responsible Medicine presents itself publicly as an association of physicians, no more than five percent of its members are doctors. It chief purpose is to promote vegetarianism and end what its calls "gruesome experiments" on animals. It recommends that children be raised as vegans (no meat *or* dairy products), promotes "non-animal methods in medical education," and acts as a "medical spokesman" for People for the Ethical Treatment of Animals. PCRM president Neal D. Barnard once worked for PETA.

The American Medical Association has strongly denounced PCRM for

> implying that physicians who support the use of animals in biomedical research are irresponsible, for misrepresenting the critical role animals play in research and testing, and for obscuring the overwhelming support for such research that exists among practicing physicians in the U.S. . . . PCRM members use the tactics of propaganda to promote their views and to distort the truth. They have manipulated facts, oversimplified complex issues and complex research, taken words out of context, omitted key facts, and misrepresented the goals of specific research projects. The overall effect of these activities has been to mislead. This is particularly true because of the apparent "scientific" credibility of PCRM.

PCRM's most recent campaign is to discourage American from supporting over 40 health charities, including the March of Dimes Birth Defects Foundation, because they fund animal research.

FOUNDED
1985

IRS STATUS
501 (c)(3)

STATED PURPOSE

To "[increase] public awareness about the importance of preventive medicine and nutrition, and [raise] scientific and ethical questions pertaining to the use of humans and animals in medical research."

MEMBERSHIP

90,000

OPERATING OFFICER

Neal D. Barnard

POLITICAL ACTION COMMITTEE

None

PUBLICATIONS

Actions Packs (includes sample letters to the editor, flyers, and other materials that criticize animal research

Alternatives in Medical Education

Eat Right, Live Longer (book by Neal Barnard)

Food for Life (book by Neal Barnard)

Foods that Fight Pain (book by Neal Barnard)

Good Medicine (quarterly magazine on preventive medicine, nutrition, and public-health policy)

Guide to Cruelty-Free Giving (lists health charities that either fund or do not fund animal research)

The Power of Your Plate

Vegetarian Starter Kit (offers advice on becoming a vegetarian)

INCOME (1997)

$1,937,375

DONORS

$20 annual membership

PROGRAMS

- Gold Plan (encourages business, hospitals, and schools to serve no-cholesterol, low-fat meals)
- New Four Food Groups (no-cholesterol, low-fat alternative to USDA dietary recommendations)
- Saving Lives (public-service announcements)

ACTIVITIES

- At a 1992 press conference in Boston, called on the government to stop recommending milk in its nutrition guideline and requiring milk in government feeding programs. A spokesman at the American Dietetic Association called the proposal "nutrition terrorism." The American Academy of Pediatrics and the American Medical Association also rejected PCRM's plan.
- With the Foundation for Economic Trends, sought a federal court injunction in 1993 to stop the National Institutes of Health from studying stunted growth in children.
- Has opposed baboon-to-human liver transplants, calling them "bad medicine and bad science."
- Stopped several medical research projects, including a U.S. Army experiment involving fatal head injuries to cats and a study at Washington State University on deprivation in monkeys.
- Through "advertising and outreach," claims to have helped persuade Oregon Health Science University, the University of Miami School of Medicine, and the medical school at St. Louis University to close their live animal laboratories. A spokesman at SLU said that although live animals are no longer used in first-year classes, they are used in later coursework. Moreover, many colleges and universities have closed their research laboratories because animals are expensive to purchase and their treatment must comply with costly federal and state regulations.
- In 1998, distributed leaflets at March of Dimes "WalkAmerica" fundraising events in 80 cities to dissuade Americans from supporting charities that fund animal research.
- In 1998, wrote to Maryland Governor Parris Glendening, urging him to drop milk as the official state drink.
- In 1998, claimed the federal government's food pyramid is racially biased because "most members of minority groups cannot digest milk easily."

APPENDIX XVI

Major Animal Rights Organizations

American Anti-Vivisection Society
American Society for the Prevention of Cruelty to Animals
Animal Legal Defense Fund
Animal Liberation Front
Animal Protection Institute of America
Animal Rights Coalition
Animal Rights International
Animal Welfare Institute
Beauty Without Cruelty
Committee for Humane Legislation
Doris Day Animal League
Farm Animal Reform Movement
Farm Sanctuary
Friends of Animals
Fund for Animals
Humane Farming Association
Humane Society of the United States
In Defense of Animals
International Fund for Animal Welfare
Massachusetts Society for the Prevention of Cruelty to Animals
National Anti-Vivisection Society
New England Anti-Vivisection Society
People for the Ethical Treatment of Animals
Performing Animal Welfare Society
Physicians Committee for Responsible Medicine
Progressive Animal Welfare Society
Psychologists for the Ethical Treatment of Animals
United Poultry Concerns
World Society for the Protection of Animals

APPENDIX XVII

Prominent Animal Rights Leaders

Neal D. Barnard, Founder and President, Physicians' Committee for Responsible Medicine,

Roger Caras, President Emeritus, American Society for the Prevention of Cruelty to Animals, New York, NY

Brian Davies, Founder, International Fund for Animal Welfare, Yarmouth Port, MA

Priscilla Feral, President, Friends of Animals, Norwalk, CT

David Foreman, Co-founder and former leader, Earth First! Tucson, AZ

Michael W. Fox, Vice President for Farm Animals and Bioethics, Humane Society of the United States, Washington, DC

Gary Francione, director, Rutgers University Animal Rights Law Center, Newark, New Jersey

John W. Grandy, Vice President for Wildlife and Environment, Humane Society of the United States, Washington, DC

Alex Hershaft, President, Farm Animal Reform Movement, Bethesda, MD

John Hoyt, President Emeritus, Humane Society of the United States, Washington, DC

Paul G. Irwin, President, Humane Society of the United States, Washington, DC

Elliot M. Katz, President, In Defense of Animals

John F. Kullberg, Former President, American Society for the Prevention of Cruelty to Animals, New York, NY

John McArdle, Scientific Director, New England Anti-Vivisection Society, Boston, MA

Ingrid E. Newkirk, Co-founder and Director, People for the Ethical Treatment of Animals, Norfolk, VA

Wayne Pacelle, Vice President of Government Affairs and Media, Humane Society of the United States, Washington, DC

Alex Pacheco, Co-founder and Chairman, People for the Ethical Treatment of Animals, Norfolk, VA

Thomas E. Regan, Founder and President, Culture and Animals Foundation, Raleigh, NC

Peter Singer, Author, *Animal Liberation: A New Ethics for Our Treatment of Animals*

Christine Stevens, President, Animal Welfare Institute, Washington, DC

Joyce Tischler, Executive Director, Animal Legal Defense Fund, Petaluma, CA

APPENDIX XVIII

Quotes by Animal Rights Leaders

Chris DeRose, director, Last Chance for Animals

"If the death of one rat cured all diseases, it wouldn't make any difference to me."– *Los Angels Times*, April 12, 1990

Gary L. Francione, professor, Rutgers Animal Rights Law Center

"Whatever educational benefits are provided by zoos cannot justify what zoos really are: prisons for animals." – "Animal Rights: The Future," 1996 essay

"Animal welfare seeks to regulate atrocity." – *Ibid.*

"Not only are the philosophies of animal rights and animal welfare separated by irreconcilable difference . . . the enactment of animal welfare measures actually impedes the achievement of animal rights." – with Tom Regan, *Animals' Agenda*, January / February 1992

"The theory of animal rights simply is not consistent with the theory of animal welfare . . . Animal rights means dramatic social changes for humans and non-humans alike." – *Animals' Voice*, vol. 4, no. 2

"Animal welfare does not work." – "Animal Rights and Animal Welfare," undated article

Michael W. Fox, vice president, the Humane Society of the United States

"The life of an ant and that of my child should be granted equal consideration." – *Inhumane Society* (1990 book)

"We are not superior. There are no clear distinctions between us and animals." – *Washingtonian,* February 1990

Dan Matthews, celebrity recruiter, People for the Ethical Treatment of Animals

On the consequences of ending the use of animals in biomedical research: "Don't get the diseases in the first place, schmo."– *USA Today,* July 27, 1994

"We're at war, and we'll do what we need to win." – *USA Today,* September 3, 1991

Ingrid Newkirk, president, People for the Ethical Treatment of Animals

"I wish we all would get up and go into the labs and take the animals out or burn them down." – speech at the Animal Rights 1997 National Convention

"Humans have grown like a cancer. We're the biggest blight on the face of the earth." – *Washingtonian,* February 1990

"Even if animal research produced a cure [for AIDS], we'd be against it." – *Vogue,* September 1989

"In the end, I think it would be lovely if we stopped this whole notion of pets altogether." – *Newsday,* February 21, 1988

"Eventually companion animals would be phased out, and we would return to a more symbiotic relationship—enjoyment at a distance." – *Harper's,* August 1988

"Pet ownership is an absolutely abysmal situation brought about by human manipulation." – *Harper's,* August 1988

"Animal liberationists do not separate out the human animal, so there is no rational basis for saying that a human being has special rights. A rat is a pig is a dog is a boy. They're all mammals."– *Washingtonian,* August 1986

Eating meat is "primitive, barbaric, and arrogant." – quoted in Charles Griswold, Jr., *Washington City Paper,* December 20, 1985.

"Six million Jews died in concentration camps, but six billion broiler chickens will die this year in slaughter houses." – *Washington Post,* November 13, 1983

Wayne Pacelle, vice president, Humane Society of the United States

"I firmly believe there is a place for civil disobedience in our movement." – "Wayne Pacelle, Unplugged," *Animals' Agenda,* n.d.

Alex Pacheco, chairman, People for the Ethical Treatment of Animals

"Arson, property destruction, burglary and theft are acceptable crimes when used for the animal cause." – *Gazette Mail* (Charleston, VW), January 15, 1989

"We feel that animals have the same rights as a retarded human child because they are equal mentally in terms of dependence on others." – *New York Times*, January 14, 1989

Tom Regan, Professor of philosophy, North Carolina State University

When asked if he would save a baby or a dog if a boat capsized: "If it were a retarded baby and a bright dog, I'd save the dog." – speech at the University of Wisconsin at Madison, October 27, 1989

"If abandoning animal research means that there are some things we cannot learn, then so be it. . . We have no basic right . . . not to be harmed by those natural diseases we are heir to." – *The Case for Animal Rights* (1983 book)

Peter Singer, author, *Animal Liberation*

"There will surely be some nonhuman animals whose lives, by any standards, are more valuable than the lives of some humans." – *Animal Liberation*

Henry Spira, former director, Animal Rights International

"My dream is that people will come to view eating an animal as cannibalism." – *New York Times Magazine*, November 26, 1989

APPENDIX XIX

Survey of Animal Rights Activists

In June of 1990, two Oregon State University researchers conduced a questionnaire survey of animal rights activits at the "March for the Animals" in Washington, D.C. Interviews with activists yielded demographic, attitudinal, and behavioral data.

Method

To assure randomization of respondents, interviewers were evenly spaced around the periphery of animal rights rallies; each interviewer entered into the crowd by an assigned number of steps, selected the closest person, then counted three persons to the right and initiated an interview. Four hundred twenty-six interviews were initiated with seven refusals and seven "incompletes," yielding a final sample of 412 (a 97 percent response rate).

Summary

The researchers concluded that "typical respondents were Caucasians, highly educated urban professional women approximately thirty years old with a median income of $33,000 . . . . Most activists think of themselves as Democrats or as Independents, and have moderate to liberal political views. They were often suspicious of science and made no distinctions between basic and applied science, or public versus private animal research. The research suggest that animal rights activism is in part a symbolic manifestation of egalitarian social and political views concerning scientific and technological change."

Demographic Data

Education

Some college or university education - 79%
Undergraduate degree - 22%
Advanced graduate or professional degree - 19%

APPENDIX XIX

Race / Ethnicity

White - 93%
Black - 2%
American Indian, Hispanic American, Asian - 3%

Gender

Female - 68%
Male - 32%

Age

19 or under - 10%
20 to 29 - 32%
30 to 39 - 29%
40 to 49 - 19%
50 or over - 10%

Income

$19,999 or under - 19%
$20,000 to $39,999 - 35%
$40,000 to $59,999 - 22%
$60,000 to $79,999 - 12%
$80,000 or more - 8%
Don't know or no answer - 4%

Population of Areas of Residence

50,000 or more - 66%
10,000 to 50,000 - 19%
Less than 10,000 - 10%
Don't know or no answer - 5%

Attitudinal and Behavioral Data

Political Ideology (1 = most conservative, 9 = most liberal)

1 - 1%
2 - 1%
3 - 4%
4 - 5%
5 - 17%

6 - 14%
7 - 26%
8 - 21%
9 - 11%

Views concerning different occupations and groups (100 = most positive, 0 = most negative)

Occupation or Group, Average Rating

Animal rights advocates - 93
Environmentalists - 88
Feminists - 70
Veterinarians - 70
Farmers / ranchers - 30
Scientist - 28
Politicians - 26
Businessmen - 25

Views concerning farm animal treatment (100 = most positive, 0 = most negative)

Animal, Average Rating

Horses - 36
Sheep - 29
Dairy Cows - 22
Pigs - 16
Beef Cows - 15
Turkeys - 11
Egg laying hens - 10
Broiler chickens - 7
Mink - 4
Veal caves - 2

"The main cause of animal exploitation is the world view that humanity has dominion over the environment."

Strongly agree - 61%
Agree - 26%
Neither agree nor disagree - 4%
Disagree - 4%
Strongly disagree - 4%
Missing data - 1%

APPENDIX XIX

Views concerning science

Science does more harm than good - 52%
Science does more good than harm - 26%
Don't know or no answer - 22%

(The researchers note that these results differ significantly from those of most Americans, almost 60 percent of whom believe that science does more good than harm; only 5 percent believe that science does more harm than good.)

Views on animal research which does not harm animals and which helps people

Disapprove - 55%
Neither approve nor disapprove - 16%
Approve - 26%
Missing date - 3%

Views on keeping pets at home

Approve - 87%
Neither approve nor disapprove - 9%
Disapprove - 3%
Missing data - 1%

Written elected representatives about animal rights

Yes - 74%
No - 26%

Campaigned for candidates who favor animal rights

Yes - 38%
No - 61%
Don't know or no answer - 1%

The researchers note that "compared to the general public, or even campaign contributors, this level of political activity is truly extraordinary . . . . Marchers were characterized by profound commitment to the movement and to continued action within the political system."

Source: Wesley V. Jamison (College of Agricultural Sciences, Oregon State University) and William M. Lunch (Department of Political Science, Oregon State University), "Rights of Animals, Perceptions of Science, and

212

Political Activism: Profile of American Animal Rights Activists," *Science, Technology, & Human Values,* Vol. 17, No. 4, Autumn 1992, pp. 438-45. Some of the data presented here are from an earlier unpublished paper, also by Jamison and Lunch, entitled "A Preliminary Report: Results from Demographic, Attitudinal, and Behavioral Analysis of the Animal Rights Movement."

Bibliography

Books

Carman, Russ. *The Illusions of Animal Rights*. Iola, WI: Krause Publications, 1990.

Day, David. *The Environmental Wars: Reports from the Front Lines*. New York: St. Martin's Press, 1989.

Finsen, Lawrence, and Susan Finsen. *The Animal Rights Movement in America: From Compassion to Respect*. New York: Twayne Publishers, 1994.

Fox, Michael W. *Inhumane Society: The American Way of Exploiting Animals*. New York: St. Martin's Press, 1990.

Henke, Janice Scott. *Seal Wars! An American Viewpoint*. St. John's, Newfoundland: Breakwater Books, 1985.

Henshaw, David. *Animal Warfare: The Story of the Animal Liberation Front*. London: Fontana Paperbacks, 1989.

Howard, Walter E. *Animal Rights vs. Nature*. Davis, CA: Walter E. Howard, 1990.

Kiley-Worthington, Marthe. *Animals in Circuses and Zoos: Chiron's World*. Basildon, England: Little Eco-Farms Publishing, 1990.

Marquardt, Kathleen, Herbert M. Levine, and Mark LaRochelle. *Animal Scam: The Beastly Abuse of Human Rights*. Washington, DC: Regnery Gateway, 1993.

Ray, Dixie Lee, and Lou Guzzo. *Trashing the Planet: How Science Can Help Us Deal with Acid Rain, Depletion of the Ozone, and the Soviet Threat among other Things*. Washington, DC: Regnery Gateway, 1990.

Regan, Tom. *The Case for Animal Rights*. Berkeley and Los Angeles: University of California Press, 1983.

Bibliography

Screaming Wolf (pseud.). *A Declaration of War: Killing People to Save Animals and the Environment*. Grass Valley, CA: Patrick Henry Press, 1991.

Singer, Peter. *Animal Liberation: A New Ethics for Our Treatment of Animals*. New York: Avon Books, 1975.

Sperling, Susan. *Animal Liberators: Research and Morality*. Berkeley and Los Angeles: University of California Press, 1988.

Strand, Rod, and Patti Strand. *The Hijacking of the Humane Movement*. Wilsonville, OR: Doral Publishing, 1993.

Swan, James A. *In Defense of Hunting*. San Francisco: Harper Collins Publishers, 1995.

Articles and Reports

American Farm Bureau Federation. "Meeting the Animal Rights Challenge." Chicago (1991).

American Medical Association. "Human v. Animal Rights: In Defense of Animal Research." Chicago (1990).

—————. "Use of Animals in Biomedical Research: The Challenge and Response." Chicago (rev. 1992).

Americans for Medical Progress. "A Wolf in Sheep's Clothing: The HSUS—PETA Connection." Alexandria, VA (n.d.).

—————. "What's Happening with Our Humane Groups? Inside the Humane Society of the United States." Alexandria, VA (Oct. 1996).

Animal Liberation Frontline. "The A.L.F. Primer." Www.animal-liberation.net (n.d.).

Geoffrey S. Becker. "Humane Treatment of Farm Animals: Overview and Selected Issues." Washington, DC: Congressional Research Service (May 1, 1992).

Bidinotto, Robert James. "Environmentalism: Freedom's Foe for the 90s." *Freeman* (Nov. 1990), 409-420.

Bibliography

Hardy, David T. "America's New Extremists: What You Need to Know about the Animal Rights Movement." Washington, DC: Washington Legal Foundation (1990).

Horton, Larry. "The Enduring Animal Issue." *Journal of the National Cancer Institute* (May 22, 1989), 736-743.

Hubbell, John G. "The 'Animal Rights' War on Medicine." *Reader's Digest* (Jun. 1990), 70-76.

Humane Society of the United States. "Summary of the HSUS Recommendations: Pet Overpopulation." Washington, DC (Mar. 24, 1993).

International Professional Rodeo Association. "To Protect an American Tradition for the Next Generation: Rodeo Looks at Its Critics." Oklahoma City, OK (1991).

Jamison, Wesley V., and William M. Lunch. "Rights of Animals, Perceptions of Science, and Political Activism: Profile of American Animal Rights Activists." *Science, Technology, & Human Values* (Autumn 1992), 438-445.

Kellert, Stephen. "Attitudes and Characteristics of Hunters and Anti-Hunters." Presented at Forty-Third North American Wildlife and Natural Resources Conference (1978).

Leader, Robert W., and Dennis Stark. "The Importance of Animals in Biomedical Research." *Perspectives in Biology and Medicine* (Summer 1987).

Macabe, Katie. "Beyond Cruelty." *Washingtonian* (Feb. 1990), 72-77, 185-198, 189-195.

—————. "Who Will Live, Who Will Die?" *Washingtonian* (Aug. 1986), 112-118, 153-157.

National Shooting Sports Foundation. "The Un-Endangered Species: It Didn't Just Happen." Newtown, CT (Sept. 1992).

—————. "What They Say about Hunting: Position Statements on Hunting of Major Conservation or Preservation Organizations." Newtown, CT (n.d.).

National Trappers Association. "Facts About Furs!" Bloomington, IL (1988).

—————. "Traps Today: Myths and Facts." Bloomington, IL (n.d.).

Newkirk, Ingrid, Gary Francione, Roger Goldman, and Arthur Caplan. "Just Like Us? Toward a Notion of Animal Rights." *Harper's* (Aug. 1988), 43-52.

Oliver, Charles. "Liberation Zoology." *Reason* (Jun. 1990), 22-27.

Oliver, Daniel T. "Animal Welfare vs. Animal Rights: The Case of PETA." Washington, DC: Capital Research Center. *Alternatives in Philanthropy* (Jul. 1997).

—————. "The ASPCA: From Animal Welfare to Animal Rights." Washington, DC: Capital Research Center. *Alternatives in Philanthropy* (Aug. 1998).

—————. "The Humane Society of the United States: Its Not about Animal Shelters." Washington, DC: Capital Research Center. *Alternatives in Philanthropy* (Oct. 1997).

Patronek, Gary, and Andrew Rowan. "Flow Chart of the US Pet Dog Population." Adopted from *Anthrozoos* (1994, 1996).

People for the Ethical Treatment of Animals. "Becoming an Activist: PETA's Guide to Animal Rights Organizing." Norfolk, VA (n.d.).

Professional Rodeo Cowboys Association. "Humane Facts: The Care and Treatment of Professional Rodeo Livestock." Colorado Springs, CO (1992).

Responsive Management. "Americans' Attitudes toward Animal Welfare, Animal Rights and Use of Animals." Harrisonburg, VA (Oct. 1996).

Salman, M., J. New, J. Scarlett, P. Kass, R. Ruch-Gallie, and S. Hetts. "Human and Animal Factors Related to the Relinquishment of Dogs and Cats in 12 Selected Animal Shelters in the USA." Unpublished (n.d.).

U.S. Department of Justice. *Report to Congress on the Extent and Effects of Domestic and International Terrorism on Animal Enterprises.* Washington, DC (Aug. 1993).

White, Robert J. "The Facts about Animal Research." *Reader's Digest* (Mar. 1988), 127-132.

Frequently Cited Periodicals

Americans for Medical Progress. *AMP News.* Alexandria, VA.

American Society for the Prevention of Cruelty to Animals. *"A" Is for Animal.* New York.

——————. *ASPCA Report.* New York.

Animal Legal Defense Fund. *Animals' Advocate.* Petaluma, CA.

Animal Protection Institute. *Mainstream.* Sacramento, CA.

Animal Welfare Institute. *AWI Quarterly.* Washington, DC.

Clifton, Merritt. *Animal People.* Clinton, WA.

Farm Animal Reform Movement. *Farm Report.* Bethesda, MD.

Friends of Animals. *ActionLine.* Darien, CT.

Humane Society of the United States. *HSUS News.* Washington, DC.

Humane Society of the United States / National Association for Humane and Environmental Education. *Student Network News.* East Haddam, CT.

International Professional Rodeo Association. *Pro Rodeo World.* Oklahoma City, OK.

National Animal Interest Alliance. *NAIA News.* Portland, OR.

People for the Ethical Treatment of Animals. *Animal Times.* Norfolk, VA.

——————. *PETA Kids.* Norfolk, VA.

Putting People First. *People's Bulletin.* Washington, DC.

Stallwood, Kim. *The Animals' Agenda.* Langhorne, PA.

INDEX

221

Health Research Extension Act, 17
Health, Safety and Research
  Alliance of New York, 137
Heflin, Sen. Howell, 126
Helmet, 186
Helping Hands, 171
Henke, Janice, iii, xiv, 55, 92, 93,
  94
Henshaw, David, 115
Herrington, Alice, 173
Hershaft, Alex, 168, 203
Herzog, Harold A., xvi
Hinkle, Judge Margaret, 116
Holland Anti-Fur Committee, 179
Hommes, Eden, 99
Horse and Chaise Carriage Rides,
  73
horses, 14, 34, 35, 66, 68, 85, 101,
  211
Horton, Larry, 1, 11, 19
Howard University, 131
Howard, Walter E., 8, 43, 44
Hoyt, John, 80, 84, 109, 113, 179,
  203
HSUS, see Humane Society of the
  United States
HSUS Wildlife Land Trust, 180
Hubel, David H., xiii, 11
Humane Farming Association, 27,
  31, 32, 91, 201
Humane Slaughter Act, 35, 36,
  163, 165
Humane Society International, 180
Humane Society of Santa Clara
  County, 55
Humane Society of St. Joseph
  (Indiana), 81
Humane Society of the United
  States, iii, viii, ix, xiv, xv, xvii, 4,
  33, 43, 44, 47, 48, 51, 53-57, 64,
  68, 69, 71, 74, 78-82, 84, 91, 92,
  94, 95, 99, 109-111, 113, 114,
  116, 131, 179, 181-183, 201,
  203, 205, 207

Hunt Saboteurs Association, 120,
  122
Hunt, George, 73
Huntingdon Life Sciences, vii, xi,
  xii, xv
Hynde, Chrissie, 193

I

IFAW, see International Fund for
  Animal Welfare
Improved Standards for
  Laboratory Animals Act, 163
In Defense of Animals, ix, 78, 91,
  103, 185, 201, 203
incurably ill For Animal Research,
  20, 104, 136
Indigo Girls, 98
Interior, U.S. Department of, 18,
  71, 182
Fish & Wildlife Service, U.S., 52,
  55, 56, 71
National Park Service, 156, 177
International Center for Earth
  Concerns, 180
International Dolphin
  Conservation Program Act, 101,
  183
International Fund for Animal
  Welfare, ix, xv, xvii, 5, 54, 91-
  94, 189, 201, 203
International League for the
  Protection of Horses, 35
International Professional Rodeo
  Association, iii, 68, 69, 138
International Society for Animal
  Rights, 114
International Whaling Commission,
  94, 95, 130, 177, 190
Scientific Committee, 94
Inuit (Eskimos), 57
Irish Republican Army, 121, 149
Irwin, Paul, 81, 180, 203
Ison, Leslie, 114
Ives, Burl, 91

J

Jackson, Michael, 90
Jam, Pearl, 186
Jamison, Wesley V., xv, 212
Jean Lafitte National Historical
Park, 177
Johns Hopkins Center for
Alternatives to Animal Testing,
160
Johnson (Robert Wood)
Foundation, 143
Jorgenson, Gunnar, 33
Justice, U.S. Department of, 119,
125

K

Katz, Elliot, 185, 203
Kentucky Fish and Wildlife
Commission, 177
Kiley-Worthington, Marthe, 65-
67, 84
King Ferdinand, 63
King Manuel the Great, 63
King, Martin Luther, Jr., 131
Kostmayer, Rep. Peter H., 73
Krantz, Gunnar, 33
Kullberg, John F., 26, 114, 203

L

L'Oréal, 195
La Renta, Oscar de, 195
Lamb, Rachael, 114
Lang, k.d., 193
Lantos, Rep. Tom, 91
Lantz, Sarah, 99
Las Vegas Sun, 70
Last Chance for Animals, 205
Lawyers' Committee for the
Enforcement of Animal
Protection Law, 146
Lazarus, 174
Lazy F Ranch, 177
Leader, Robert W., 14

least tern, 55
Lee, Ronnie, 43, 115, 120-122, 149
Lewis & Clark College
Northwestern School of Law, 146
light-footed clapper rail, 55
Linck, Peter, 90
Lindgren, Astrid, 163
Linscombe, Greg, 55
llamas, 66
Loma Linda University
Medical Center, 152
Lomasky, Loren, 49
Los Angeles Board of Animal
Commissioners, 82
Los Angeles Times, 205
Lowey, Rep. Nina, 53
Lucci, Toni, 152
Ludd, Ned, 7
Lunch, William M., xv, 212
Lush, 186
Lyman, Howard, 114

M

MacGregor, Lisa, 73
Macy's, 174
Maehr, David, 49
Magendie, 11
Makah Indians, 157
Manitoba Ministry of Agriculture,
34
March for the Animals, 90, 209
March of Dimes Birth Defects
Foundation, 197, 199
Marine Mammal Protection Act,
67, 130, 163, 165, 173, 176
Marine World / Africa USA, 157
Marshall, Peter, 90
Martin, M.P. "Humanities Dick," 1
Martin's Act, 1
Mason Neck National Wildlife
Refuge, 182
Mason, James, 142, 168
Massachusetts Farm Bureau, 36
Massachusetts Fisheries and
Wildlife Board, 147

New York Post, 160
New York Times, 159, 173, 207
New York Times Magazine, 207
Newkirk, Ingrid, xii, xiii, 7, 11, 16, 78, 103, 109, 116, 122, 123, 126, 153, 191, 192, 194, 203, 206
Newsday, 206
Newsweek, 160
Nicholas Turkey Breeding Farms, 124
Nickum, John G., 52
Nilsson, Greta, 164
North American A.L.F. Press Office, 150
North American A.L.F. Supporters Group, 150, 151
North Carolina State University, 207
nutria, 55

O

O'Regan, Frederick, 189
Ohio Wildlife Council, 55
Oregon Cooperative Fishery Research Unit, 52
Oregon Health Science University, 199
Oregon State University, 152, 209
  College of Agricultural Science, 212
  Department of Political Science, 212

P

Pacelle, Wayne, 50, 114, 131, 183, 203, 207
Pacheco, Alex, xiii, 5, 95, 96, 116, 122, 123, 126, 153, 191, 192, 203, 207
Palestine Liberation Organization, 121
Palo Alto Humane Society, 18
Paris, Peter, 112

Patent and Trademark Office, U.S., 147
Patronek, Gary, 78, 84
PCRM, see Physicians Committee for Responsible Medicine
Peace, Adam Troy, 126
Peninsula Humane Society, 83, 116
People for the Ethical Treatment of Animals, iii, vii-ix, xi-xv, xvii, 5, 7, 8, 11, 16, 18, 20, 25, 26, 33-36, 49, 51, 52, 64, 69-71, 73, 77, 78, 84, 90, 91, 95-97, 99, 100, 103, 104, 109, 114-116, 122-124, 126, 130, 131, 145, 149, 150, 153, 191, 192, 194, 195, 197, 201, 203, 206, 207
  Aspen Hill Sanctuary and Memorial Park, 100, 194
Pepper, John, 195
Perdue Farms, 159
Perdue, Frank, 29, 161
Performing Animal Welfare Society, 70, 71, 201
Pet Safety and Protection Act of 1998, 16
PETA, see People for the Ethical Treatment of Animals
Peter, Rev. Val, 97
Pfizer, Inc., 143
Phoenix, River, 90, 98
Physicians Committee for Responsible Medicine, ix, xvii, 14, 116, 197, 201, 203
pigs, 66, 211
Pils, Charles, 55
Point Defiance Zoo, 72
Premarin, 34-36, 90, 103, 157
Presumed Consent Law, 156
Primus, 186
Probst, Marian, 175
Procter & Gamble, xi, 186, 187, 195
Professional Rodeo Cowboys Association, iii, 68, 69, 139
Progressive Animal Welfare Society, 72, 81, 201

Veterans Administration, 171
Victoria Street Society, 3
Vogue, 206

W

Wahlberg, Sven, 33
Wall Street Journal, 98
Walsh, Edward J., 97, 98
Washington City Paper, 206
Washington Humane Society, 3,
  67, 114
Washington Post, 103, 160, 206
Washington State University, 199
Washington Times, 160, 161
Washingtonian, 205, 206
Watson, Paul, 94
Weber, Vin, 19
whales, 94, 95, 130, 157
Wherwall Estate, 124
White Zombie, 186
White, Ben, 185, 186
White, Betty, 20, 193
White, Robert J., 16
Wieczorek, Deurita, 73
wild turkey, 45
Wildlife 2000, 43
Wildlife Conservation Fund of
  America, 138
Wildlife Legislative Fund of
  America, 53
Wise, Steven, 125
Woolf, Norma Bennett, 81, 130
World Society for the Protection
  of Animals, xv, 35, 111, 114,
  179, 201
World Week for Animals in
  Laboratories, 19
World Wildlife Fund (Sweden), 33
Wright State University, 195
Wu Wang, 63
Wyeth-Ayerst Laboratories, 34, 35
Wyngaarden, James, 19

Y

Yellowstone National Park, 50,
  177
Yerkes Primate Research Center,
  19
Young, Peter D., 126

Z

Zawistowski, Stephen, 29
zebras, 66
Zoocheck Canada, 73
Zoological Society of London, 63

Capital Research Center (CRC) was established in 1984 to study nonprofit organizations, with a special focus on reviving the American traditions of charity, philanthropy, and voluntarism.

Since the launching of the Great Society, thousands of nonprofit advocacy groups have emerged, often promoting more government welfare programs in areas once considered the domain of families, charities, neighborhood associations, and other voluntary organizations. The growth of government has increasingly supplanted the voluntary action and community-based problem-solving that the great observer of early American society, Alexis de Tocqueville, recognized as a defining feature of our country.

CRC specializes in analyzing organizations that promote the growth of the welfare state–now almost universally recognized as a failure–and in identifying viable private alternatives to government programs. Our research forms the basis for a variety of publications:

Organization Trends, a monthly newsletter that reports on and analyzes the activities of advocacy organizations.

Alternatives in Philanthropy, a monthly newsletter that examines major issues and trends in philanthropy.

Philanthropy, Culture & Society, a monthly newsletter highlighting the work of small, locally based charities that help the needy.

Studies in Organization Trends, a series of monograph's focusing a advocacy groups, their agendas, sources of funding, and effectiveness.

For the public-spirited Americans who provide the backbone of American philanthropy—individuals as well as corporate and foundation personnel—CRC provides perspective on organizations that shape public policy. For the media, CRC provides insight into the world on nonprofit advocacy so that reporters and editors can better judge the credibility of nonprofit spokesmen.

CRC is a nonprofit, tax-exempt, education and research organization operating under Section 501 (c)(3) of the Internal Revenue Code. Our programs are financed through gifts from foundations, corporations, and individuals and through the sales of publications. We accept no government contracts or grants.

CAPITAL RESEARCH CENTER
1513 SIXTEENTH STREET, NW
WASHINGTON, DC 20036
TELEPHONE: (202) 483-6900
http://www.capitalresearch.org